D0765691

The French Enlightenment in America

PAUL MERRILL SPURLIN

The French Enlightenment in America

Essays on the Times of the Founding Fathers

The University of Georgia Press
Athens

© 1984 by the University of Georgia Press
Athens, Georgia 30602
All rights reserved

Designed by Sandra Strother Hudson
Set in Linotron 202 Galliard
The decorations in this book are enlargements of
French typographic ornaments from the eighteenth
century.

The paper in this book meets the guidelines for
permanence and durability of the Committee on
Production Guidelines for Book Longevity of the
Council on Library Resources

Printed in the United States of America
88 87 86 85 84   5 4 3 2 1

Library of Congress Cataloging in Publication Data

Main entry under title:

The French Enlightenment in America.

    Includes index.
    1. United States—Intellectual life—18th century—
Addresses, essays, lectures. 2. United States—
Civilization—French influences—Addresses, essays,
lectures. 3. Enlightenment—Addresses, essays,
lectures. 4. France—Intellectual life—18th
century—Addresses, essays, lectures. I. Spurlin,
Paul Merrill, 1902–   II. Title.
E163.F84   1984   973   84-233
ISBN 0-8203-0721-1

TO

ALIX

PAULA AND PAMELA

JUDITH SUTHER AND CECIL TAYLOR

Contents

Preface

 The French Enlightenment in America is an imposing subject. I have begun this book several times, and on occasion have been tempted to abandon it. Inward pressure to complete it, however, has never weakened. And a desire to convey to others something of the absorbing interest the subject has for me has never diminished.

I address this cross-cultural study to the scholar, to the curious but largely uninformed general reader, and to anyone interested in the history of American civilization. It offers, within modest bounds, an overview of French-American cultural relations, science generally excluded, in the period under consideration. One other comment is appropriate here. Theseus needed a thread to extricate himself from the Cretan labyrinth. I am convinced that many advanced students and scholars, not to speak of the inquisitive general reader, also need guidance in making their way through nebulous areas of this important interdisciplinary field. One does not always know which way to turn, where to look for help. It is my hope that the bibliographical documentation provided in these pages will assist those seeking information to find their way more easily through the maze.

My principal concern in this book is with the literary presence of French authors in America between 1760 and 1800 and with the reception of their writings by the Founding Fathers and other Americans, particularly of the writings of major *philosophes* of the French Enlightenment whose names turned up rather often in my research. It hardly need be said that while the presence of French books in private libraries may indicate interest, their presence does not necessarily imply influence. Thomas Jefferson's library is a case in point. I have not hesitated, however, to cite when appropriate the conclusions of various scholars about the action exerted by French thought on Americans.

These essays derive from intensive reading in, and close scrutiny of, all sorts of printed sources. Much material comes from eighteenth-century newspapers published in important cities. I have not dealt with the French enclaves in America. If spellings and punctuation in some of the quotations from the past look odd, or lack French accents, they are like that in the original documents. Research on the subjects treated could go on through the years. The result, however, would differ very little in kind, I think, from what is presented here. *Half a loaf is better than no bread.*

The writings of Gilbert Chinard, Bernard Faÿ, and Howard Mumford Jones, to name only these scholars, clarify numerous and important aspects of this cultural relationship. I would like to pay tribute especially to Professor Chinard, my mentor at the Johns Hopkins University. He was a pioneer in the study of eighteenth-century intellectual relations between France and America. He inspired and directed fellow workers in new academic territory.[1] He had the knowledge, the enthusiasm, and the diligence to cultivate in masterly fashion not only the French-American field but also the fields of French and comparative literature, literary history, the history of ideas, and American history and biography. His contribution is a vast one. Bernard Faÿ's major contribution is a synthesis of the moral and intellectual relations between France and the United States from 1770 to 1800.[2] Howard Mumford Jones's well-known book spans the long period between 1750 and 1848.[3] Neither Faÿ nor Jones gives a sufficient account of the fortunes of the French *philosophes* here in the times of the Founding Fathers. Nor did either author claim to do so. And neither one has much to say about French literature in itself in the United States.

For editorial permission to use, in whole or in part, articles of mine which have appeared elsewhere, I am grateful to the editors of *Actes du Congrès Montesquieu* (Bordeaux: Delmas, 1956) for "L'Influence de Montesquieu sur la constitution américaine"; *Studies on Voltaire and the Eighteenth Century* for "Diderot, Alembert, and the Encyclopédie in the United States, 1760–1800"; *The World of Voltaire* (Ann Arbor: University of Michigan Museum of Art, 1969) for "Voltaire and the Enlightenment"; *France and North America: Over Three Hundred Years of Dialogue* (Lafayette: University of Southwestern Louisiana, 1973) for "French-American Cultural Relations, 1760–1800"; the *French Review* for "The World of the Founding Fathers and France"; and the *Modern Language Journal* for "The Founding Fathers and the French Language."

I am especially indebted to the United States Educational Commission for France for the award of a Fulbright grant to lecture at the Universities of Lille and Grenoble and to the Horace H. Rackham School of Graduate Studies of the University of Michigan for a Faculty Research Fellowship. These generous grants, which I acknowledge with many thanks, gave me leisure, support, and encouragement in the initial stages of this project.

Appreciated also are the many courtesies and help extended to me by staff members of the American Philosophical Society, the Historical Society of Pennsylvania, the Library Company of Philadelphia, the Library of Congress, and the William L. Clements Library and the Harlan Hatcher Graduate Library at the University of Michigan.

Introduction

 Carl Becker, in his review of Howard Mumford Jones's *America and French Culture 1750–1848*, wrote that he could not "avoid the feeling that detailing the contacts of Americans with things French is one thing; that estimating the influence of French culture on American culture is another; and that between the two is a gulf extremely hazardous to cross. 'Influence' in this connection is so uncertain a quantity to calculate, so illusive a quality to estimate!" I agree. In matters involving Western civilization, I lean toward the view expressed by Charles and Mary Beard: "In reality the heritage, economics, politics, culture, and international filiations of any civilization are so closely woven by fate into one fabric that no human eye can discern the beginnings of its warp or woof."[1]

American culture, until well into the nineteenth century, derived mostly of course from Great Britain. But France, it goes without saying, had always played a powerful role in the development of western European civilization. From the end of the seventeenth century she had engaged in a two-way commerce in intellectual relations with Britain. In the eighteenth century a cosmopolitan-minded France became the center of one of this civilization's most influential philosophical movements. The possibilities, then, of French contribution to eighteenth-century American culture, direct or indirect, can by no means be disregarded.

Scholars on both sides of the Atlantic have long been interested in, or concerned with, the question of the impact of French Enlightenment thought on the United States. But disagreement persists, despite unwearying inquiry into the origins of American institutions and perennial concern with intellectual currents here in the formative period. A half-century of controversy concerning Rousseau is a case in point.[2]

Pitfalls await the unsuspecting and the incautious in attributions of influence. Here are five: over-intellectualization of the past, scholarly myopia, inadequate knowledge of the cultural background, generalizations from insufficient data, and national pride. These pitfalls must be avoided if we are ever to know the approximate truth.

It is easy for the scholar to over-intellectualize the past. He is a man of the book and here lies a great danger. James Truslow Adams described it in commenting on the importance of literary sources to the American Revolution: "As time passes, books remain, whereas the gossip of the village tavern and the unspoken emotions in the heart of the mass are lost forever. But although it follows that the tendency is always to overemphasize the intellectual aspect of any great movement of the past, it is a mistake to consider that man's political actions necessarily or even mainly spring from reasoned premises."[3]

Myopia is also a formidable handicap when one enters the complex ideological maze of the eighteenth century. The same idea or similar ideas were expressed by many writers. Let me illustrate. Rhetorical happenstance hardly explains the inclusion in the Declaration of Independence of the phrase "the pursuit of happiness" as one of the inalienable rights of mankind. Jefferson admitted as much when he wrote that all the authority of the document rests on "the harmonizing sentiments of the day." The Declaration's phrase is an exact translation of "la recherche du bonheur," which expression, as Robert Mauzi points out in a massive study,[4] had a "valeur quasi obsessionnelle" in eighteenth-century France. His bibliography is replete with titles of essays, treatises, and other writings in French devoted to the idea of happiness. With regard to the ideological background of "the pursuit of happiness," especially in England, Scotland, France, and Italy, one should consult a generously documented book by Garry Wills.[5] Wills calls it "the phrase considered most vulnerable or indefinable" in the Declaration. Happiness was one of the great *idées en l'air* in the eighteenth century, a time when authors, in their attacks upon every stronghold of the established order, did not hesitate to use the ammunition or brandish the intellectual weapons of others. American pamphleteers and writers of controversial newspaper articles had almost a mania for quoting. Writers and editors would frequently cite more than one writer on the same point, and often without acknowledgement. Like lawyers they would avidly make use of authorities whose reasoning buttressed their arguments. Such practices have serious implications for scholarship because the hazards inherent in deductions from ideological or verbal parallelism are only too obvious.

Inadequate knowledge of the cultural background is still another factor in the perpetuation of error. Too little is known by too few about the dissemination and availability of French literature in eighteenth-century America. I shall cite only one instance. A historian of an older generation, in a book which has been reprinted, presumed to write, "By French literature the colonists were unaffected, because with few exceptions, they knew nothing about it. The number who could read French was small, the number who did read French to any extent was smaller. . . . the political theories of Montesquieu and of Rousseau, the wit of Voltaire, the infidelity of the encyclopaedists, had no influence upon men, the most of whom did not know these writers even by name."[6]

Generalizations from insufficient data, or the universal sport of jumping to conclusions, another pitfall, needs no documentation. One swallow does not make a summer and a *post hoc ergo propter hoc* judgment is a trap into which the best may stumble.

National pride is still another snare. It does occasionally becloud a scholar's vision. One can be too dogmatic in asserting belief concerning influences. Undue stress on one's own history and literature promotes insularity, misunderstanding, and ultimately intolerance. On the other hand, a more international outlook, and a wider knowledge, solidly grounded on fact, make for better understanding and mutual forbearance. Greater understanding tends to obviate sweeping generalizations, products of provinciality, limited experience, and prejudice.

The importance of the objectively written and carefully documented monograph can not be overstated. Scholars working in eighteenth-century French-American intellectual relations need make no apology, however, for their occasional inability to arrive at firm conclusions about questions of influence, or for raising questions to which they have not found the answers. Thanks to the efforts of a great many researchers, almost every phase of French-American relations of that century is in clearer focus than ever before.[7] My study deals with this relationship in the last four decades of the century.

About 1760 British colonials in North America began to ponder earnestly the meaning of liberty under the English constitution. By 1763, when the Treaty of Paris brought an end to the French and Indian War, "the colonies," according to Louis B. Wright, "had come of age, and their citizens had indeed become Americans."[8] The terminal year, 1800, rounds off the period. Jefferson's accession to the presidency in March of the following year brought to a close the first great era of controversy regarding the Constitution of the United States.

It is hardly necessary to stress the crucial nature of these decades both in America and in France. It was a time of social and political upheaval. Parties and party strife emerged. Conflicts, hostilities, and revolutionary wars marked these years, which witnessed the beginning of a new order of things. In the New World, to speak only of it, this was a period of intense discussion—of such subjects as natural and constitutional rights, political and religious liberty, the relationship between church and state, theories and machinery of government, orthodoxy, deism, economics, education, humanitarianism, the human habitat, penological reform, progress, the perfectibility of man, and science.

The four decades comprise the times of the Founding Fathers.

This was the age of enlightenment in the United States.[9] Influential men of a far earlier day have, of course, every right to be considered founders. One need only recall the Pilgrim Fathers and the Mayflower Compact. But my concern is with the molders of opinion in the last forty years of the century. The leaders and influential participants in such momentous undertakings and events as the two Continental Congresses, the Declaration of Independence, the War of Independence, and the Constitutional Convention were the Founding Fathers of the Republic. In all, according to Saul K. Padover, "a list of one hundred names, without claiming inclusiveness, would give an approximate idea of the number of Founding Fathers who were most active and prominent in the fields of political organization, military affairs, oratory, writing, diplomacy, administration, and jurisprudence."[10] Padover prints at the beginning of his book the names of thirty-one of the more eminent members of this group. With the exception of Franklin, the Fathers were, generally speaking, "young" men.[11] In 1787, the year of the Constitutional Convention, Hamilton, Madison, and Gouverneur Morris were in their thirties. In that year Jefferson, forty-four, was minister to France. When Jefferson learned the names of these and the other fifty-two delegates from the thirteen colonies who met in Philadelphia in 1787 to draw up a constitution for the United States, he remarked that the Constitutional Convention was "an assembly of demi-gods." The convention could boast of a good company of Founding Fathers. The reader will come upon the names of many of them in these pages on the French Enlightenment in America.

One

The Enlightenment

 The Enlightenment, like the Renaissance and the Reformation, was no localized phenomenon.[1] Called the Age of Reason or the Age of Enlightenment in England, the *Siècle des lumières* in France, the *Aufklärung* in Germany, the liberating force that the word *enlightenment* suggests stopped at few frontiers. Italy had its *Illuminismo,* the Spanish world its *Ilustración,* and America its era of the Founding Fathers.

A vast movement of ideas, the Enlightenment had its real beginning in seventeenth-century Europe. It did not, of course, pass from one place to another simultaneously. The United States, for example, lagged behind France by several decades. Herbert Dieckmann, in his essay "Themes and Structure of the Enlightenment," summarizes the views of Herman Hettner, Ernst Cassirer, and Paul Hazard on the Enlightenment and its origins. One can find here a blanket explanation of this lack of synchrony. Paraphrasing Hettner, Dieckmann writes that "the seeds of that great movement can be found in all three countries [England, France, and Germany] alike, but they germinate at different times and in different ways, owing to combined philosophical, scientific, political, and cultural factors."[2] But the Enlightenment "can be understood only as a whole of which the parts are interrelated." This last statement is Dieckmann's rendering of another of Hettner's views. In context, its immediate reference is to the countries just mentioned. The thought expressed, however, is universally valid. Neither nations nor individuals exist, nor have they ever existed, in an ideological vacuum.

Peter Gay speaks of the Enlightenment as "a family of philosophes." Among the more illustrious members of the family were
Sir Isaac Newton, John Locke, David Hume, Adam Smith, Montesquieu, Voltaire, Rousseau, Diderot, Helvétius, Holbach, Condillac, Condorcet, Kant, Lessing, Beccaria, Benjamin Franklin,
and Thomas Jefferson. The Enlightenment family was composed
of rationalists. Its members differed in many respects. They did
not all think alike. Voltaire's views on society and luxury were
quite different from those of Rousseau. And certainly Rousseau's
notion of property was not Jefferson's.

Eighteenth-century France, until 1789, was the principal
theater of the Enlightenment.³ The climate of ideas in France had
undergone a radical transformation in a hundred-year period
which began around 1650. Whether right or wrong concerning
the swiftness of this change, Paul Hazard described it vividly. "A
majority of the French people thought like Bossuet," he wrote,
referring to the eminent and ultraorthodox seventeenth-century
prelate, but "suddenly they began to think like Voltaire: it was a
revolution." This is hyperbole, but the statement contains much
truth. Rationalism coursed through eighteenth-century France
like a mighty tide, followed, however, by a heavy ground swell of
that emotion known as sensibility—a reaction to the overempha-
sis upon reason.

It is hazardous to generalize about the Enlightenment and its
leaders in France, and presumptuous to expect to bring forward
anything particularly new on subjects about which so much has
been written. But one can link these leaders, the *philosophes,* in
terms of somewhat common interests and goals. At the risk of
oversimplification, one can say that they were humanitarians and
reformers, intellectuals committed to improving man's lot. They
opposed every form of tyranny and cruelty, did their best to
depose blind faith, combat credulity, and stamp out superstition.
They worked to enthrone reason, promote humaneness, and better the government of mankind.

Voltaire, archapostle of reason and "genius of mockery," was an awakener of consciences. Rousseau, a rationalist *and* an apostle of sensibility, sought to form consciences. These two writers, and many more, lashed out against intolerance, corruption, and hypocrisy under the Old Regime. Each, in his own inimitable way, castigated abuses of power wherever found—in church, state, or society. Voltaire and Rousseau stirred men's minds and helped to put an end to authority based solely on tradition or divine right. They anticipated revolution. Rousseau, in 1762, declared, "We are approaching a state of crisis and the century of revolutions." And Voltaire, in a letter of 1764, said, "Everything I see sows the seeds of a revolution which will not fail to come, but which I shall not have the pleasure of witnessing." Condorcet, far more optimistic than either of the two, wrote later, "Everything tells us that we are now close upon one of the great revolutions of the human race."

The American Revolution, which in turn greatly influenced the revolutionary movement in France, was itself the consequence of a fundamental shift in traditional modes of thought. Vividly symbolic of the changed outlook, though hardly typical, is a remark of Jefferson's. Reflecting on the momentous event at home, he wrote from Paris in 1787, "What country before ever existed a century and a half without a rebellion? . . . The tree of liberty must be refreshed from time to time with the blood of patriots and tyrants." In America, as in France, the rationalistic and critical currents had become ever more powerful as the eighteenth century progressed. By 1760 the old dikes of religious and political orthodoxy had been breached. Intellectually, the climate in the second half of this century—the period of the Enlightenment in the United States—differed markedly from that of the first half.

Any study of the impact of French thought on eighteenth-century America must take into account the American cultural heritage. It is often very difficult to say what is French thought and what is not. In an essay entitled "Jefferson Among the Philosophers," Gilbert Chinard wrote, "I have often proposed that our ignorance and neglect of [the] classical background vitiates most of our studies on eighteenth-century thought. To the age of enlightenment we attribute an originality and a boldness which the philosophers of the eighteenth century themselves did not presume to possess. This would certainly be true of Bolingbroke . . . it is no less true of Voltaire, Diderot, Helvétius, and D'Holbach. From this point of view, it would be more correct to call the eighteenth century the Second Renaissance rather than the age of enlightenment. At any rate, if the *philosophes* were the torchbearers of their age, they had received the sacred spark from the ancient philosophers."[4] America was "a peece of the Continent, a part of the maine." At least 130 alumni of Oxford and Cambridge had come to New England before 1646. Up to 1793, some 2,300 students had been graduated from Yale alone. Many well-educated men came from Europe in the twenty-five years preceding the American Revolution. Four of these became college presidents. They had received a classical education. They too were part of the "Atlantic community," to use an expression of Michael Kraus, whose book *The Atlantic Civilization: Eighteenth-Century Origins* (1949) is the authority for these figures. As members of the "Atlantic community," Americans were subject to the same general climate of ideas that brought about the Enlightenment in Europe. The basic reading of educated Americans, Englishmen, and Frenchmen was substantially the same. Americans read classical literature.[5] They too were obliged to react to the awesome impact of the Newtonian discoveries and the scientific revolution, dangerous to traditional patterns of thought.

When information is sought on the origin or origins of the Enlightenment in America, a tangled skein of opinion meets the eye. One has only to look at the antithetical conclusions of Daniel J. Boorstin and Henry Steele Commager. In a chapter entitled "The Myth of an American Enlightenment,"[6] Boorstin refers to the Enlightenment itself as "that miasma." He strongly objects to "the academically stereotyped 'system' of eighteenth-century thought," disapproves of "homogenizing the mind of the past," and stresses "the myriad particularity of the thinking of different men in different places in the eighteenth century." Commager, at a symposium held at the Library of Congress, said, "My theme can be put simply and succinctly, though I am aware that simplicity is deceptive and succinctness suspect. It is this: that the Old World imagined the Enlightenment and the New World realized it. The Old World invented it, formulated it, and agitated it; America absorbed it, reflected it, and institutionalized it."[7] But the American Enlightenment, in his judgment, was "an Enlightenment that differed strikingly from the French and English versions in that (unlike these) it found support in experience as well as in philosophy, vindicated itself by reference to environment and circumstances, as well as to imagination and logic."[8] Here is a sampling of other views. Gerald Stourzh would direct our attention to an introductory phase, preceding the major period of American Enlightenment. In an essay, "Sober Philosophe: Benjamin Franklin,"[9] he insists that the "roots" of Franklin's thought are to be found in "earlier developments" in America, in the first half of the eighteenth century. Russel B. Nye believes that the Enlightenment here "was late, eclectic, and American. It is misleading to assume that eighteenth-century America was merely a reflection of eighteenth-century Britain, or Europe."[10] And finally, this opinion of Bernard Bailyn, "The political and social ideas of the European Enlightenment have had a peculiar importance in American history. More universally accepted in eighteenth-century America than in Europe, they were more completely and more permanently embodied in the formal arrangements of state and society . . . they have lived on more vigorously into later periods, more continuous and more intact. The peculiar force of these ideas in America resulted from many causes. But originally, and basically, it resulted from the circumstances of the prerevolutionary period and from the bearing of these ideas on the political experience of the American colonists."[11]

From this brief presentation it is obvious that scholars differ rather widely in their views concerning the origins of the Enlightenment in the United States.[12] I hope that the essays which follow will give a better idea of the role of French thought in the American Enlightenment.

Two

The World of the Founding
Fathers and France

 Henry Thomas Buckle believed that the "junction of the French and English intellects, . . . looking at the immense chain of its effects, [was] by far the most important fact in the history of the eighteenth century." Why? Because the French, wrote the English historian, had sought liberty in England, "where alone it could be found."[1] He was right with regard to the first half of the century. But the rest seems to be an exaggeration. Liberty, as if one could forget, was also the leitmotif in what we may call the New World Symphony. The Founding Fathers made the proper orchestration of this theme their principal task. Inasmuch as eighteenth-century France became the principal theater of Enlightenment, it is appropriate to shift attention away from England and toward the "junction" of the French and American intellects.

Many scholars have written about the ideological impact of the United States on France in the latter half of the eighteenth century. Let me cite in this connection only the studies of Gilbert Chinard on the American antecedents of the French *Declaration of the Rights of Man*,[2] R. R. Palmer's *The Age of the Democratic Revolution*,[3] and Durand Echeverria's *Mirage in the West*.[4] My inquiry moves in the opposite direction. I am concerned with the image of France and the French held by Americans in the years between 1760 and 1800.[5] Knowledge of this concept is basic to any consideration of the role of French thought in the American

Enlightenment. This essay deals with the coming together of the American and French minds in these four critical decades.

Today Americans find it difficult to visualize their country and its people in the decisive years of its history. In 1790, the year of the first census, the population totaled 3,929,625.[6] Contrast this with the population of France at that time. The first French census did not take place until 1801, but the number of its inhabitants in 1789 has been variously estimated at from 26 to 27 million. The American census figures included whites, free Negroes, and slaves. The whites numbered 3,172,444. The southern states had 48.5 percent of the entire population. The remainder was distributed almost equally between New England and the middle Atlantic states. Virginia had the greatest number of people. Massachusetts was second in number and Pennsylvania third. The nonurban population was widely dispersed. "The four millions of people in the country in 1790," Frank J. Klingberg writes, "were sparsely settled over a misshapen rectangle some twelve or thirteen hundred miles from its northeastern corner to the southwest, and with primitive homes extending a thousand miles to the west into the Ohio Valley, and beyond the Alleghenies into Tennessee and Kentucky."[7] In 1790 just 5.4 percent of the people lived in towns.

Philadelphia, New York, Boston, Charleston, and Baltimore were, in descending order, the five largest cities. Their combined population at the time of the first census amounted to only 123,475. Even so they were, as Thomas J. Wertenbaker called them, "crucibles of culture." Merle E. Curti wrote that "the towns were the chief centers of intellectual activity because they enjoyed closer relations with Europe and because they offered great opportunities for social contacts and the discussion of events and ideas."[8] The new federal government began its operations in New York in March 1789. Philadelphia was the nation's capital from 1790 to 1800. Washington became the seat of government in the latter year.

Urban centers along the eastern seaboard were by no means

impervious to outside influence. Boston, Newport, New York, Philadelphia, and Charleston were cosmopolitan cities, "oases of culture and taste," writes Carl Bridenbaugh.[9] According to Michael Kraus, "in the 1760s some two hundred [ships] a year sailed from London alone for the thirteen colonies." And "more than 1,800 ocean-going vessels arrived at New York and Philadelphia in 1788."[10] Reading matter from England and the European continent flowed into the ports and thence trickled into the interior. Abundant information on the book trade, book ownership, and libraries in the United States, from colonial times on, is easily available. French books in the original and in translation were in a great number of eighteenth-century collections. The importance of the printed word, not to speak of personal contacts and conversations, in effecting a meeting of minds and in the formation of opinion requires no comment. Accounts of the difficulties of travel and communication within the country are also plentiful.[11] But America, manifestly, was no hermetic "Iland, intire of itselfe."

The foreign news columns in the American gazettes kept readers posted on events in Europe, with due allowance for a time lag. How much was it? Atlantic crossings were of different lengths, of course, depending on various factors. An interesting sidelight is to be found in the *Maryland Journal* for September 22, 1789. The editor announced that he stopped this issue in the press to report the first news of the storming of the Bastille. The news, he said, had arrived in Philadelphia on September 18: July 14 in Paris, September 22 in Baltimore! Kraus, however, mentions speedier crossings in his book. And Elkanah Watson, about whom more later, in his *Memoirs* wrote, "After a sail of twenty-nine days, I was standing on a quay in France. What a transition!" His voyage had taken him from Boston to Saint-Martin-de-Ré. The year was 1779.

Before 1776 the American attitude toward France had been one of distrust. France had long been the age-old foe of the mother country. Americans also looked upon France as a nation of papists and as a land of religious intolerance. The presence of the Huguenots[12] in New England, New York, and South Carolina and the activities of French missionaries in Canada lent cogent support to this view. "The savage years" of the French and Indian War had also left the colonials with bitter memories of their French enemies. But a new order was in the making. The Declaration of Independence would mark the end of an era and the beginning of another. The times change and people change with them. Only two years after the Declaration the United States and France signed a treaty of amity and commerce and a treaty of alliance.

In 1768 the American Philosophical Society, the country's oldest scientific academy, elected Buffon to its membership. He was the first French member. By the year 1800 the society had elected fifty-eight more French men of science and *philosophes* and had honored France by the election of still other persons of note.[13] Brissot de Warville, journalist and Girondist, visited the Harvard library in 1788 and was moved to rapture when he discovered that it contained French books.[14] On the Yale campus in the 1790s, students used names of French *philosophes* as nicknames.[15] These instances of American concern with French thinkers and French literature may appear to be isolated events or fortuitous occurrences. But they are not. One might compare them to the small designs one sees in unrolling a large tapestry—tiny parts of a logically developing pattern of great interest.

"There are multitudes of Frenchmen come over," noted Princeton's president, John Witherspoon, in February 1777, "and almost everybody is ambitious of learning the French."[16] But the great influx of Frenchmen began only in 1778, after the signing of the treaties between the two countries.[17] Some forty-six thousand French soldiers, sailors, and officers participated in the War of the Revolution. The names of these men and their place of origin have been set down in a lasting record.[18] The names of such distinguished commanders as Lafayette, Rochambeau, Chastellux, Estaing, and De Grasse remain firmly secured in memory. The presence of the French offered ample opportunity for acquaintance and even fraternization. "I doubt much," wrote General Washington on the completion of military operations, "whether there ever was an instance before, where the Troops of two Nations which have served together in the Field, have parted with such sentiments of sincere affection and mutual regret."[19] There were other important consequences of the wartime connection. The presence of the French armed forces and their contribution to the defeat of England greatly stimulated American interest in the language and literature of France. One need but recall a similar situation—this time in reverse. More than two million American soldiers went to France in World War I. Their contribution to victory gave a decisive impetus to French curiosity about the United States and its literature. It is worthy of notice that Charles Cestre, first incumbent of the chair of American literature and civilization at the Sorbonne, began his lectures there in 1918. The association of Americans with the French in the Revolutionary War also helped promote growth of a more tolerant spirit in the United States. Samuel Breck, in his "Recollections," wrote of an abrupt change in attitude which took place in New England "after a few years intercourse with the French army and navy." In 1789 he attended a celebration of the Mass in Boston, held in a building in which Huguenots had once worshipped. "I can bear witness, that not the smallest opposition took place; neither was there a hostile remark from the press. Puritan jealousy and intolerance had wholly disappeared. Not a vestige of former austerity remained." Only fourteen years before, Breck recalled, the pope had been burned in effigy in New England, "as a token of the hatred borne by the people, to the Roman C. Religion."[20]

The French Revolution itself facilitated further contacts between the two peoples. It has been estimated that "well over ten thousand" refugees came to the United States from France and Santo Domingo to escape the violent disruption it caused. The author of the monograph from which this figure is taken writes that "they began to arrive in 1792, and in the following years 'thousands upon thousands of Frenchmen crowded into the American seaboard towns.' But this immigration was not confined to the East. One group formed a project to found a new city, Gallipolis, on the Ohio, and some six hundred of them not only reached the Ohio wilderness but survived in it. They were people of humble rank, and a fair proportion of the émigrés in the East were artisans and shopkeepers. The majority of those from metropolitan France, however, were aristocrats."[21] Among these were Chateaubriand, Talleyrand, and the future king of the French, Louis-Philippe.

French architects and artists came also to the new Republic— among them L'Enfant, Houdon, and Saint-Mémin. Pierre Charles L'Enfant rests today in Arlington National Cemetery, close to the great federal city he planned. Houdon spent about two weeks at Mount Vernon, modeling Washington's face, shoulders, and hands. He took the models back to France, where Gouverneur Morris posed for the rest of the general's statue, which is in the Virginia capitol. Févret de Saint-Mémin executed hundreds of portrait medallions of prominent Americans, a collection of which can be seen in the Corcoran Gallery of Art.[22] Quesnay de Beaurepaire, who fought here in the War of the Revolution, proposed to establish an academy of arts and sciences in Richmond, with branches in Baltimore, Philadelphia, and New York. His ambitious project to strengthen the cultural relations between France and America did not succeed.[23]

French travelers went here and there, noting their impressions, collecting material for the accounts of their American tours.[24] French newspapers issued from presses in the United States.[25] Meanwhile, in France, Americans were gathering information firsthand about that country.

English visitors by the thousands crossed the Channel into France in the last half of the eighteenth century.[26] A voyage across the Atlantic to France in those long-ago days was a much more difficult undertaking. But the number and character of those Americans who braved the high seas will doubtless come as a surprise to many readers. With no pretension to give an exhaustive account, I would like to direct attention to some of these travelers. First, there were the accredited representatives of government—commissioners, envoys, ministers or ministers plenipotentiary, consuls. Then there were students, doctors, tourists, businessmen, and artists. All sorts of people, in fact, made their way from the New World to the Old. Their contacts and novel experiences, it goes without saying, proved highly instructive to them, and through them, to Americans at home. Many became important intermediaries between the two countries.

Benjamin Franklin lived in France from 1776 to 1785. While there he exercised responsibilities of the utmost importance to the success of American arms and to the future of the United States. He and Conrad-Alexandre Gérard helped negotiate the treaties between the two countries. In 1778 Louis XVI named Gérard minister to the United States, and the Continental Congress appointed Franklin minister to France. Franklin's diplomatic and personal triumphs abroad are too well known to require mention. His circle of acquaintances included Voltaire, Turgot, Condorcet, Cabanis, Marie Antoinette, Comtesse d'Houdetot, and a host of others.[27] Voltaire's blessing in 1778 of a grandson of Franklin's, at the latter's request, needs no recounting. Whether Voltaire used the words "Dieu et la liberté" or "God and Liberty" in his invocation is a moot point.[28] John Adams, hardly a friend of Franklin's, wrote glowingly of the high esteem in which he was held throughout France. Albert H. Smyth, one of his biographers, declared that "a list of the names upon the visiting cards found among Franklin's private papers would be an index of the society of Paris before the Revolution." Franklin was "the American personality most frequently depicted on the stage" during the French Revolution.[29] However prodigious his political activity in Paris, it was not all work and no play for Dr. Franklin. The gallantry of the septuagenarian ambassador in the French capital also commands admiration. The story of his amorous disposition, especially toward Madame Brillon and Madame Helvétius, widow of the *philosophe,* is a source of perennial amusement and delight.[30] "The French are an amiable People to live with," wrote the good Doctor in 1783. "They love me, & I love them. Yet I do not feel myself at home, & I wish to die in my own Country."[31] Thomas Jefferson succeeded Franklin. He was minister from 1785 to 1789, and saw the beginning of the French Revolution. Much has been written by Jefferson and others on his sojourn in France. For the general reader two or three references are enough. They will provide information concerning his acquaintances, attitudes, interests, life, and travels in that country.[32] In his *Notes on the State of Virginia*, written in 1781, Jefferson had said, "We are but just becoming acquainted with her [France], and our acquaintance so far gives us high ideas of the genius of her inhabitants." In a letter from Paris in 1786, two years after his arrival in the foreign capital, he wrote, "We have no idea in America of the real French character. With some true samples, we have had many false ones."[33] He met and knew many well-known persons. According to Chinard, "There is no doubt that, during his stay in France, Jefferson formed personal friendships with Morellet, Mably, Démeunier, Condorcet, young Cabanis, whom he met at the house of Mme. Helvétius, and with the last survivors of the old philosophical guard."[34] Jefferson left France in 1789. Here is what he wrote in his *Autobiography:*

> I cannot leave this great and good country, without expressing my sense of its pre-eminence of character among the nations of the earth. A more benevolent people I have never known, nor greater warmth and devotedness in their select friendships. Their kindness and accommodation to strangers is unparalleled, and the hospitality of Paris is beyond anything I had conceived to be practicable in a large city. Their eminence, too, in science, the communicative dispositions of their scientific men, the politeness of the general manners, the ease and vivacity of their conversation, give a charm to their society, to be found nowhere else.

Gouverneur Morris, James Monroe, and William Vans Murray, in that order, succeeded Jefferson as ministers to France in the closing years of the century. A witness to the Revolution, Morris concluded his *Diary* with a letter to Jefferson, then in Philadelphia. In it he gave the Virginian a description of the execution of Louis XVI.[35]

John Adams, though never a minister to the French court, had first gone to Paris in April 1778 with an appointment by the Continental Congress as commissioner to France in his pocket. He returned home the following year. In the 1780s he was again in and out of the capital, while acting in various official capacities abroad. At one time or another, the conservative Adams made the acquaintance of various *philosophes*. The caustic comments in his writings and correspondence on the ideas of some of the *philosophes* are unforgettable. The diary of his life in France makes good reading.[36] And so do the letters of his wife, Abigail, commenting on the French scene. The New England woman's reactions to such things as customs, dress of ladies, and the scanty clothing of girl dancers etch themselves on the mind. The letter in which she describes the appearance and behavior of Madame Helvétius at a dinner at Dr. Franklin's has become a minor classic.[37] "I own I was highly disgusted, and never wish for an acquaintance with any ladies of this cast," Abigail declared. "I hope, however, to find amongst the French ladies manners more consistent with my ideas of decency, or I shall be a mere recluse," said she.

Boys from Maryland Catholic families early went to study at the Jesuit English College of Saint Omers in French Flanders. Charles Carroll of Carrollton, a future signer of the Declaration of Independence, left Annapolis for France in 1748. He was eleven at the time. His cousin Jacky, two years older, accompanied him. After Saint Omers, Charles Carroll studied at Rheims, Paris, and Bourges. He lived in France for ten years. John Carroll would become the first Roman Catholic bishop in the United States and the founder of Georgetown University.[38] John Quincy Adams, sixth president of the United States, in his youth, studied French in Passy. Samuel Breck, a leading citizen of Philadelphia and a member of Congress from Pennsylvania, as a boy, studied in the 1780s for more than four years at the Collège de Sorèze, not far from Toulouse. But some four decades before Breck went to Sorèze, Thomas Bond, a Marylander, had "completed his medical education in Europe, chiefly at Paris." Bond helped found the Pennsylvania Hospital, oldest in the United States. He was also a founder of the American Philosophical Society.[39] In 1751 John Jones had obtained his M.D. at the University of Rheims. Jones, from Jamaica, Long Island, became a professor of surgery and obstetrics at King's College (Columbia) and is said to have written the first textbook on surgery in the American colonies. All these men were in the vanguard of the multitude of Americans who, as time rolled on, would go to France for study.

French medicine also interested other American doctors who traveled or studied in France. Among them were William Shippen, Jr., who visited the medical schools at Paris and Montpellier, John Morgan, Benjamin Rush, Solomon Drowne, and George Logan. Logan attended anatomical lectures in Paris in the winter of 1779–80.[40] Morgan and Rush, particularly, command our attention.

John Morgan was medical director of the Continental Army. Early on he had been an apprentice in Philadelphia under Dr. John Redman, who had done some study in Paris. After receiving his M.D. at Edinburgh in 1763 John Morgan studied anatomy for a while in the French capital. He was admitted to the Académie Royale de Chirurgie de Paris in 1764. One Sunday afternoon in this same year, accompanied by Samuel Powel, he called upon Voltaire at Ferney. Morgan quotes Voltaire as saying, "If ever I smell of a Resurrection, or come a second time on Earth, I will pray God to make me born in England, the land of Liberty." Morgan's account of their conversation is captivating.[41] Of Voltaire's linguistic ability he made this observation, "We meet with few french Men who pronounce english better."

Benjamin Rush, another renowned Philadelphia doctor and a signer of the Declaration of Independence, went to Paris in 1769.

He was received by Diderot in his library, heard the Abbé Nollet lecture, met Jussieu and others.[42] Professionally, Rush's trip was a disappointment. He had received his M.D. at the University of Edinburgh only the year before. "I visited most of their hospitals and conversed with several of the principal physicians in Paris, and was sorry to find them at least fifty years behind the Physicians in England and Scotland in medical knowledge."[43] In his diary, *Traveling Through France,* which holds the attention, the genial Rush comments at length on French manners.[44] He even thought of a number of ways to compare the French to the North American Indians.

The French capital was always the great magnet. "It is amazing," declared one writer, "how many Americans there were in Paris during those brief years when revolution had ended in America and not yet commenced in France."[45] I have already dealt with a few of the persons he mentions. The reader will come across the names of some of the others in the ensuing comments touching on tourists, businessmen, and artists.

Foster Rhea Dulles calls Elkanah Watson "the first [American] tourist." Born in Plymouth, Massachusetts, Watson initially landed in France, as indicated above, in 1779. Unlike most tourists, he established a mercantile house, at Nantes, in the very year of his arrival. His *Memoirs,* in which he narrates his travels and reactions while in France, make pleasurable reading. "I trust," wrote Watson, "that our alliance and intercourse with France may enable us, as a nation, to shake off the leading-strings of Britain—the English sternness and formality of manner, retaining, however, sufficient of their gravity, to produce, with French ease and elegance, a happy compound of national character and manners, yet to be modeled. The influence of this alliance will tend to remove the deep prejudice against France."[46] A number of Americans, in addition to those previously mentioned, went to Paris in the 1780s, either as tourists or in other capacities. Dulles's book provides us with brief information concerning these travelers.[47] Among them were John Paul Jones, Thomas Paine,

Louis Littlepage, David Humphreys, William Short, John Ledyard, Thomas Lee Shippen, John Rutledge, Jr., and Mr. and Mrs. William Bingham, who cut a wide swath in the French capital. During the French revolutionary period itself many Americans resided in Paris or lived somewhere in France. Bizardel has established a list of more than two hundred who were in the country in the years 1789–99. Among them were the inventors James Rumsey and Robert Fulton. Several became officers in the French army. Quakers from Nantucket lived in Dunkerque and fished for whales. Some even knew the insides of Paris prisons because they were mistaken for Englishmen.[48] William Henry Vernon, of Rhode Island, spoke formally to the National Assembly on July 10, 1790.[49] He swore "amitié éternelle aux François." Eleven other citizens of the United States, among them Joel Barlow and John Paul Jones, signed this address. In response to it the president of the Assembly exclaimed, "Que les Américains & les François ne fassent qu'un Peuple: réunis de coeur, réunis de principes. . . . L'Assemblée Nationale vous offre les honneurs de sa Séance." In his *Diary* Robert C. Johnson, a Connecticut lawyer and tourist, wrote, "I mixed with the citizens and *saw Lewis the Sixteenth beheaded.*"[50] His underscoring still produces a mild shock.

As early as 1793 American businessmen and merchants began to buy properties that the state had taken over from the church and émigrés. Some even made money on their purchases of hôtels and châteaux, paying with devalued assignats, selling for gold or cash. One American won two houses in Paris in the national lottery and another a house that had belonged to Lafayette.[51]

Paris, of course, attracted American artists. Benjamin West arrived in 1763, John Singleton Copley ten years later. John Trumbull landed in France for the first time in 1780. Joseph Wright and John Vanderlyn, among others, also made their way to the capital.[52]

The National Assembly bestowed French citizenship upon George Washington, Alexander Hamilton, and James Madison.

Only Madison accepted it.[53] The National Convention made Thomas Paine and Joel Barlow citizens of France. Paine was elected to the convention. Barlow, a Yale graduate and one of the Connecticut Wits, campaigned for election to it from Savoy, but he was defeated.[54]

I have set down a few of the circumstances that brought Americans and French people together in revolutionary times. The associations were innumerable. For instance, we forget or may not be aware of the fact that Franklin knew Turgot and Beaumarchais, that John Adams was acquainted with the Abbé de Mably and Condorcet. "Did I know Baron Grimm while at Paris?" wrote Jefferson to Adams. "Yes, most intimately. He was the pleasantest, and most conversible member of the diplomatic corps while I was there: a man of good fancy, acuteness, irony, cunning, and egoism: no heart, not much of any science, yet enough of every one to speak its language. . . . I always supposed him to be of school of Diderot, D'Alembert, D'Holbach."[55] All these connections—personal, artistic, commercial, educational, military, and political—had a role to play in the creation of a somewhat different image of France from that formerly held in the United States. Protestant Americans, we have seen, had long feared, among other things, the Catholicism of the French. But despite their misgivings it was thought, as Gilbert Chinard pointed out so many years ago, that they had something to gain from the study of French economists, political thinkers, and scientists. The increase in travel abroad, and the presence of a large number of Americans in *la Ville lumière* and elsewhere in France advanced French-American cultural relations, helped allay old fears.

Americans hailed the French Revolution at the outset. Noah Webster wrote, "When the revolution in France was announced in America, his [Webster's] heart exulted with joy; he felt nearly the same interest in its success, as he did in the establishment of American Independence."[56] John Adams, writing later than Webster, declared, "The enthusiasm for . . . France and the French revolution, was at that time [1793], almost universal throughout the United States, but, in Pennsylvania, and especially in Philadelphia, the rage was irresistible. . . . . Marat, Robespierre, Brissot, and the Mountain, were the constant themes of panegyric and the daily toasts at table."[57] And, according to Cushing Strout, "in staid Boston Sam Adams, hero of the American Revolution, presided over a typical banquet in the middle of the winter of 1793 in which mass fervor for Liberty and Equality, mingled with a voracious appetite for food and liquor, so moved the people that in an ecstasy of civic good will the city's criminals were liberated from prison for a day." Strout goes on to say that "when Citizen Genêt, minister of the new Republic to the United States, arrived in the spring of that year, seeking American aid, he was greeted with elaborate enthusiasm, and his journey from Charleston was so studded with fêtes and ovations that it took him twenty-eight days to reach Philadelphia."[58] This widespread enthusiasm, however, would dwindle.[59]

The French Revolution, someone has said, "drew a red-hot ploughshare through the history of America as well as through that of France." The news of the execution of Louis XVI jarred emotions everywhere. Genêt's undiplomatic behavior as ambassador, his interference in their domestic affairs, infuriated many citizens of the United States. Washington's Proclamation of Neutrality (1793) in the war between France and England strained the alliance, angered many others here. Americans began to take sides. Party cleavage in the United States deepened. The sympathies of the Federalists (conservatives) under the leadership of Alexander Hamilton would lie with Great Britain and those of the Republicans (liberals, democrats), under Jefferson, with France. "Within an all too short period," Nathan Schachner writes, "the division between Francophobes and Francophiles, corresponding almost exactly with the split between Federalists and Republicans, grew so wide, deep and passionate that for the remainder of the era the more extreme of the participants on both sides were darkly certain that a similar revolution impended here."[60] Struggles between parties in both countries, political events, and the increasing abhorrence of American conservatives to the French Revolution itself would, by the end of the century, wipe out almost all the hard-earned gains in French-American understanding. Cultural relations inevitably suffered.

"Le grand schisme." This is the phrase Bernard Faÿ used to characterize the rift between the United States and France in the years 1795–1800. And such was indeed the case. The treaty negotiated in 1795 by John Jay with England antagonized the French. The publicity over the XYZ Affair in 1798 antagonized the Americans. An undeclared naval war with France between 1798 and 1801 smothered the spirit of good will and fraternity generated by the Alliance of 1778.[61] The Alien and Sedition Acts, passed by Congress in 1798, frightened French aliens in the United States and caused many of them to leave. Volney and Moreau de Saint-Méry, the Philadelphia bookseller, were among those who departed. A faction of the Federalist party pressed for a declaration of war on the allied nation. The United States repealed the treaties with France in 1798.

Conservative Americans would hold the "infidel philosophers" responsible for the coming of the French Revolution. In the decade following its outbreak, they were unsparing in the expression of their aversion to them. Some connected the French *philosophes* with the Illuminati, feared a conspiracy to destroy Christianity, overthrow governments, and exalt reason. Contemplating France in 1790 even John Adams said, "I know not what to make of a republic of thirty million atheists." There also appeared here a "literature" of hate, hatred of the French "monsters," numerous examples of which can be found in articles in the conservative gazettes. Such writings as *The Bloody Buoy* and *A Bone to Gnaw*, by William Cobbett, a British and pro-Federalist journalist, also helped arouse hateful emotions. Authors of this kind of literature sometimes wrote in gory detail of French revolutionary "atrocities."

It is easy to understand the attitude of many American clergymen toward Voltaire and certain other French writers of his time. We can accept the sincerity of their censures. But our understanding of the often heated opposition of some ministers to the *philosophes* is complicated by another factor—the political. Herbert M. Morais wrote, "Although French deists exerted some 'influence' upon a relatively small section of the American public, their 'influence' was exaggerated by Dwight [Timothy Dwight, president of Yale and a clergyman] and Payson [Seth Payson, also a clergyman], who, because of their Federalist affiliations, viewed with alarm the rise of Jeffersonianism which they sought to check by using the French bugaboo."[62]

The French Revolution was "refought" on this side of the Atlantic in the 1790s. Newspapers, the political platform, colleges, and even pulpits were the battlefields. Some Americans wore partisan badges on their hats—Federalists the black rosette, Republicans the tricolored cockade. Sympathizers with the Revolution organized Democratic clubs, drank countless Gallic toasts, sang martial songs—"La Marseillaise," the "Ça ira"—and, on occasion, addressed one another as "Citizen." Federalists sang "Yankee Doodle" and said "Mister." Phrases such as "the French mania" and "the French faction in this country" became clichés. Torrents of invective against France, Jefferson, and his fellow Republicans flowed from Federalist newspapers. Republican papers published vehement denunciations of the Federalists and defended France. Contention in the United States over French Enlightenment philosophy itself came about mainly in the years from around 1789 to 1801, approximately four decades later than was the case in France. But the smoke of battle between the pro-British and anti-French and the pro-French and anti-British partisans obscures our view of philosophical considerations and makes most difficult a proper assessment of the impact various French thinkers may have had here in this period of party strife.

John Fiske, historian and essayist, long ago wrote, "In 1800 the Federalists believed that the election of Mr. Jefferson meant the dissolution of the Union and the importation into America of all the monstrous notions of French Jacobinism. . . . New England clergymen entertained a grotesque conception of Jefferson as a French atheist, and I have heard my grandmother tell of how old ladies in Connecticut, at the news of his election, hid their family Bibles because it was supposed that his very first official act, perhaps even before announcing his cabinet, would be to issue a *ukase* ordering all copies of the sacred volume throughout the country to be seized and burned."[63]

Jefferson's accession to the presidency in 1801 marked the defeat of federalism, but his election did not put a stop to name-calling nor did it absolve him from continued accusations of guilt by association.

Three

The Fathers' Knowledge of French

 An amusing story is told of an experience James Madison had while a student at Princeton. As the only "French scholar" easily available, he was once called upon to act as interpreter for a Frenchman who had come to the college. According to the anecdote, Madison, "listening with all his might, was able to catch a few words . . . a glimmering" of what the "forlorn, way-worn" Frenchman was saying. Even more frustrated, Madison could not make himself understood. "I might as well have been talking *Kickapoo* at him!"[1] In 1776 the Continental Congress sent one of its members, Silas Deane, to France to seek crucial aid for the American colonies. There, Deane was obliged to work with Beaumarchais, secret agent of the French government. Deane assured Beaumarchais that he never spoke with English people in Paris. "We must conclude from this that he is the most silent man in France," wrote Beaumarchais to Vergennes, the French foreign minister, "for I defy him to say six consecutive words before Frenchmen."[2] Even Patrick Henry, on one occasion at least, was left speechless. As governor of Virginia, he received the visit of a Frenchman who could speak no English. The fiery patriot and orator could speak no French.[3] Shortly before the Declaration of Independence, John Adams lamented his own deficiency in French. "I every day see more and more that it will become a necessary accomplishment of an American gentleman or lady."[4] And so it went, in a time of crisis, in the little world of the

American forefathers. Inability to speak French was a cause of frustration to many. Some historians, moreover, have charged the forefathers with another shortcoming. I shall cite only one. Carl Becker wrote that "it does not appear that Jefferson, or any American, read many French books."[5]

In any attempt to assess the literary and intellectual impact of France on America in the time of the Founding Fathers questions with regard to the American knowledge of the French language inevitably arise. There is no desire on my part to exaggerate or to minimize the role of French here. There are indications enough, however, that we must be wary of assertions about the supposed unfamiliarity of eighteenth-century Americans with the language. And we must also be on guard against uncritical statements concerning the competency in spoken French of some of the American statesmen. Nor is there any desire to duplicate the fine work of Howard Mumford Jones[6] and many others. I too have collected over the years information similar to theirs. I intend rather to take a comprehensive view of the subject, and not to enter overmuch into detail. The French enclaves in America, it goes without saying, are excluded from this inquiry. I shall trace the fortune of the French language in the United States up to the end of the eighteenth century, point out or comment on whatever seems appropriate, and conclude with a series of linguistic portraits of some of the great public figures of the time.

First one can say that American interest in the French language developed only slowly in the eighteenth century. There were a number of reasons for this. Protestant Americans, at one time or another, feared both the Catholicism and the infidelity of Frenchmen. There was also the question of morals. Maurice Le Breton put it all very succinctly: "The main obstacle to a development of French culture in New England was of a religious character. Neither the Catholicism of the France of Louis XIV nor the deism of later days could escape the censure of the Puritans. The word French with them was too closely allied to extreme narrowness of views or loose morals, and often both. So, while quite willing to learn the language, because so 'useful' and so 'distinguishing' they were not at all disposed to let French ideas be preached to them under that disguise."[7]

In the light of Le Breton's remarks, it is hardly surprising to read that in 1724 Harvard refused a gift to its library by Thomas Hollis of London of Pierre Bayle's *Dictionnaire historique et critique* because, it was said, students could not read French. The college authorities made it clear, furthermore, that they wanted no more French books.[8] In 1778, still annoyed at the thought of his personal difficulties with French while abroad, Silas Deane wrote a letter to President Stiles of Yale in which he urged the establishment of a professorship of the French language in the college. Said Deane, "The French Language is spoken in great purity in most of the Swiss Cantons, particularly so at Geneva, whence a Professor might be obtained, whose principles as well as manners could not fail of being agreeable." President Stiles began consultations on the matter of the professorship, and in his *Diary* one finds this notation, "Mr. C—violently against because of Popery—others doubtful."[9]

Not all Protestant clergymen, however, were opposed to the learning of French. As far back as 1726, Cotton Mather, in his *Manuductio ad Ministerium,* had encouraged prospective ministers to undertake the study of French, saying "there is no Man who has the *French Tongue,* but ordinarily he speaks the neater *English* for it."[10] Mather of course was interested in the writings of French Protestants. Much later, President Witherspoon, of Princeton, recommended French as helpful in the ministerial calling because of the "sound calvinistic, reformation divinity" written in that language.[11]

With regard to Le Breton's comment concerning loose morals, let me point out that this fear was by no means limited to New England. As late as 1786 in Norfolk, Virginia, "the principal of the school was to appoint his assistants, all except the French tutor, who was to be appointed by the trustees."[12] And from Paris, Thomas Jefferson wrote in 1789, "The French language is unquestionably an important object of education. The habit of speaking it can only be acquired by conversation. This may be done either in France or Canada. . . . While learning the language in France a young man's morals, health and fortune are more irresistibly endangered than in any country of the universe: in Canada he would be acquiring a knoledge of the country and it's inhabitants which cannot fail to be useful in life to every American. On this point I have long ago made up my mind, that Canada is the country to which we should send our children to acquire a knoledge of the French tongue."[13]

Greek, Latin, and Hebrew requirements also delayed the development of the study of French in American colleges. These languages were core subjects in higher education. The classics had long enjoyed a monopoly. In the last half of the eighteenth century, Greek and Latin came under heavy attack. As early as 1749, Benjamin Franklin, in his *Proposals Relating to the Education of Youth in Pensilvania,* had insisted that "all should not be compell'd to learn *Latin, Greek,* or the modern foreign languages." The attacks on, as well as the defenses of, the teaching of the classical languages appear to have been more frequent in the late 1780s and in the 1790s. In 1782, Harvard had permitted students to substitute French for Hebrew, if they obtained special approval.[14] And in 1797, Harvard required students who had been excused from the study of Hebrew to take French.[15]

Political considerations also hindered the progress of French language study, at least until the American Revolution. But the Declaration of Independence meant a new beginning. The American insurgents were in desperate need of financial and military help. With the signing of the treaties between the United States and France in 1778 the old enemy became the ally. American interest in the French language indeed quickened. It was high time, for Le Breton affirms that "when the French officers of the army and navy came to Boston in the days of the Revolution, conversation with the American authorities had to be held in Latin."[16] Alluding to the close proximity of the French fleet, John

Eliot wrote to Jeremy Belknap in September 1782 that "it is necessary to talk French, or you would be a stranger in the streets of Boston."[17]

In a Baltimore newspaper in 1786 a writer, commenting on a plan for an academy, said, "*French* is the language most generally used. Boys should be taught to speak and write it with fluency and accuracy, after which they will seldom have cause to regret the want of other modern tongues."[18] The following year another newspaper writer ventured to say of French that in Philadelphia and New York "almost every youth speaks it more or less" and many men in Boston speak it well.[19] In its issue for February 1791, the *New York Magazine or Literary Repository* printed a five-page extract from Rivarol's celebrated essay *Of the Universality of the French Language*.

The influx of thousands of émigrés from France and Santo Domingo into the United States, beginning around 1792, increased concern with the idiom. The *New York Magazine*, in its March 1794 number, printed a "Histoire," three and a half pages in French, extracted from Saint-Evremond. The editor said, "As many of our young friends are now studying that language, which is daily becoming more interesting to us, we should be pleased with an exercise of their talents in a translation of this elegant story." A reader promptly came forth with a translation, which appeared in the next month's issue. A Boston minister's advice to a Harvard student in 1796 points up the momentous changes that time and circumstance had wrought. "An acquaintance with the French language is essential to a modern education. The [American] revolution has introduced us to the politest people on earth. Even before that event, there was a prevailing inclination to study their language. And long before a French instructor was employed by the university, some of the scholars added this to their other accomplishments."[20]

Despite the "prevailing inclination" and a long history of tutors and extracurricular instruction in the language, Harvard did not appoint its first "salaried" French instructor until 1787.[21]

The first Department of Modern Languages had been established at the College of William and Mary in 1779 and the second at Columbia College in 1784.[22] In 1784 also, the College of Rhode Island, today Brown University, solicited the aid of Louis XVI in establishing a professorship "of the French language and history in this our infant seminary."[23] At Princeton, French had been offered as an elective subject to the undergraduates as early as 1770.[24] At Yale the teaching of French was irregular, and the language was not officially recognized until 1825.[25]

Outside the colleges there was no scarcity of French teachers. Newspapers in the last half of the century are strewn with their advertisements.[26] Many also proposed to give lessons in dancing and *maintien* (posture). Instruction in the language, however, had been available here even in colonial times.[27] French was also considered by some to be important in the education of girls.[28] But others disagreed. This became a subject of controversy in the press.

We shall never know how many Americans studied, spoke, or read French in the eighteenth century. Compared with the total white population the number was surely small. But the prestige of French was great in the last half of the century. Much more attention was paid to it than to any other modern foreign language. Its growth in popularity was steady.

Chastellux, a major general and a traveler here, particularly in New England and Virginia, noted that a speaking knowledge of the language was far from common in America in the early 1780s, but "at least the importance of it is beginning to be felt."[29] Jefferson, writing from Paris in September 1785, made reference to "our country where the French language is spoken by very few."[30] Even in 1795 Jefferson would mention to Madame de Tessé as one of the obstacles to her coming to America the "little use here of your language."[31]

It is a fact that encouragement was not everywhere given to the learning of French. Many people regarded such learning merely as an "accomplishment." But the amount of earnest advice to young men particularly to acquire a knowledge of the language is both impressive and significant. Cotton Mather, Franklin, Thomas Jefferson repeatedly, John Clarke, all recommended the study of French. And so did others, among them William Smith, provost of the College of Philadelphia, Stephen Girard, John Witherspoon, Noah Webster, and Benjamin Rush. The study of the language was urged for many reasons—commercial, economic, jurisprudential, literary, medical, political, practical, scientific, social, and theological. There were competent American translators of French: Joel Barlow, Philip Freneau (for the State Department), Jefferson, John Quincy Adams, Noah Webster, Benjamin Franklin Bache, Charles Brockden Brown.

The weight of the evidence of a broad concern with French, given the small population of the country, is such that it is impossible to accept *obiter dicta* such as "we were practically limited to one language—the English," and "it was still a rare individual who could read any modern foreign language." To contest sweeping generalizations of this sort, I am constrained to acquaint the reader with a few particulars. I do so with reluctance because of the risk of distorting the picture by citing a handful of cases.

Charles Carroll of Carrollton, a signer of the Declaration of Independence, as a very young boy, had studied at a Jesuit college in France. John Witherspoon, also a signer, championed the study of French for several reasons, its utility in a new country being one of them. He himself taught the language for a while at Princeton. According to his biographer, "he spoke and read French easily." He could write letters in the language. But his pronunciation apparently left something to be desired. The marquis de Chastellux, who visited Princeton in 1780, wrote that "in accosting me he [Witherspoon] spoke French, but I easily perceived that he had acquired his knowledge of the language from reading, rather than conversation, which did not prevent me, however, from answering him, and continuing to converse with him in French, for I saw that he was well pleased to display what he knew of it."[32] The prince de Broglie, here with the French fleet, wrote of the Reverend Samuel Cooper of Boston that "although he expresses himself with difficulty in French, he understands it perfectly well, knows all our best authors."[33] Cooper was a leader of American political thought before 1776. Chastellux, in his *Travels in North America*, observed that William Bingham of Philadelphia, who had been an agent of the Continental Congress in Martinique, returned home with a "tolerable knowledge of French," and that John Laurens, an officer in the American Revolution, "speaks very good French." Alexander Graydon, also an officer in the army and an author, wrote in his *Memoirs* that he was able to read the language "with tolerable facility." A Swedish officer noted that John Paul Jones spoke "tolerably good French."[34] Robert Morris of Philadelphia, a signer, "financier of the American Revolution," and a member of the Federal Convention, sent sons to study at Passy. George Mason recommended a Marylander, Richard Harrison, to James Madison for a consular appointment in Spain. Harrison, said Mason, learned French in Martinique, where he "transacted a good deal of business for Virginia and some other of the United States in a manner that gave general satisfaction."[35] Mason, later to become a member of the Federal Convention from Virginia, urged his two sons in France to make the most of their opportunity to learn to speak French. John Jay, the first chief justice of the United States, studied French in his youth with Huguenots at New Rochelle. It is reported that Aaron Burr was probably "able to speak French quite fluently, but he commonly wrote it badly, and in a careless and slovenly manner."[36] Fisher Ames, Massachusetts statesman, could read but not speak French.[37] William Short, a Virginian, a founder of Phi Beta Kappa, and a diplomat, was Jefferson's private secretary when the latter was minister to France. When Jefferson returned home in 1789, Short became chargé d'affaires. He is reported by more than one scholar to have achieved a mastery of French. Jefferson said that Short wrote letters for him in that language. But as will be seen farther on, Short had not made any appreciable progress in spoken French in his first year in France. James Monroe was appointed minister to France in 1794. "All the members of the Minister's family learned to speak French fluently; by 1796 Monroe was sufficiently at ease to dispense with an interpreter at official interviews."[38] Noah Webster, as editor of the New York Federalist paper, the *Minerva,* "spent countless hours translating from French books, pamphlets, and newspapers, making abstracts and writing editorials for his columns."[39] "Benny" Bache, grandson of Dr. Franklin, was editor of the powerful democratic organ, the *Aurora.* According to Bernard Faÿ, "Bache spoke good French; one-third of the advertisements of his newspaper were in French. . . . [He] translated endless French documents and books. . . . He could translate readily and print quickly news and articles from the French papers, and he was the only newspaperman who could do so in Philadelphia."[40] Many another American was attracted to the study of French—such men as Ethan Allen; John Randolph of Roanoke; Charles Brockden Brown,[41] the novelist, mentioned above as a translator; and William Dunlap, the playwright.[42]

Well-known people—as well as lesser- and little-known—were far from being "practically limited to one language—the English." Many an American studied French. There is much that I must leave out. But the advertisements of textbooks, their availability,[43] and a solicitude about foreign language learning bear witness to an ever-increasing interest in French.

The earliest French textbook published in eighteenth-century America, to my knowledge, was *Some Short and Easy Rules Teaching the True Pronunciation of the French Language* (Boston: S. Kneeland, 1720). Its author was Thomas Blair, a tutor at Harvard. The most renowned, I believe, was published toward the end of the century. This was Joseph Nancrède's *L'Abeille françoise; ou, Nouveau recueil de morceaux brillans, des auteurs françois les plus célèbres* (Boston: Belknap and Young, 1792). Nancrède, Harvard's first "salaried" instructor in French, brought the book out for the use of the college's students. Faÿ pointed out that it had only eighty-two subscribers, but they included John Hancock, John Quincy Adams, James Lowell, Elisha Ticknor, and others—"tout le beau monde de Boston."[44] Other books directed to Americans learning French, also published here in the 1790s, might be mentioned. One was Bernardin de Saint-Pierre's *Voyages of Amasis* (Boston: I. Thomas and E. T. Andrews, 1795). Part of a more extensive work, *Voyages* has French and English texts on opposite pages. Another was Moreau de Saint-Méry's *Idée générale ou abrégé des sciences et des arts à l'usage de la jeunesse* (Philadelphia, 1796). And Nancrède published a book addressed "To the American Youth of Both Sexes." This was his edition of Fénelon's *The Adventures of Telemachus* (Philadelphia: G. Decombaz, 1797). In two volumes, this work too has French and English texts on opposite pages.

How best to learn modern languages was a question that evoked innumerable comments and responses. One or two instances will suffice. Noah Webster, in his essay *On the Education of Youth in America* (1790), wrote that French and other modern languages "should be learned early in youth, while the organs are yet pliable; otherwise the pronunciation will probably be imperfect." Benjamin Rush expressed the same sentiments, more or less, later on. In his essay *Of the Mode of Education Proper in a Republic* (1798), Rush said, "The state of the memory in early life is favorable to the acquisition of languages, especially when they are conveyed to the mind, through the ear. It is, moreover, in early life only, that the organs of speech yield in such a manner as to favour the just pronunciation of foreign languages." Good pronunciation was expected, as this criticism of an oration in French at a Harvard commencement, printed in the Boston *Columbian Centinel*, July 19, 1794, makes clear: "The French *Oration* was a good composition; but the delivery of it would have done honor to an Aboriginal Sachem, or a Hebrew Rabbi."

Countless individuals learned French here in the course of the century, however good, bad, or quaint their pronunciation might have been. And many people obviously could and did read the language. Books in French in various private libraries, the gradual accumulation of French titles in the catalogs of college libraries, and the occasional acquisition of books in the language by library companies and societies afford evidence of this. There are, moreover, other indications of readership, all of which contradict the statement above that "it was still a rare individual who could read any modern foreign language." Nancrède, for example, edited a weekly French newspaper, *Le Courier de Boston,* which began publication in April 1789 and ran for six months. He said that "three quarters of our subscribers are Americans."[45] And with reference to the some 250 novels and romances in French in Hocquet Caritat's circulating library in New York City at the turn of the century, George G. Raddin, Jr., wrote, "Certainly the attempt to circulate these books . . . bespeaks a representative public able to read French."[46]

So far I have been mostly concerned in this essay with the French language in the times of the Founding Fathers. In one connection or another I have had occasion to refer to a number of the Fathers: John Adams, Ames, Burr, Carroll, Franklin, Hancock, Henry, Jay, Jefferson, Madison, Mason, Robert Morris, Rush, and Witherspoon. Let me now direct attention, with regard to their knowledge of French, to some of the principal Founding Fathers. Selected for consideration, and based almost entirely on published sources, are the cases of Washington, Franklin, John Adams, Jefferson, James Madison, Benjamin Rush, Alexander Hamilton, and Gouverneur Morris.[47]

In an essay on "Washington and the French" Jules Jusserand pointed out that "Washington's acquaintance with things French began early" and that he was "a pupil of the French Huguenot Maryes, who kept a school at Fredericksburg."[48] Washington had many French titles in his library in the original and in translation.[49] He encouraged the study of French within the family circle. He was most solicitous concerning the progress of his stepson and his nephews in this language. As early as 1771 he wrote that "to be acquainted with the French Tongue, is become a part of polite Education; and to a Man who has any [prospect] of mixing in a large Circle absolutely [necessary.]" And as late as 1797, advising a relative on his studies, he pointed out that "the French language is now so universal, and so necessary with foreigners, or in a foreign country, that I think you would be injudicious not to make yourself a master of it."

Washington himself bought French dictionaries and books. But in spite of his great interest the "Father of his Country" could not understand, read, or speak French. His own correspondence is sufficient proof. To Philadelphia bookdealers Boinod and Gaillard he wrote: "Your Books [are] chiefly in a foreign Language (which I do not understand)." And in a letter to the marquis de Chastellux, thanking him for presenting him with a copy of the enlarged and corrected French edition of his *Voyages*, he speaks of Colonel Humphreys, then a visitor at Mount Vernon, having put into his hands "the translation of that part [of the *Voyages*] in which you say such, and so many handsome things of me." A letter to Lafayette is the most candid of all.

> You are pleased my dear Marquis to express an earnest desire of seeing me in France (after the establishment of our Independency) . . . but remember my good friend, that I am unacquainted with your language, that I am too far advanced in years to acquire a knowledge of it, and that to converse through the medium of an interpreter upon common occasions, especially with the *Ladies* must appr. so extremely aukward, insipid, and uncouth, that I can scarce bear it in idea.[50]

It was precisely with the ladies that Benjamin Franklin's French was perhaps at its best. He wrote, or endeavored to write, *billets doux* in this language when past the canonical age of seventy. Of greater significance was his own recognition of the prestige and power of French in the eighteenth century. Franklin knew full well the service French could render to the American revolutionary cause. "As French is the political Language of Europe," he wrote, "it has communicated an Acquaintance with our Affairs very extensively."[51] And in a letter to Noah Webster in 1789 Franklin acknowledged the cultural universality of the

French language, noting at the same time that "our English bids fair to obtain the second place."[52]

Franklin had begun the study of languages at the age of twenty-six. "I soon made myself so much a master of the French as to be able to read the books in that language with ease." This self-evaluation concerning his reading skill, to be found in the *Autobiography*,[53] was entirely just. His subsequent career and correspondence prove that his reading knowledge of French served him often and well. In this connection it is of interest to note that he did not like translations; translations, he felt, never did justice to the originals.

In serious matters Franklin did not trust himself to write French. Great caution should be exercised before accepting as authentic some letters in this language, purportedly of Franklin's composition. It is not burdensome to copy in one's own hand, and sign, a letter which has been translated or drafted by an obliging French friend. There exist a number of letters in French in Franklin's handwriting. Some of these letters are neat, well written; others are filled with erasures and corrections. One can safely say that the latter were of Franklin's own composition.[54] He was not unduly inhibited, however, when composing, or trying to compose, letters and *bagatelles* in French sent to ladies such as Madame Brillon de Jouy and Madame Helvétius.[55] Witty and amorous, these make very amusing reading despite the imperfect French.

Franklin lived in France almost a decade, from 1776 to 1785. He was named minister plenipotentiary in September 1778. He had also been in France on two occasions prior to 1776. How well, really, could he speak and understand French? Some light is thrown on this question by John Adams, who, with an appointment as commissioner of the Continental Congress in his pouch, had arrived in Paris in April 1778. In the very month of his arrival Adams jotted down in his *Diary:*

> Dr. Franklin was reported to speak french very well, but I found upon attending critically to him that he did not speak it, grammatically, and upon my asking him sometimes whether a Phrase he

had used was correct, he acknowledged to me, that he was wholly inattentive to the grammar. His pronunciation too, upon which the French Gentlemen and Ladies complemented him very highly and which he seemed to think pretty well, I soon found was very inaccurate, and some Gentlemen of high rank afterwards candidly told me that it was so confused, that it was scarcely possible to understand him. Indeed his Knowledge of French, at least his faculty of speaking it, may be said to have commenced with his Embassy to France. He told me that when he was in France some Years before, Sir John Pringle was with him, and did all his conversation for him, as his Interpreter, and that he understood and spoke French, with great difficulty, untill his present Residence, although he read it.[56]

Seven years after Adams had recorded his own observations in his *Diary,* Franklin himself disclosed his difficulties with French, revealed something of his progress, or lack of it, in the language. Less than two months before his final departure for America, after nine long years in France, the good doctor wrote a letter on the subject of glasses. It was he, one recalls, who invented bifocals. Hear what he had to say:

As I wear my [bifocal] Spectacles constantly, I have only to move my Eyes up or down, as I want to see distinctly far or near, the proper Glasses being always ready. This I find more particularly convenient since being in France, the Glasses that serve me best at Table to see what I eat . . . [and] the best to see the Faces of those on the other Side of the Table who speak to me; and when one's Ears are not well accustomed to the Sounds of a Language, a Sight of the Movements in the Features of him that speaks helps to explain; so that I understand French better by the help of my Spectacles.[57]

Franklin and Adams provide a study in contrasts. Franklin was leisurely, tolerant, and unpretentious; Adams was aggressive, morally rigorous, and ambitious. Adams's approach to French was typical of the man. His first stay in France lasted little more than a year. He was in his forties at the time. During this comparatively brief residence he made a frontal attack on the French language. The record of his year's work in French is one of mortification and hope, dejection and pride, frustration and disillusionment, and of high linguistic resolve for the future.

When he arrived in the French capital Adams confessed that he was looked upon as "a Man of whom Nobody had ever heard before, a perfect Cypher, a Man who did not understand a Word of French." Feverishly, he set out to get a working knowledge of the language. He proposed to learn spoken French in his own way. "I had not been a month, as yet, in France, nor three Weeks in Passi, but I had seized every moment that I could save from Business, company or Sleep to acquire the language. I took with me the Book to the Theatre, and compared it line for Line and word for Word, with the pronunciation of the Actors and Actresses, and in this Way I found I could understand them very well. Thinking this to be the best course I could take, to become familiar with the language and its correct pronunciation, I determined to frequent the Theatres as often as possible." Adams also made other plans in order to become conversant with French. But he came to regret that he had not employed a teacher—this was "an egregious Error."

Adams's assiduity apparently bore fruit. Less than a year after his arrival he made this notation in his *Diary:* "Went to Versailles, in order to take Leave of the Ministry. Had a long Conversation, with the Comte De Vergennes, in french, which I found I could talk as fast as I pleased." He hated to leave France, and he did not mind telling why. "I have just acquired enough of the Language to understand a Conversation, as it runs at a Table . . . to conduct all my Affairs myself . . . and understand all the Prattle of the Shop keeper—or I can sit down with a Gentleman, who will have a little Patience to speak a little more distinctly than common, and to wait a little longer for my Sentences than common, and maintain a Conversation pretty well."

But leave France he must. Reluctantly therefore, Adams departed but not without taking with him some well-considered opinions as to the quickest and best means of learning French. Musing, for example, on the "two ways of learning french commonly recommended—take a Mistress and go to the Commedie," he concluded, "Perhaps both would teach it soonest, to be sure sooner than either. But . . . the Language is no where better spoken than at the Comedie." To plays then he would go as often as possible, to the law courts to hear cases, and to churches to hear sermons. He would eat at taverns because "after a few Coups du Vin [peoples'] Tongues run very fast," and he would frequent the shops because "the female Shop keepers are the most chatty in the World." John Adams was sure that "these are the Ways to learn the Language, and if to these are Added, a dilligent study of their Grammars, and a constant Use of their best Dictionaries, and Reading of their best Authors, a Man in one Year may become a greater Master in it."

Sailing homeward, Adams engaged in shipboard conversations with Barbé-Marbois, a newly appointed member of the French legation in the United States. Adams, in one of these conversations, said "that it was often affirmed that Mr. Franklin spoke French as fluently and elegantly, as a Courtier at Versailles, but every Man that knew and spoke sincerely, agreed that he spoke it very ill. Persons spoke of these Things, according to their affections." Barbé-Marbois, Adams relates, "said it was Flattery. That he would not flatter, it was very true that both Mr. F. and I spoke french, badly."

Adams's *Diary* is a treasure trove of information pertaining to his French and that of others. He noted, among other things, that his fellow commissioner to seek aid in France for the American revolutionary cause, Arthur Lee, "spoke french with tolerable ease."[58]

Jefferson yielded to none of his contemporaries in his awareness of the political, scientific, and cultural importance of French. He encouraged its study in his family and among his friends and protégés. His successful efforts in support of the study of French and other modern languages in the curriculum of higher education in America are well known. He was interested in linguistic methodology.[59] And his library shelves were crowded with books in French.

Jefferson began his study of the language early. At the age of nine he was placed by his father in the Latin school. "My teacher, Mr. Douglas, a clergyman from Scotland, with the rudiments of the Latin and Greek languages, taught me the French."[60] Dumas Malone, in *Jefferson and His Time,* has little good to say about William Douglas as a modern language teacher. When Jefferson left William and Mary College at the age of eighteen, he was said to have been "remarkably proficient" in French.[61] His reading ability is of course incontestable. He also showed himself to be an able and discerning translator of the language.[62] What of his ability to speak and write French?

Jefferson represented the United States as special envoy and as minister to France during the years 1784–89. One year after his arrival there, he revealed in a letter his difficulties with the spoken language. "Patsy [his daughter Martha] . . . speaks French as easily as English, whilst Humphries, Short and myself are scarcely better at it than when we landed."[63] Jefferson, according to Kenneth Umbreit, "was unwilling to trust himself to oral negotiations in French. . . . He usually wrote in English."[64] Whatever his progress in speaking and writing the language in the latter part of his stay in Paris, Jefferson, two years after he had arrived in the capital, still lacked confidence in his ability to express himself clearly in French when putting pen to paper. This diffidence is seen in a letter that he wrote to Hector St. John de Crèvecoeur from Paris on July 11, 1786: "Being unable to write in French so as to be sure of conveying my meaning, or perhaps any meaning at all, I will beg of you to interpret what I now have the honour to write."[65] But Jefferson did compose some "informal letters" in the language.[66]

James Madison owned, ordered from Europe, and borrowed from Jefferson many books in French.[67] The "Father of the Constitution" made good use of them. As a boy of eleven he had entered a school kept by a Scotsman, Donald Robertson, where he studied French—reading it, he said, "*as a dead language.*" Even worse was the pronunciation acquired. "From Donald Robertson, as Madison discovered to his subsequent chagrin and ultimate amusement, he learned to speak French with a broad Scotch accent. Knowledge of this fact caught up with him at Princeton, though not from any superior French scholarship at that institution."[68] Madison's knowledge of the spoken language must have been exceedingly shaky. Jefferson wrote from Paris in 1787 urging him to "learn French" from Madame de Bréhan, then a visitor here.

Benjamin Rush, the distinguished Philadelphia physician and signer of the Declaration of Independence, knew French. In 1774, Benjamin Franklin addressed a letter to Rush from London, saying, "I now write to you as one of the Secretaries of our Philosophical Society [the American] who understands French, to request your Attention to the enclos'd Papers and that you would translate them for the Use of the Society."[69] In 1779, John Adams wrote to Rush saying, "You speak French so perfectly . . . that I wish you to be acquainted with the Chevalier De la Luzerne, and Mr. Marbois."[70]

Rush had studied French when a student in Britain. He stated that he made himself a "master" of it in a summer and part of a fall, having as a teacher "a man of uncommon genius."[71] He received his medical degree at the University of Edinburgh in 1768. Many years later he would write to John Adams that "I have found much more benefit from the French than I ever found from the Latin or Greek in my profession."[72]

Rush was a great advocate of the study of French—by male Americans. For several reasons set forth in his *Thoughts upon Female Education* (1787), he did not believe that French should be made a part of the education of American ladies. Noah Webster did not think so either. Except for the American woman, Benjamin Rush did not tire of publicly recommending the study of both French and German. In 1788 he proposed *A Plan for a Federal University*. These languages should be taught in this university, and a knowledge of them should become "an essential part of the education of a legislator of the United States."[73] In his essay *Of the Mode of Education Proper in a Republic* (1798), he insisted that the two languages be taught in all colleges and "that a degree should never be conferred upon a young man who cannot speak or translate them."

Alexander Hamilton and Gouverneur Morris both began to learn French early in life—Hamilton in the West Indies and Morris at New Rochelle. The mother of each was of Huguenot extraction. Hamilton, according to his son, "wrote and spoke [French] with the ease of a native."[74] Morris, on the authority of one of his biographers, "knew the French language as few of his contemporaries knew it, and wrote it with somewhat prolix but often spritely grace."[75]

Both men's French served them and their country well in the American Revolution. Hamilton's "command of the French language . . . made him useful and welcome" in contacts with foreign officers.[76] Morris acted as interpreter for his chief, Robert Morris, superintendent of finance (and no relation), in all of Robert Morris's dealings with the chevalier de la Luzerne, French minister to the United States.[77] Gouverneur Morris, the "Penman of the Constitution," would find his knowledge of French especially valuable when he assumed office as United States minister to France in 1792.

In retrospect, many factors influenced the development of interest in French in eighteenth-century America. Americans had first to surmount prejudices, often deeply ingrained, against France and Frenchmen before there could be any extensive concern with the language itself. The industrious French-speaking Huguenot population surely served as a leaven in moderating bias. Swiss from the French cantons also contributed in some measure to the advancement of the foreign idiom. Albert Gallatin, for instance, was born in Geneva. As a young man he taught French for a year at Harvard and later became secretary of the treasury under Thomas Jefferson. The Scotch teachers of French likewise had a hand in breaking down old barriers that had obstructed the progress of French here—Thomas Blair in Cambridge, clergymen such as William Douglas and Donald Robertson in Virginia, and especially John Witherspoon, the Scottish-American Presbyterian minister who became president of Princeton. He was an enthusiastic advocate of the study of French. Perhaps the Quaker example also helped. Quakers and their children studied the language.

The Declaration of Independence and the American Revolution brought a reversal of traditional opinion and policy. War was the paramount factor in influencing change. Just as the American contribution to victory in World War I gave a decided impetus to French curiosity about the United States, its literature and language, so in the War of the Revolution the French contribution to American victory over England heightened American interest in the language and literature of France. The growth and spread of this interest here is an incontrovertible fact.

Unfortunately, political events at the end of the century, referred to in the preceding essay, produced a contrary result. Jay's Treaty with England angered France. The machinations of Talleyrand, French foreign minister, in the XYZ Affair, an attempt to bribe and intimidate American envoys in Paris, when publicized, infuriated this country. The undeclared naval war with France worsened the now fragile connection. And finally, as we have seen, great numbers of people in the United States had long and vehemently opposed what they considered the ungodly French Revolution.[78] All these occurrences caused a heavy surf of Gallophobia. The repeal in 1798 of the treaties with France terminated the alliance. Cultural relations inevitably suffered. In many if not most places, the desire to learn French disappeared. The language was dropped from college curricula.[79] In America, French undoubtedly lost much ground as the century drew to a close.

Four

French Literature

Caritat's great circulating library on Pearl Street, later Broadway, must have been, for browsers and lovers of French fiction, one of New York City's more attractive spots. Opened in 1797, the library published a catalog of its holdings in 1804. It lists more than two hundred titles in this category of literature.[1] One could find at Caritat's Laclos's *Les Liaisons dangereuses* in French or English, a French edition of Restif de la Bretonne's *Le Paysan perverti,* and a copy in English of *Le Sopha,* by Crébillon *fils*. The knowledge of the early availability of such novels as these is tantalizing. It leads one to question seriously the correctness of assertions by some scholars that eighteenth-century Americans knew little or nothing about French literature. Harvey Gates Townsend, for instance, writes, "Before the Revolutionary War . . . we were practically limited to one language—the English. . . . Even at the time of the transcendental movement, it was still a rare individual who could read any modern foreign language."[2] And Carl Becker, as previously noted, felt constrained to assert, "It does not appear that Jefferson, or any American, read many French books." A sweeping statement, and especially with regard to the third president of the United States. On the list of books Jefferson proposed in 1771 to Robert Skipwith as a library, there were many names of prominent French authors.[3] Jefferson was then only twenty-eight. The books recommended were to be read in English translation. In his own collection, he had a great number of books in French. Their titles are arrayed in the five volumes of E. Millicent Sowerby's *Catalogue of the Library of Thomas Jefferson.*

One could write another monograph on John Adams's, the second president's, knowledge of French authors.[4] James Madison, the fourth president, read French books constantly from his youth until his death.[5] The reading of innumerable American contemporaries of these men was by no means confined solely to English. For instance, James Kent, a Columbia University law professor, jurist, and author of the *Commentaries on American Law,* wrote that he had begun the study of French in 1789, that by the year 1793 he had become a master of the language "and read the authors with facility." Among the authors whose writings he mentioned as having read were Corneille, Sévigné, Fénelon, Montesquieu, Rousseau, Marmontel, and Barthélemy.[6] And William Dunlap, the playwright, noted in his *Diary* on November 9, 1797, "I bought . . . an Octavo close printed French edition of Buffon." On the following page he jotted down, "Read in Buffon."[7]

American culture, until well into the nineteenth century, was derivative. The greater part of the books purchased in the United States in the eighteenth century came from or via England. But acquaintance with the literary productions of France was far more extensive than some have been ready to admit. To belittle the acquaintance of Americans with the literature of France, without taking the American cultural background into account, is presumptuous and profitless. An awareness of readership, reading interests, and book availability is indispensable. I have dealt with these subjects elsewhere.[8] But whether Americans read this literature in the original language or in English translation does not greatly matter. Far more important was their introduction to French writers.

Bookstores and booksellers abounded. Russel B. Nye writes that Boston had fifty bookstores in the 1770s and Philadelphia "probably thirty or more."[9] The catalog of a Boston bookseller, Benjamin Guild, published about 1790 offered "nearly a thousand titles of books of English, French and classical origin," and the catalog of books for sale or circulation by a Salem bookdealer in 1791 was "larger than Guild's in size, but much the same in content."[10] Moreau de Saint-Méry was a prominent Philadelphia bookseller and publisher. Albert Schinz has analyzed a catalog of books which he offered for sale in 1795.[11] Thirty of its seventy-six pages are devoted to French books.

The catalogs of libraries of various sorts—private, college, social, and circulating—provide firsthand information concerning French book holdings. The circulating library was a particularly serviceable institution. Michael Kraus found that by 1800 Connecticut alone had more than a hundred such libraries.[12] Two large New York City libraries of this type were those of Garrat Noel and Hocquet Caritat. Even as early as 1763 Noel's library was thought "to contain several thousand volumes."[13]

The anthology, however limited the number of readers, cannot be ignored in any cultural survey. *L'Abeille françoise* (Boston: Belknap and Young, 1792) is a classic example. This is a collection of prose extracts from French authors. Containing 339 pages of reading matter, it is one of the earliest French textbooks printed in the United States for American students.[14] Michel Martel's *Elements* (New York: C. C. Van Alen, 1796) is also an example. This textbook, dedicated to Theodosia Burr, Aaron's daughter, who had studied French with Martel, was intended for young people, especially *demoiselles*. Others were Robert Bell's *Illuminations for Legislators, and for Sentimentalists* (Philadelphia, 1784), and Mathew Carey's *The School of Wisdom* (Philadelphia, 1800). So much now for collections of literary pieces.

Howard Mumford Jones, in one of his many articles, said that "the character and amount of American interest in French literature during the last half of the eighteenth century is among the difficult problems of comparative literature." A partial solution of this problem, particularly as it relates to literature other than philosophic and scientific, is offered here. Philosophic writings are dealt with elsewhere. Let me first point out a few bibliographical sources that one may consult on matters concerning this literature during the American Enlightenment. *Qui scit ubi scientia sit, ille est proximus habenti* (F. Brunetière). Mention of and comments on the French authors whose books were well and widely received follow. My conclusions as to the character and amount of American interest in French literature in the last forty years of the century come afterward.

For literature in English and French published in the United States see especially Clifford K. Shipton and James E. Mooney, *National Index of American Imprints Through 1800: The Short Title Evans* (1969). This is an excellent tool to which I am much indebted for information contained in these pages. For translations from the French printed in America through 1820, consult the admirable work of Forrest Bowe.[15]

The newspaper is an invaluable research tool. Scholars have examined the papers of cities, towns, colonies, and states for their own purposes and projects. Two instances shall suffice. Howard Mumford Jones used New York and Philadelphia papers in studies on the importation of French literature into these cities.[16] His two articles merit careful consideration. Mary E. Loughrey also made good use of newspapers in her book *France and Rhode Island, 1686–1800* (New York: King's Crown Press, 1944). Booksellers' advertisements appear rather regularly in the papers. See, for early examples, the long lists of books for sale in the *Boston Gazette,* November 30, 1761, and in the *Maryland Gazette* (Annapolis), August 26, 1762. They included writings of Rabelais, Ninon de Lenclos, Fénelon, Le Sage, and Voltaire. Anecdotes about French authors, paragraphs concerning them, and quotations from their works also enliven the pages and articles of these weekly and daily publications. One could read much later, for instance, a biography of Malesherbes in the *Gazette of the United States* for February 10, 1798. Editors sometimes printed even lengthy excerpts from French books, in English translation of course, to amuse, instruct, or fill up space—and all too often without acknowledgment of source. This practice alone rules out the feasibility of any undertaking to identify the authors;

polymaths are not available for such work. An examination of newspapers is rewarding, but time-consuming because of the absence of indexes, or at least indexes broad in scope. Anyone with a particular project in mind must go through them anew. Frank Luther Mott has found that "in all, 202 papers were being published January 1, 1801."[17] Would that there were comprehensive indexes for all the more important American newspapers during the Enlightenment! I know of only one: Lester J. Cappon and Stella F. Duff, *Virginia Gazette Index 1736–1780* (Williamsburg: Institute of Early American History and Culture, 1950). This is an excellent historical work of reference in two volumes.

Magazines also provide valuable information. Mott in his book *A History of American Magazines 1741–1850* (1957) states that about seventy-five of them were begun during the years 1783–1801. For some findings from studies of these periodicals see Adrian H. Jaffe, *Bibliography of French Literature in American Magazines in the Eighteenth Century* (East Lansing: Michigan State College Press, 1951). Jaffe's booklet must be supplemented by the *Index to Early American Periodicals to 1850*, edited by Nelson F. Adkins (New York: Readex Microprint, 1964). An older study is that of Charles Dean Cool, "French Literature in American Magazines Prior to 1830" (Ph.D. dissertation, University of Wisconsin, 1909).

There is no statistical standard by which one can compare quantitatively the reception of French authors and their writings in the United States in our period. But David Lundberg and Henry F. May have attempted to develop statistical information on the reception of certain major authors of the European Enlightenment. To do this they used booksellers' auction or sales catalogs, and libraries of all sorts in the period from 1700 to 1813.[18] Much more important than statistics of course is the nature of a writer's impact. Let me turn, then, to the French authors whose writings were well and in many cases widely received. With very few exceptions this general survey does not aim to establish any order of precedence of one writer over another.

Fénelon was highly esteemed. Magazines printed biographical sketches of the author.[19] A number of editions of his great didactic novel, *Les Aventures de Télémaque* (1699), in both French and English, as well as a bilingual edition, were published here.[20] Newspapers up and down the Atlantic coast carried advertisements of it.[21] Copies were everywhere. *Télémaque* was, for example, on the shelves of Maryland libraries.[22] It was "popular" in colonial Virginia.[23] Interest in this Homeric novel was indeed widespread and of long duration. Its first American reader whose name I know was Richard Hickman of Williamsburg. An inventory of his books, recorded in 1732, shows that he owned "Telemachus, French."[24] *Telemachus* was listed in the 1744 edition of "A Catalogue of Some of the Most Valuable Authors . . . Proper to Be Read by the Students" at Columbia.[25] The son of a president of Harvard "was reading" it with Nathaniel Gardner, "a resident graduate" at the college in 1748.[26] Many years later, a Massachusetts minister, John Clarke, wrote to another Harvard student, said to have been John Pickering, "I hope soon to hear that you have made considerable progress in Telemachus, delighted equally with the style as with the sentiment."[27] A Philadelphia poet, Elizabeth Graeme Ferguson, had long since translated the entire novel into English heroic couplets.[28] From Dumfries, Virginia, on May 21, 1797, Parson Weems, peddler of books in the South for Mathew Carey, Philadelphia publisher and bookseller, sent this message to Carey: "Telemaque Eng. & French are *much, much* Wanted . . . it were well to put them for Dumfries as soon as possible."[29] In this same year, a New York publisher brought out another edition of the novel in English, in two volumes. George Washington's library contained the publisher's presentation copy of this edition.[30] There is good justification for having gone into such detail concerning this masterpiece. In his study of the popular book in the United States, James D. Hart writes, "Voltaire may have been the most popular French author, but no single book of his seems to have been so well read as was Fénelon's *Télémaque*."[31] Agreed! Said one reader, "I have entertained myself all day reading *Telemachus*. It is really delightful, and very improving."[32] People the country over must have found it so. A few of Fénelon's minor pieces were also published here before the eighteenth century came to a close. But not his treatise, *Traité de l'éducation des filles* (1687). John Witherspoon, president of the College of New Jersey (Princeton), cited it in writing on education.[33] According to V. L. Collins, "Fénelon appears to have been carefully studied by him and is easily his favorite author after Montesquieu."[34]

Rousseau's novel *La Nouvelle Héloïse*, first published in French in 1761, was one of the two greatest *succès de librairie* in eighteenth-century France. This novel, in English translation, was also highly successful here. And his pedagogical novel, *Emile*, enjoyed a vogue in the United States.

Another favorite author was Bernardin de Saint-Pierre, an immediate disciple of Rousseau. His famous exotic and "idyllic" novel *Paul et Virginie* (1787) was widely liked, found on the shelves of private, circulating, and other types of libraries. It was published in the United States in a bilingual edition, French and English on opposite pages, and in French and English editions, two of which appeared under the title of *Paul and Mary* instead of *Paul and Virginia*. Parson Weems called it a book of "high fame," a "sweet and improving piece." In February 1801 he berated Mathew Carey for not having sent him books like this, saying, "I ought . . . to know at this time of day, what books will suit & sell well."[35] Saint-Pierre's *Etudes de la nature* (1784), in Henry Hunter's English translation, was also read by many. Isaiah Thomas printed an edition of this work in English for Joseph Nancrède in 1797.[36] This three-volume set was dedicated to George Washington, as president. The book furnished arguments to combat atheism. In an advertisement of it by William Young, a Philadelphia bookseller, in the *Gazette of the United States,* June 2, 1798, one reads, "The avidity with which the clergy and other learned characters in New-England have purchased the English edition of this delightful performance, and the opinion entertained by them, and warranted by experience, that although written before the 'Age of Reason,' a part of it contains a more solid and compleat refutation of it, than any thing published since, are perhaps a sufficient recommendation of the STUDIES OF NATURE, in which the Botanist, the natural and christian Philosopher, the friend of order and government are equally interested, and by which they will be equally gratified." Magazines printed extracts from this work.[37] John Clarke wrote in the letters to a student at Harvard cited above, "The Studies of St. Pierre will afford you much entertainment. If his philosophy is sometimes lame, his language is good." William Dunlap, the playwright, having the *Studies* in mind, found Saint-Pierre "very shallow" as a "reasoner." Some of the French writer's ideas on science did not go down well with Americans, particularly his rejection of Newton's theory of tides, and his own explanation of them. Said Samuel Miller, "Surely this and some other of his doctrines are utterly unworthy of a mind which had been conversant with the inquiries and the writings of the great practical philosophers of the eighteenth century."[38] I shall mention only two other publications of Saint-Pierre in the United States, the *Voyages of Amasis* and the *Indian Cottage (La Chaumière indienne)*. With French and English texts on opposite pages, this edition of *Amasis* was offered to those learning French as an alternative to a similar edition of *Telemachus*. The translators suggested that it might be better suited, prove of greater utility, to this country than Fénelon's novel "designed for the education of a prince." Samuel Miller, minister and polymath, probably spoke for most Americans in saying, "The fictitious writings of M. De St. Pierre, Madame Genlis, and M. Florian are worthy of particular distinction, especially on account of their pure moral tendency."[39]

Alain René Le Sage was also a favored author. *The History and Adventures of Gil Blas de Santillane* turns up almost everywhere. It was advertised in the *South Carolina Gazette* in 1753. It was "popular" in Virginia.[40] In Maryland in the years 1700–1776, this pica-

resque novel was apparently "the most read foreign book except-
ing Voltaire's historical works, judging from the number of
times it was mentioned."[41] In Boston in 1786 the manager of a
circulating library complained in the *Independent Chronicle* that
Gil Blas, along with a few other titles, "had been absent more
than two months, to the 'great disappointment of the Subscribers
and disgrace of the establishment.' "[42] In the Philadelphia *General
Advertiser,* August 14, 1792, one finds a long paragraph of criticism, which could be indigenous, devoted to Le Sage. The writer
asserts that *Gil Blas* will be read "long after Voltaire's physical
and metaphysical novels and romances shall be forgotten." English translations of *Gil Blas* were published here, as was *Le
Diable boiteux; or, The Devil upon Two Sticks,* an edition of the
latter novel having French and English texts on opposite pages.
According to Frank Luther Mott, *Gil Blas* was a "better seller" in
this country in the year 1790.[43] He finds that of all French fiction
published in English translation in the United States before the
end of the eighteenth century only this novel of Le Sage and
Rousseau's *The New Eloisa,* in 1796, attained to such distinction.

Madame de Genlis was a prolific author of novels, children's
books, plays, and writings on education. Several of her things
were published in English in the United States in the period
under consideration. The reader can find the titles in Bowe,
French Literature in Early American Translation. Ruth Halsey
writes, "Many educated people regarded [her books] as particularly suitable for their daughters, both in the original text and in
the English translations."[44] Mary S. Benson finds that Madame
de Genlis was one of the very few writers who were considered
here as "authorities on female character and education" and
whose works "exerted marked influence on American thought"
in the 1780s and 1790s.[45] Her play, *Zélie,* was translated and
adapted by Mrs. Elizabeth Inchbald. Entitled *The Child of Nature,* it was performed many times in different cities along the
eastern seaboard.[46] Her *Theatre of Education* and *Sacred Dramas,*
as well as writings of many other French authors mentioned in

these pages, were listed in Thaddeus M. Harris's *A Selected Catalogue of Some of the Most Esteemed Publications in the English Language, Proper to Form a Social Library, With an Introduction upon the Choice of Books* (Boston, 1793). Harris was the librarian of Harvard.[47]

Young people read *The Children's Friend* and *The Looking-Glass for the Mind*, translations of writings of Arnaud Berquin. A number of editions of these books were printed here. "For half a century [*The Looking-Glass for the Mind*] was to be found in the shop of all booksellers, and had its place in the library of every family of means."[48]

Americans read history with avidity. Charles Rollin and Voltaire stood in the forefront in this category of the "literature of knowledge." As early as 1749, Franklin recommended Rollin's "Ancient and Roman Histories" for consideration by the trustees of the Philadelphia Academy for "The Third Class."[49] A Boston bookseller advertised Rollin's "Ancient History 10 vol" in the *Boston Gazette,* November 30, 1761, and a Maryland bookdealer offered his "Roman History, 16 Vols." for sale in the *Maryland Gazette,* August 26, 1762. Smart found the *Ancient History* "fairly common" in libraries in colonial Virginia. For its fortune in the private libraries of North Carolina, consult the thorough study of Stephen B. Weeks.[50] The *Ancient History* seems to surface more often in this country than Rollin's other books, even though his *The Life of Alexander the Great* was published in Providence in 1796. In this same year John Clarke, advising the Harvard student, wrote, "The name of Rollin is well known and respected at the university. You will read his ancient history with the care due to a work so well-intended; and which displays such various learning."[51] Thaddeus Harris included the *Ancient History* in his *Selected Catalogue.* And Frank Luther Mott determined that it was a "better seller" in 1796.

The histories of Voltaire were everywhere. Expressing admiration for the French author, a writer of that time made this telling statement in a Massachusetts periodical: "In our country he is best known as a historian."[52] Present-day findings bear him out.[53] After Rollin and Voltaire came the Abbé Raynal and the Abbé Barthélemy, whose "histories" catered to the tastes of many. Raynal's *A Philosophical and Political History of the Settlements and Trade of the Europeans in the East and West Indies* was included in Thaddeus M. Harris's *Selected Catalogue.* In his *Letters* (p. 66), John Clarke said, "Raynal's account of the East and West-Indies was read and admired, when it first made its appearance." Only Raynal's *The Revolution of America* was published here in the years under study. Robert Bell printed a lengthy extract from Raynal in his compilation *Illuminations for Legislators, and for Sentimentalists* (Philadelphia, 1784), and Mathew Carey included brief extracts from the French author in his own collection, *The School of Wisdom* (Philadelphia, 1800). Mary E. Loughrey, in her book mentioned above, found that after Voltaire, there were a few more allusions to Raynal than to Rousseau or Montesquieu in Rhode Island newspapers of the eighteenth century. And a colleague, Edward Seeber, regarding his work on Charleston newspapers in the last half of the century, informs me that "considerable attention was paid also to Raynal." The Abbé Barthélemy's *Travels of Anacharsis the Younger in Greece* was also well received. Clarke called this book a production of "acknowledged merit." And the *American Universal Magazine* (Philadelphia), for example, printed extracts from it, as well as an account of Barthélemy's life, in various numbers of three of its four volumes, published in the years 1797–98.

The erudite Samuel Miller had a high opinion of eighteenth-century French historians. Close to the time of which he writes, here is how he placed some of them in the order of their popularity among Americans. He ranked Rollin first. Rollin, in his *Ancient History,* paid respect "to the government and providence of God, and to Revelation," and he was "more generally perused and praised than most other historians of the age." Next came Vertot, obscure to the modern reader, then Voltaire. Miller considered Voltaire a historian "partial, uncandid, grossly defective in authenticity, and disposed, upon every pretext, to depart from probability, truth, and decorum, for the purpose of reviling the religion of Christ." The Abbé Millot, also obscure today, succeeded Voltaire. And finally, Miller mentions Raynal, whose *History of the East and West Indies,* "though not generally respected as authentic, drew much of the attention of the literary world."[54] So much for the French novelists and historians who were downstage on the eighteenth-century American literary scene. Who were the most prominent figures upstage? I exclude the *philosophes* in this essay.

According to one scholar, "Rabelais and Montaigne were probably the best-known sixteenth-century writers."[55] My findings corroborate this statement. The works of Rabelais were advertised in the *South Carolina Gazette* in 1756 and in the *Boston Gazette* on November 30, 1761, and March 15, 1762 (in this latter issue an advertisement of a five-volume edition in French). Rabelais was "among the foreign titles" Joseph T. Wheeler found in his study of books owned by Marylanders. I shall not go into details of individual ownership, and one allusion to the author will have to suffice. In a reprint in the *Gazette of the United States,* September 20, 1798, "The Lay Preacher," deriding some of the English romantic writers, included an appreciative mention of Rabelais. Some of the Founding Fathers had Montaigne's *Essays* on their bookshelves, as did other libraries of various types.[56]

Among seventeenth-century writers, Molière was the most conspicuous. His *Works* were offered for sale in Williamsburg in 1765.[57] "Molière in French & English" was advertised in the *South Carolina Gazette* in 1767, and again in the same paper, "Molière," in 1768. Smart found Molière, Corneille, and Racine in a few private libraries in colonial Virginia. Joseph T. Wheeler came upon Molière's comedies in two personal libraries in Maryland.[58] "Molière's Works" were available at the Library Company of Philadelphia.[59] And French editions of Molière, as well as of Corneille, were in Caritat's circulating library. James Bowdoin, to cite only one name, had plays of Molière, "fr. &

Eng.," in his library in 1775.[60] Bowdoin became a governor of Massachusetts. A Philadelphia periodical printed a life of the great comic playwright, "embellished with a portrait."[61] Almost no Racine was come upon in private libraries, and even less Corneille. A bookseller advertised "Racine, 3 tom." in the *Boston Gazette*, March 15, 1762. A three-volume French edition of Racine's works, along with an eight-volume edition in French of Molière, were offered for sale in the *Maryland Journal*, September 10, 1782. Gilbert Chinard, who edited *The Literary Bible of Thomas Jefferson: His Commonplace Book of Philosophers and Poets* (Baltimore: Johns Hopkins Press, 1928) found that "Racine is the only French writer represented here."

Library holdings aside, many Americans had the opportunity to see performances of English adaptations of plays by the three illustrious classical dramatists and others. Performances of Molière outstripped those of all other French playwrights in eighteenth-century America. After Molière with some 160-odd performances came Destouches, followed very closely by Corneille, Dancourt, and Voltaire, in descending order.[62] Few plays were presented in French. In light of this record, it is surprising to read that "despite more than a century and a quarter of traditional friendship between France and the United States, American production of Molière's plays had to await the era of the First World War."[63]

Other writers of the classical period were known only to a few. The Library Company of Philadelphia had "Boileau's Works" and "Pascal's Thoughts."[64] Mentions of La Fontaine are surprisingly rare. Wreg offered "Fontaine's Fables" for sale in Williamsburg in 1765. La Rochefoucauld's name does turn up, but very infrequently even though editions of his *Maxims and Moral Reflections* were published in the United States toward the end of the century. V. L. Collins, in his book *President Witherspoon: A Biography*, writes that Witherspoon "scored" La Rochefoucauld in his *Address to the Senior Class* at Princeton, and that he "barely named" Boileau and Pascal.[65] "Pascal's Thoughts on Religion and other curious Subjects" was advertised in the *Virginia Gazette*, November 25, 1775, in a very long and interesting "Catalogue of Books for Sale" in Williamsburg.[66] The *New York Magazine* devoted two pages to a reprint of "Remarkable Particulars in the Life and Conduct of Pascal" in its issue for May 1790. Pascal was quoted on religion in the Philadelphia *General Advertiser*, June 4, 1792. James Kent, proud reader of French, owned *Les Pensées*.[67] In a recent book by John Barker, there is an appendix on "Pascal in America." Here one can find information concerning John Adams's, Madison's, and Jefferson's acquaintance with Pascal's writings, as well as information on library holdings of these.[68] Barker finds no real influence of Pascal on the development of American thought.

Eighteenth-century French authors upstage, dramatic and philosophic literature excluded, were Marmontel and Florian. Editions of Marmontel's novel *Belisarius* were published here in 1770 and 1796. Several of his minor pieces, in English, also appeared. In 1771 Jefferson recommended "Marmontel's moral tales" and *Belisarius* to Robert Skipwith as desiderata for his library.[69] *Belisarius*, for instance, was advertised for sale in the *Maryland Journal*, May 6, 1777, and in the *General Advertiser*, July 28, 1791. Under the rubric "Tales of an Evening," the *American Universal Magazine* (Philadelphia) printed five stories from "Marmontel's new Moral Tales" in its first volume (1797). A writer in the *Gazette of the United States*, February 4, 1797, in announcing the performance of a play in the City of Brotherly Love, referred to the inclusion in it of "the pathetic Tale of CORA and ALONZO, from Marmontel's Incas." The Library Company of Philadelphia, according to Reitzel, owned both the *Tales* and *Belisarius*. Writings of Marmontel and Florian in English and French were available in Caritat's circulating library. Florian's *Galatea: A Pastoral Romance*, was published in Boston in 1798, and his brief piece, *A Very Entertaining and Affecting History of Claudine*, at Whitestown, New York, in 1800. Thaddeus M. Harris included "Florian's Select Tales" in *A Selected Catalogue of Some of the Most Esteemed Publications in the English Language*.

What does the evidence show with regard to the character and amount of American interest in French literature up to 1800? A concern with it on the part of a select few goes back to the seventeeth century. The fine library of John Winthrop, Jr., governor of Connecticut, contained French books.[70] William Byrd's great library at Westover, in Virginia, contained three hundred volumes in French embracing the complete works of some famous authors.[71] Cotton Mather was interested in, and most familiar with, the literature of French refugee writers published toward the end of the *Grand Siècle*.[72] According to Forrest Bowe, the first translation of a French text printed in the colonies, at Cambridge in 1668, was a small work by Guy de Brès pertaining to one of the radical religious movements of the Reformation. "Between 1668 and 1775," Bowe adds, "the printing of translations of French works was limited; indeed, for sixty-four of those years, none have been located. During this period, of course, most translations were published in England and exported to the colonies."[73] The contrast between the lack of publication in these sixty-four "empty" years and the numerous translations printed in the United States toward the end of the century could hardly have been greater. But much had happened in the intervening time. As the exercise of reason waxed, puritanism and intolerance waned. Ancient enmity against France had begun to weaken. The Franco-American alliance would be created in 1778, and the myriad contacts during the War of Independence would engender fraternity and arouse interest in things French.

Most American readers of books were urban residents—generally people of the middle class who were able to buy them or who had fairly easy access to collections in cities and towns. French books were advertised in both northern and southern newspapers. After the French and Indian War (1754–63), their acquisition by all kinds of libraries gradually increased as the century advanced. The private libraries in the period 1760–1800 were generally quite small. But the number of books by French authors in some collections commands attention, and especially in such private libraries as those of James Bowdoin,[74] a governor of

Massachusetts; Charles Carroll, a signer of the Declaration of Independence; James Madison,[75] "Father of the Constitution"; William Duane,[76] editor of the *Aurora General Advertiser,* a powerful Philadelphia democratic newspaper; and James Kent,[77] the distinguished jurist. The great libraries of Jefferson and John Adams require no further remarks.

The growth of the circulating library was phenomenal. J. H. Shera writes that it "was concurrent with and in large measure dependent upon the rising popularity of the novel as a literary form."[78] According to James D. Hart, "Novels were the reading matter of the lower middle class which rose to prominence after the Revolution, of nearly all the younger generation, and of women of every age and station, but older, more sober, or more religious citizens were generally horrified at the degradation of morality and intellect that they associated with fiction."[79] Both Shera and Hart agree that the circulating library had become a middle-class institution by 1800. It would be onerous to search out the numerous titles of French fiction available to American readers in the eighteenth century, which the Reverend Samuel Miller called the "Age of Novels." Had it been in his power, he would have wholly prohibited the reading of this literary genre.[80] And so would have many others.

The importance of newspapers as vehicles of Enlightenment thought can hardly be overstressed. One example is enough. In a study of the fortune of Montesquieu in America, I made extensive use of newspapers. The editors, my findings show, were wont to print entire chapters of the *Spirit of Laws.* I concluded that the most important parts of this masterpiece could be reconstructed, verbatim, from the eighteenth-century papers. They were the most popular and certainly one of the least expensive forms of reading matter. When William Cobbett announced in the *Gazette of the United States* on February 1, 1797, his intention to publish *Porcupine's Gazette* to combat the pro-French journals, he said that "thousands who read them [American newspapers] read nothing else." And John Ward Fenno, the well-informed publisher of the *Gazette of the United States,* declared in this paper on March 4, 1799, that "more than nine-tenths of the scanty literature of America is made up of newspaper reading." The magazines were also highly useful intermediaries. They did much to acquaint their readers with the literature of France. I can say that almost any French author of note was represented, referred to, made the subject of an anecdote, or quoted in the periodicals, and to a lesser degree, I think, in the newspapers. Here are a few random examples. Anecdotes concerning Piron, Argens, Crébillon *fils,* and Gresset can be found in the *Boston Magazine,* April 1784. The *Charleston Morning Post,* on May 17, 1786, contained citations from Mercier's *Tableau de Paris.* The *New York Magazine; or Literary Repository* included Montesquieu's *Arsace and Ismenia: An Oriental Story* in four of its numbers in 1791. This magazine also printed *The History of Apheridon and Astarte,* from Montesquieu's *Persian Letters,* in May 1795. *Aucassin and Nicolette* ran in issues of the *South Carolina Weekly Museum* between January and July of 1797. The *American Universal Magazine* carried a page of appreciation of Pierre Corneille in August of this year. And in 1798 this same magazine printed *Selico: An African Tale,* by Florian. The *Lady's Magazine and Repository* (Philadelphia) had already published *Selico* in 1793. Charles Dean Cool, whose unpublished dissertation on the magazines was referred to at the outset, calls the years before 1800 their "extract period." His tabulation shows that the incidence of extracts from French literature was far greater from 1789 to 1799 than at any time preceding. Adrian H. Jaffe's study of the magazines, also previously mentioned, corroborates Cool's findings concerning this decade.

From the information I have amassed over the years I can only conclude that countless American readers had, at the very least, some familiarity with French writing. The evidence is everywhere. In addition to what has been brought forward for consideration, I could cite innumerable references to, and quotations of, French authors in then contemporary addresses, books, biographical sketches, essays, lectures, letters, orations, sermons, records, and printed matter of almost every kind. Available statistics on the circulation of newspapers and magazines will throw some light on readership. But we shall never have an accurate conception of the number of readers of French books in private, college, social, and circulating libraries. With regard to the character or sort of French literature that appealed to these readers one may safely conclude, from what has been adduced in this essay, that they were certainly interested in novels, histories, and moral tales. I cannot affirm, however, that they showed a marked preference for one type of literature, imaginative as opposed, say, to philosophic, at a given time or period. There were different levels of readers in the American Enlightenment. But they were not, of necessity, mutually exclusive.

There was some criticism of this literature. Not much. John Witherspoon thought that "in general, there is to be found a greater purity, simplicity and precision in the French authors than in the English."[81] John Clarke wrote that "France has produced numberless writers who do honour to human genius."[82] An expression of this sort today would strike us as hackneyed in the extreme. But coming as it does from a Boston clergyman at the end of the eighteenth century, it is far from trite. In addition to Clarke, Samuel Miller[83] and Jefferson[84] had more to say about the merits and faults of many of the *littérateurs* discussed in this section than any others to whom I can point.

Literature from France increased in volume as the century approached its end. This can be seen, among other indications, in the number of translations printed in the United States in the 1780s, and especially in the last decade of the century. Among these were Le Sage's *Gil Blas*, Rousseau's *The New Eloisa*, and Rollin's *Ancient History*, all "better sellers" in the 1790s, according to Frank Luther Mott. Mott's concern was with first editions published in America. As a criterion for the designation of a book as a best seller, he sets the sales figure at one percent of the entire population of the continental United States for the decade in which the book was published.[85] To be an "over-all best seller" in the decade 1790–99 he stipulates as a requirement total American sales of forty thousand copies. "Better sellers," Mott writes, were "runners-up." They came close to, but did not reach, he believes, the total sales required to be a best seller. His calculations arrest our attention, especially when we reflect that in the first census in 1790 the white population numbered 3,172,444. Mott's figures with regard to the sales of books at that time, if compared with the sale of books in proportion to the population of the United States today, are quite significant.

Five

Buffon

 In a review of Bernard Faÿ's book, *L'Esprit révolutionnaire en France et aux Etats-Unis à la fin du
XVIIIe siècle*, Gilbert Chinard expressed disappointment that the author had not included a
chapter on French science in America, in which he
might have discussed, among other things, the vogue of Buffon's
Histoire naturelle.[1] In Chinard's opinion, this was not merely a
matter of fleeting fashion; he believed that Buffon and his collaborators exerted a durable influence here. Somewhat paradoxi-
cal is the opinion of a recent investigator who affirms that "the
more popular works of Buffon, although available in several English translations, seem [not] to have attracted American booksellers."[2] He concludes that Erasmus Darwin was "the favorite
European writer on natural history, judging from the number of
American editions of his writings." I wish to address myself to
this question of Buffon's vogue in the United States.

The life and extraordinary labors of the illustrious French scientist have received the attention of many scholars.[3] The first
three volumes of the *Histoire naturelle* had appeared in 1749. The
vast project was not to be completed, however, until after Buffon's death, which occurred in 1788. Ultimately, there were forty-
four quarto volumes. An English translation of part of the bold
undertaking, entitled *The Natural History of Animals, Vegetables,
and Minerals, with the Theory of the Earth in General*, in six volumes, was published in London in 1775–76. Various other editions in English also made their appearance there before 1800.

Buffon became famous in the Old World in his lifetime. His

epoch-making work enjoyed an immense vogue in France. What was the case in the New World? It goes almost without saying that other investigators have been concerned with Buffon and America.[4] Some have written at length on the controversy that the eminent naturalist initially provoked here. Of this more later. Buffon was the first Frenchman elected to membership in the American Philosophical Society. The election took place in 1768. Subsequently, he made donations of his books to the society.[5] In 1782 the American Academy of Arts and Sciences elected him a member.[6] As early as 1762 William Shippen, an eminent Philadelphia physician and teacher, had gone to the Jardin du Roi (today the Jardin des Plantes) in Paris to see Buffon, who was its superintendent.[7] Franklin and Jefferson were friends of Buffon.[8] Jefferson considered him "the best informed of any Naturalist who has ever written." Daniel Webster once enjoyed hearing the Virginian describe his visit to Buffon's residence in the country.[9] John Adams tells of visiting the British Museum one day in 1786 where the keeper of the collection of natural history gave him an earful about Buffon. Such gossip, Adams writes, "is partly national Prejudice and Malignity, no doubt."[10]

The *Histoire naturelle* was one of the first great popular scientific successes, Michael Kraus writes, and it was "scattered" over Europe and America.[11] Although no work by Buffon was published in the United States in the eighteenth century, one could order his tomes from abroad, as some did. Or one could purchase them in a number of American bookshops. "Buffon's natural history, 9 vols with plates," for example, was advertised by William Young, a Philadelphia bookseller, in the *General Advertiser,* May 8, 1793. In 1795 Moreau de Saint-Méry, also in Philadelphia, published an extensive catalog of books for sale, which included editions of Buffon in both French and English.[12] A Baltimore dealer offered the naturalist's "Works" in an advertisement which appeared for the first time in both the *Federal Intelligencer* and the *Maryland Journal* on October 22, 1795. Robert Campbell, another Philadelphia bookseller, advertised "Buffon's Natural

history of Birds, 9 vol. 8 vo." in the *Gazette of the United States,*
December 27, 1796. His "System of Natural History" was available at Caritat's circulating library in New York City, as was an
edition of his complete works in French.

Harvard College was well supplied with volumes of the *Histoire naturelle* in French and with other writings of Buffon.[13] The
Yale library had no copy of the monumental work.[14] The University of Pennsylvania received the *Histoire naturelle* (thirty volumes) in a gift of books made to it by Louis XVI.[15] "Buffon in
Quo. complete" was among the books which the king also gave
to William and Mary College.[16] The Charleston Library Society
ordered Buffon.[17] The Hartford Library Company owned his
Natural History, in nine volumes.

Washington had an abridged edition of the *Natural History.*
There were many volumes of the great work, in French, in the
library of John Adams. Jefferson's 1815 library contained much
more of it than did Adams's, also in the original. Around 1767
Jefferson had recommended Buffon as reading for the "Education of a Lawyer."[18] He was among the French writers most often
mentioned by James Madison.[19] Madison was very concerned
with Buffon.[20] He possessed much of the *Histoire naturelle,* and
made notes on, and translations from, several volumes of it.[21]
James Logan in Philadelphia owned books by Buffon.[22] William
Short, Jefferson's secretary of legation, had a French edition of
his writings in fifty-eight volumes. A Baltimore resident, Mr.
Parkin, possessed seventy-six volumes by the great naturalist.[23]
William Dunlap, a New Yorker, recorded in his *Diary* that he
"bought . . . an Octavo close printed French edition of Buffon"
and that he read in him.[24] In the forests of New York State, a
misanthropic bachelor, Mr. Seagrove, said, "To console me in
these sad reflections, I study Buffon, the outstanding painter of
nature."[25] The evidence indicates that many others either owned
or had access to volumes of the *Natural History.* Charles Nisbet,
president of Dickinson College, cited Buffon in his lectures on
"Moral Philosophy."[26] At Union College students in the philo-

sophical class, before completion of the undergraduate curriculum, had to be "acquainted" with a number of subjects. *"Instead of the Greek"* they could substitute "Buffon's *Natural History, in French, or some other approved French author."*[27] The naturalist was quoted on "Les Modes" in the collection of prose extracts which Joseph Nancrède prepared for the use of Harvard students.[28] And John Clarke, in *Letters to a Student* (1796) at Harvard, wrote, "In the works of Buffon, You will find the beauties of language with the wonders of nature." A Harvard commencement speaker placed Buffon and Voltaire in a category of "extraordinary geniuses."[29]

The French naturalist was mentioned and quoted in periodical literature. In 1787 the *Columbian Magazine* (Philadelphia) printed a memoir, "Method of Preserving Birds, and Other Subjects of Natural History,"[30] which Buffon requested to be sent to Franklin. In a recommendation of books to a young lady, the author of an article on women's education appearing in this periodical said, "Buffon [in the pursuit of natural history] will claim superior attention."[31] In its December 1788 issue the magazine reprinted in translation, from the *Journal de Paris,* an apparently well liked eulogy on the "Beautiful Characters of Montesquieu, Voltaire, Rousseau, and Buffon."[32] In July 1797 the *American Universal Magazine* devoted several pages to "Biographical Anecdotes of the Count of Buffon." The *New York Magazine* reprinted from Buffon a "Description of the Sensations and Ideas of the First Man, on His Coming into Existence."[33] This magazine also printed selections from his *Natural History of Birds.*[34] In the *Philadelphia Monthly Magazine* one finds "A View of Nature. From Buffon," and again in this publication the "Description of the Sensations and Ideas of the first Man."[35] Incidentally, I. W. Riley believed that Buffon was influential here because his *"View of Nature* fortified the American deists."[36] I cannot validate this.

Let me turn to the question of Buffon's impact on Americans who were particularly interested in the sciences. I have not found any reference to the Frenchman by Cadwallader Colden, the prominent colonial scholar and botanist. John Bartram sent a message to Peter Collinson in 1755, in which he mentioned Buffon's name. Collinson, a London horticulturist, had introduced Bartram, by letter, to Buffon.[37] Bartram's son, William, attacked certain theories of Buffon.[38] Brooke Hindle points out that David Rittenhouse published anonymously in the *Columbian Magazine* around 1786–87. "Some Observations on the Structure of the Surface of the Earth in Pennsylvania and the adjoining Countries" was the title of one of his articles. In such writings, according to Hindle, Rittenhouse "gave no indication whether he had read Buffon."[39] From 1791 on, according to another scholar, Charles Willson Peale "maintained a correspondence" with Buffon. "In all this the subject of interest to him was not so much natural history as museum administration, particularly the character and progress of the European institutions."[40] Peale would soon open his own museum in Philadelphia. Another investigator finds that Peale "identified his exhibits according to the writings of Buffon and classified them according to the system of Linnaeus."[41] Madame Necker sent Peale "a portrait of the sainted Buffon shown surrounded by representatives of all nature, including a little depiction of Rousseau kissing in adoration the threshold of the great man's *cabinet*."[42]

I have alluded above to the controversy that Buffon stirred up by some of his theorizing in the *Histoire naturelle*. There are excellent and detailed accounts of this lengthy polemic, which took place in the latter half of the century, over the question of the degeneracy of animals and men in the New World.[43] I shall only touch upon the debate here. The chief European detractors of America were Peter Kalm, Cornelius de Pauw,[44] Buffon, Raynal, and William Robertson. Franklin, Jefferson, and John Adams were the principal defenders. They replied to the detractors with facts, not theories. "The opinion advanced by the Count de Buffon," Jefferson wrote, "is 1. That the animals common both to the old and new world, are smaller in the latter. 2. That those peculiar to the new, are on a smaller scale. 3. That those which have been domesticated in both, have degenerated in America: and 4. That on the whole it exhibits fewer species. And the reason he thinks is, that the heats of America are less; that more waters are spread over its surface by nature, and fewer of these drained off by the hand of man. In other words, that *heat* is friendly, and *moisture* adverse to the production of large quadrupeds."[45] In a letter to Chastellux in 1785, Jefferson said, "As to the degeneracy of the man of Europe transplanted to America, it is no part of Monsr. de Buffon's system. He goes indeed within one step of it, but he stops there. The Abbé Raynal alone has taken that step."[46] It was also the abbé who, writing in French of course, remarked in his most celebrated work that "one must be astonished that America has not yet produced one good poet, one able mathematician, one man of genius in a single art or a single science." In the *Notes on the State of Virginia,* Jefferson marshalled fact after fact in order to refute Buffon.[47] He sent or had sent to the naturalist specimens of American animals. He defended the Indians and the white population of North America against the charges of degeneration. Both Buffon and Raynal later "modified," to use Chinard's expression, their opinions of this continent. Apropos of the biological specimens Buffon received from Jefferson, Harlow Shapley affirms that the French scientist "was generous enough to write, 'I should have counseled you, sir, before publishing my Natural History, and then I should have been sure of the facts.' "[48] I have not been able to locate the source of Shapley's quotation.

The charges of degeneracy provoked other Americans and called forth many responses.[49] There was an element in the controversy, however, that went beyond arguments over such matters as friendly or unfriendly heat and "adverse" moisture. Michael Kraus, for instance, in his book *The Atlantic Civilization,* cites eighteenth-century evidence of belief that America was a healthy place, not one of degeneracy. "This was more than an academic question," Chinard writes, "and its political implications grew apparent as the British colonies progressed towards independence and finally formed a new nation."⁵⁰ At issue was civilization itself. Ultimately, the controversy was a dispute between the adherents of Old World culture and the supporters of a new order of the ages. Commager and Giordanetti affirm that for Europeans "America was merely a kind of stalking-horse for their own domestic problems" and that "to attack or to defend America were methods of criticizing the evils of government and economy and society in the Old World."⁵¹ To sum up, one can say, speaking generally, that the French critics of America were the champions of French culture and civilization, and the French champions of America were those critical of France. The quarrel lingers on! So much for the controversy and Buffon's role in it. The great naturalist was much admired for his "elegant pen." He had a vogue here, and the *Histoire naturelle* exerted an influence of sorts. He and his work were both praised and criticized, as the two following quotations from Americans of that age attest.

In an address at the University of Pennsylvania in November 1800, Charles Willson Peale expressed himself in this manner:

> Although he is so much celebrated, yet, I think it my duty to say, however dazzling and captivating the stile of Buffon, such theoretical writers should be read with caution: we ought always to suspect an author, when he suffers his thirst for variety of language to lead him into unjust comparisons of the operations of nature; or to use irreverend [*sic*] expressions of the Creator, when through shortsightedness things appear strange, or unaccountable.
> In the course of these lectures, in the description of American animals, some such instances will be illucidated; and although I may not spare his faults, I shall with candour always acknowledge how very serviceable his works have been to me in my studies.⁵²

Samuel Miller had this to say of Buffon:

> As a writer, in which he excels all other natural historians, [he] is far less accurate and philosophical. His neglect of regular systematic arrangement is a great defect, and must ever lessen the value of his works. He was a zealous cultivator of zoology, and by his splendid

publications and captivating style made himself admired throughout the scientific world. And though many of his hypotheses are whimsical, extravagant, and delusive, it must yet be allowed that he did much to encourage and forward the study of nature; that he made many observations of great value; that he collected a multitude of interesting facts; and that his works hold a very important place in the zoological history of the age.[53]

For the prevalence of the study of natural history in the second third of the eighteenth century, wrote the knowledgeable Mr. Miller, "we are, perhaps, indebted to the genius, labours and influence of no two individuals so much as to those of Linnaeus, and the Count de Buffon."[54]

Six

The Philosophes

Montesquieu, Voltaire, Rousseau, and Diderot were the principal French *philosophes* of the Enlightenment. The writings of Voltaire were more widely advertised and disseminated in this country than those of any of the others. A few, including the *Philosophical Dictionary,* were published in the United States before 1800. Diderot's writings were the least known. With regard to Rousseau, I have not much hesitancy in affirming that he was as well known as Montesquieu, whom Robert Shackleton calls "a *philosophe* before the *philosophes* had formed a party."[1] But Rousseau was the author of several masterpieces whereas Montesquieu was really known in America only for one. Rousseau's influential novel and his *Social Contract* were both published here near the end of the century. The *Social Contract* contains one of the world's most eloquent enunciations of the doctrine of popular sovereignty. Yet it had no influence on the Declaration of Independence. Montesquieu, on the other hand, exerted an influence on the Constitution of the United States. The *Spirit of Laws,* however, did not have the honor of an eighteenth-century American imprint.

"Who Were the *Philosophes?*" This is the title of a judicious article[2] by John Lough in which he seeks "to bring out into the open a question which lurks at the back of one's mind whenever one speaks or writes about eighteenth-century French thought." Lough identifies as *philosophes* of the first order Voltaire, Diderot, Raynal, D'Alembert, Helvétius, Holbach, and Condorcet. Noticeable omissions in this list are the names of Bayle, Fontenelle,

Montesquieu, and Rousseau, about all of whom he has reservations, which others, past and present, have not had. Differences of opinion arise in part from lack of clear distinctions, in some cases, among *philosophes,* encyclopedists, and ideologues. Lough's exclusions and tentative conclusions will not, of course, be acceptable to everyone.

What is meant by a *philosophe?* We would expect to find a satisfactory definition under the entry "Philosophe" in Diderot's *Encyclopédie,* the authorship of which has been attributed variously to Diderot, Dumarsais, and others. But Lough finds little help here, and I agree. Lough includes in his article several eighteenth-century definitions of the term. Most useful of all, he finds, is a statement by Condorcet in the ninth stage of his *Esquisse d'un tableau historique des progrès de l'esprit humain.* In this place, the *philosophe* speaks of a class of men in Europe who took *reason, tolerance,* and *humanity* for their battle cry.

These shibboleths, these beliefs, are central. But the French philosophic creed, it goes without saying, contained many other tenets. Among them was belief in natural law, the natural goodness of man, natural religion, a social contract, liberty, equality, and the pursuit of happiness, education by the state, science, progress, the indefinite perfectibility of mankind, empiricism, behaviorism, enlightened self-interest, the relativity of ethics, and utilitarianism.

All the *philosophes,* of course, did not assent to, much less discuss, every one of these tenets. Most of them accepted many of the doctrines; others only a few. There was no concerted philosophic program. But whether optimists, meliorists, or pessimists, they strove through their writings to bring about a new and better social order—in politics, economics, education, and morality. Some looked to the New World. They were imbued with the American experiment, enamored of the American Dream.[3] But all looked to the future, not to the past.[4]

Bayle and Fontenelle were the most prominent French precursors of *le mouvement philosophique,* and Helvétius and Holbach were two thoroughgoing and outstanding *philosophes*. Recorded here is some evidence concerning the reception by Americans of these men's writings, a matter about which little or nothing is known.

Pierre Bayle was a "master of doubt" and a great apostle of tolerance. Voltaire held him in the highest esteem, called his writings "the library of the nations." Bayle published his *Pensées diverses sur la comète* in 1682, and his famous *Dictionnaire historique et critique,* the "Old Testament" and arsenal of the philosophic movement, in 1697. An English translation of the former was available as early as 1708, of the latter in 1710.

James Bowdoin, Massachusetts statesman, owned Bayle's "Works."[5] Harvard had the *"Oeuvres diverses,"* the *Pensées diverses sur la comète,* and three sets of the *Pensées* in English.[6] A Philadelphia bookseller advertised the *"Oeuvres."*[7] Bayle's masterpiece, the *Dictionary,* was by no means unknown. The first book order made by the Library Company of Philadelphia, a list completed in March 1732, included the "Critical Dictionary."[8] Harvard College, as pointed out elsewhere, had refused a gift of a French edition of the great work in 1724, allegedly because the students could not read the language. Jonathan Edwards knew of the *Dictionary.*[9] It was in the Rhode Island College (Brown University) library, on the shelves of the Providence Library Society and of individual Rhode Islanders.[10] It was among the books of a Maryland clergyman.[11] In 1771 Jefferson proposed its purchase to Robert Skipwith for his library.[12] John Randolph of Roanoke had a "noble" French edition of the *Dictionary* as well as an English translation in five volumes.[13] Benjamin Rush seemingly quoted Bayle's *Miscellaneous Reflections Occasion'd by the Comet of 1680.*[14] Samuel Miller thought the *Dictionary* a "work of great labour and learning." And the writer of an antifederal editorial in the *Baltimore American and Daily Advertiser,* December 4, 1800, praised Bayle and others as "disciples" of political freedom.

Fontenelle, a prolific writer and the second great precursor of the Enlightenment in France, was known in the United States for two of his books, the *Dialogues des morts* (1683) and *Entretiens sur la pluralité des mondes* (1686). Both were early available in English translations, the first in 1685, the second in 1688. One could purchase his *Dialogues of the Dead* and *New Dialogues of the Dead* in Williamsburg in 1765.[15] A catalog of books advertised for sale by other dealers in this city appeared in the *Virginia Gazette*, November 25, 1775. It contained *Dialogues of the Dead*, but did not mention the name of an author.[16] The Redwood Library Company in Newport, Rhode Island, had listed *Dialogues of the Dead*, most likely Fontenelle's, in its 1764 catalog.[17] The Library Company of Philadelphia had his *Dialogues* and also his *History of Oracles*.[18]

Fontenelle's *Entretiens sur la pluralité des mondes* appeared in 1686. "Coming as it did . . . just one year before the publication of Newton's *Principia* was to assure the success of the Copernican system," writes Leonard M. Marsak, "the *Entretiens* provides a cogent and smoothly flowing argument for that system, and particularly for the Cartesian interpretation of it."[19] Significant and most readable, this work of popularization consists of six evenings of talks between the author and a supposed marquise. The "Plurality of Worlds" was advertised in the *South Carolina Gazette* in 1753, in the *Maryland Gazette*, August 26, 1762. The first president of King's College (Columbia), founded in 1754, read the book in 1739–40.[20] Donald Robertson, the Scot whose school in Virginia James Madison once attended, owned a copy.[21] The book was in the Redwood Library Company in 1764, and in a circulating library in Providence in 1789.[22] An excerpt from the work appeared in the *National Gazette*, June 28, 1792.[23] The "Plurality of Worlds" was praised in an article of foreign origin reprinted in 1798 in the *American Universal Magazine*.[24] The year before, this same periodical had offered its readers a full-page engraving of Fontenelle.[25] One could buy the author's *Oeuvres* at Moreau de Saint-Méry's bookstore in Philadelphia in 1795.[26] John Adams had an edition of the *Oeuvres* in his library. And the "*Works* of M. d'Fontinelle" were on a list of books to be auctioned in Providence.[27] Samuel

Miller wrote that Fontenelle, along with Voltaire, Rousseau, and Buffon, deserves to stand in the "first rank" of the eighteenth-century writers who contributed to the enrichment and refinement of the French language.[28]

Helvétius and Holbach were arch materialists. The Parlement de Paris condemned Helvétius's *De l'Esprit* to be burned publicly. Holbach was called the "personal enemy of God." John Lough has made a study of the two *philosophes* to show how far they were in agreement and where they differed on certain fundamental questions.[29] He found that they had much in common: they were rigid determinists and disciples of John Locke, they "base their utilitarian ethics on physical sensation," and both believe that "the object of society is the happiness of the greatest number, founded on the union of public and private interest."

Helvétius attracted the attention of more American readers than did Holbach. His major work, *De l'Esprit* (1758), appeared in English in 1759 as *Essays on the Mind*. His book *De l'Homme* was published posthumously in 1772. The translation, *A Treatise on Man*, was printed in London in 1777. I have noted few offers of Helvétius's books in the gazettes. A Baltimore dealer advertised his "Works" in the *Federal Intelligencer* from October 22 to November 2, 1795. This advertisement is doubtless the same as the one that ran concurrently in the *Maryland Journal*. Moreau de Saint-Méry, the Philadelphia bookseller, listed the *Treatise on Man* and the author's *Poésies* in an extensive catalog of books for sale published in 1795. "Helvetius on Man, 2 vols." could be had at Boston's Salem Book-Store and Circulating Library in 1796.[30] And this work was available in French at Caritat's circulating library in New York.[31] H. M. Jones noted an advertisement of "Helvetius's 'Treaty of Man' " in this city's *Royal Gazette* as early as November 11, 1778.[32] Joseph Nancrède's anthology, *L'Abeille françoise*, Martel's *Elements*, and Mathew Carey's collection, *The School of Wisdom*, contained very brief extracts from the author's writing. The *American Universal Magazine*, in its December 5, 1797, issue, favored its readers with a full-page engraving, an

"Elegant Head," of Helvétius, together with a ten-page biography of the *philosophe.*

The author's writings were on the shelves of various types of libraries. *De l'Esprit* was among the books left to the College of Charleston by a benefactor.[33] The Library Company of Philadelphia had *De l'Esprit* and *A Treatise on Man* before or by 1789.[34] The library later acquired, according to its catalog published in 1807, two copies of *De l'Esprit* in English translation. "Helvetius on Man, 2 vols." was in the New York Society Library in 1793.[35] And the *Records of the Union Library of Hatborough* (Pennsylvania), show that this library bought the latter title in 1794. A literary society at the University of North Carolina purchased "Helvetius on the Human Mind" shortly after the opening of the university in 1795.[36] "Helvetius on Man" was in the Warren Library Society (Rhode Island) in 1799.[37]

His books were in private libraries. John Adams owned the *Treatise on Man.* So did the southerner John K. Read.[38] William Duane, the Philadelphia newspaper editor, had this work in French. Solomon Drowne, a Rhode Island College graduate and future professor, owned *De l'Esprit.*[39] Jefferson's second library contained the *Oeuvres d'Helvétius,* an edition in five volumes published in 1781.

The author was quoted or referred to in newspapers. Mary Ellen Loughrey points out quotations from *De l'Homme* in three issues of the *Newport Herald* in the 1780s. These involved morality and religion.[40] In the *Gazette of the United States,* October 31, 1795, one finds this sarcastic apostrophe: "Dear Helvetius! How I love thy memory! Thou has *unsouled* us all—All the little Jackanapes about me also admire thee. Not because they *understand* thy *principles,* but because they love thy *maxims.* The very ladies of my acquaintance are beginning to praise thee!—I hope it is for the *freedom* thou art pleased to recommend in the *commerce of the sexes.*" And on this subject, the writer of the article supplies his readers with exact page references. In an oration before the Tammany Society, a speaker praised Helvétius as one who "accelerated the epoch of the French Revolution [but] despaired of the restoration of liberty to his country."[41]

According to the evidence, Americans were by no means indifferent to the *philosophe*. Benjamin Franklin, in a letter to the Abbé de la Roche in 1779, said, "I have often remarked, in reading the works of M. Helvetius, that, although we were born and educated in two countries so remote from each other, we have often been inspired with the same thoughts; and it is a reflection very flattering to me, that we have not only loved the same studies, but, as far as we have mutually known them, the same friends, and *the same woman*."[42] It does not seem likely that Franklin ever met Helvétius personally.[43] But he was well acquainted with, and very fond of, his widow—"the same woman." It has been generally considered that he proposed marriage to her. Her refusal of his offer inspired Franklin to write the *Elysian Fields*, one of his most famous bagatelles.[44]

Jefferson called Helvétius "one of the best men on earth." He quoted *De l'Esprit* on egoism or self-interest as the source of moral action, and said that the author was "the most ingenious advocate of this principle." But for Jefferson self-interest was not enough. In his opinion, the source of altruism is to be found in man's "moral instinct."[45] Early on the French philosopher had evoked the Virginian's interest. Gilbert Chinard, in the introduction to his edition of Jefferson's *Commonplace Book*, wrote that Jefferson "was impressed by at least two theories of Helvétius." He found that Jefferson copied into his book three rather lengthy passages from *De l'Homme*. They deal with the soul, accusations of atheism, and federative republics.[46] Chinard was inclined to believe that Jefferson made these entries before going to France.

One mention of John Adams's reaction to the *philosophe* will suffice. "I have never read Reasoning more absurd, Sophistry more gross," he wrote Jefferson, "than the subtle labours of Helvetius and Rousseau to demonstrate the natural Equality of Mankind."[47] On this subject, James Madison was not so sweepingly condemnatory of Helvétius as Adams.[48]

Noah Webster, according to Allen O. Hansen, was influenced in some fashion by Helvétius in the period following the American Revolution.[49] If so, he later changed his mind. "Helvetius and other profound philosophers may write as much as they please, to prove man to be wholly the *creature of his own making*, the work of *education*; but facts occur every hour to common observation, to prove the theory false."[50] At the very end of the century, Webster wrote, "The theories of Helvetius, Rousseau, Condorcet, Turgot, Godwin and others, are founded on artificial reasoning, not on the nature of man; not on fact and experience."[51]

In Helvétius's philosophy education and legislation were basic principles. Samuel Miller could not accept the notion of the "intellectual and moral *omnipotence*" of education, "first distinctly taught by M. Helvetius."[52] In a thumbnail sketch of the *philosophe*, Miller writes, "Helvetius may be regarded as one of the earliest and most conspicuous of the advocates for that system of *materialism*, and of *atheistical reveries*, usually called the *new philosophy*."[53] And to his sons he wrote, "Were I to hear that, under the guise of enlarged and liberal reading, you were, in your leisure moments, poring over the pages of *Voltaire*, *Helvetius*, and other similar writers, I should . . . be ready to weep over you, as probably lost to virtue and happiness, to say nothing of piety."[54] He calls these writers "vile men."

The Paris Parlement condemned several books by Holbach to be lacerated and burned by the public hangman. It declared them "impious" and "blasphemous," and the parlement threatened all French readers with punishment for "lèse-majesté human and divine."[55] Among the books were *Le Christianisme dévoilé; ou, Examen des principes et des effets de la religion chrétienne* (1761) and the *Système de la nature* (1770). William M. Johnson, an American medical student, translated the former book. This translation was printed in New York in 1795.[56] A condensation of the latter work was also published in New York in the same year under the title of *Common Sense; or, Natural Ideas Opposed to Supernatural*. Johnson made the only English translation of *Le Christianisme dévoilé* in the eighteenth century. He felt remorse for having done so. "Persuasion and poverty induced me to translate this work of Boulanger [pseudonym of Holbach]." And in the same letter to a friend from which the preceding is taken, Johnson wrote, "I do not believe that Boulanger's sentiments concerning the Christian religion are just. I believe the most prominent features of the monster in question are sophistry and rancour."[57]

The Reverend Uzal Ogden excoriated Holbach in "Remarks on Boulanger's Christianity Unveiled," which he prefixed to his book *Antidote to Deism*.[58] And a Baltimore newspaper printed an extract from "The Lay Preacher" (Joseph Dennie) in which he says, "Boulanger, an audacious Frenchman, in his 'Christianity Unveiled,' has presumptuously attempted to sap the Christian's fortress."[59] Such denunciations of Holbach would long continue. Timothy Dwight, Congregational minister and former president of Yale, writing after the close of the eighteenth century on religion in New England in the period of the French Revolution, had this to say, "From the Système de la nature and the Philosophical Dictionary, down to the Political Justice of Godwin and the Age of Reason, the whole mass of pollution was emptied on this country. . . . On the people of New England their influence [that is, of Holbach, Voltaire, Godwin, and Paine], though sensibly felt, was not extensive; on other parts of the Union, it is declared, as I believe with truth, to have been great."[60]

Benjamin Franklin visited Holbach in his home.[61] Jefferson's second library had "The System of Nature, Eng. 1st vol. 8vo." William Dunlap, the playwright, purchased the book, and made this notation in his diary: "Read in System of Nature."[62] Joel Barlow, according to Leon Howard, owed much to Holbach. One statement concerning this indebtedness will suffice. Barlow's "deterministic materialism . . . derived from Holbach and the Encyclopedists, dominated his mature mind and his major literary works."[63] Elihu Palmer will refer to Holbach and quote the *System of Nature* on motion in his book *Principles of Nature,* published shortly after the century's end.

In the last decade of the century, Caritat, proprietor of the big bookshop in New York City, did his best to disseminate books in French by leading authors of the French Enlightenment. Among these, according to Raddin, were writings of Holbach (including the *Système de la nature*), Helvétius (*De l'Homme*), Montesquieu, Voltaire, Rousseau, D'Alembert, Condorcet (*Esquisse*), and Volney.[64] Raddin cites numerous other offerings by Caritat of less well known French authors. He does not, however, mention any book by La Mettrie. Yet Riley, in his old but classic work on American philosophy, speaks of the coming of La Mettrie's materialism to the United States.[65] The writings of this *philosophe* were conspicuously absent on the American scene. I can only point to the possession by Harvard of *L'Homme machine* (Leyden, 1748) and *L'Homme plus que machine* (London, 1748).[66]

The duke of La Rochefoucauld-Liancourt, who traveled here and in Upper Canada in the years 1795–97, commented on the habit of referring to the United States as "the most enlightened nation in the world." And Bernard Faÿ, the French historian, expressed the opinion that in the last thirty years of the eighteenth century, "the average man seems to have read more than was the case in Europe."[67] The increase in readership in America in this century had been extraordinary. Long before its close, Americans had the opportunity to buy and to read, in English or in French, important writings of the principal *philosophes*.

The fortunes in the United States of Bayle, Fontenelle, Helvétius, and Holbach have become clearer. In the pages that follow I shall deal with Montesquieu, Voltaire, Diderot, Condorcet, and the reception of certain philosophies. I have written on Rousseau elsewhere.[68]

Seven

Montesquieu and the American Constitution

 America has long been interested in Montesquieu. From those remote days in the eighteenth century when his books found their slow way by sailing vessel across the Atlantic to a comparatively recent time when an assumption was prevalent that some of his ideas had exerted an influence on the Constitution of the United States, many Americans have been concerned with this writer. Some scholars have claimed for him a significant role in the development of American political thought. Others have vigorously denied the validity of their claims. The most astonishing fact of all is that two hundred years after the foundation of the Republic disagreement still persists as to Montesquieu's importance in the crucial years of American history.

Gladstone affirmed that the American Constitution was "the most wonderful work ever struck off at a given time by the brain and purpose of man." This language may strike us as inflated, but the statement is not unsupported. The document is girded with the triple and ingeniously twisted strands of separation of powers, balance of powers, and checks and balances. The checks and balances buttress the Constitution's interior structure.[1] They counterpoise its exterior structure, the separation of power into legislative, executive, and judicial branches, which Madison referred to as "parchment barriers." This Constitution, the Federal Constitution of "the compound republic of America," to use the Virginian's words,[2] unites both experience and theory.

Montesquieu's impact, or lack of impact, on early American constitutional thought is, as indicated above, a subject that has provoked much controversy. Between the extreme and conflicting statements of some scholars, one finds numerous and sundry views of others. A survey of this mass of scholarly opinion leads only to an impasse. Many years ago I concluded that the role of Montesquieu in the most critical period of our national history would continue to be a matter for speculation and debate if there were no other avenues of approach to the subject than those hitherto traveled. It seemed obvious that a satisfactory solution of what I then saw as only a conceptual problem hinged on the acquisition of some very basic information—in short, that conclusions about influence could not be validly arrived at until many facts were in hand concerning the extent of American acquaintance with the French thinker. These facts I brought together in my book *Montesquieu in America, 1760–1801.*[3] Written solely from the literary historical point of view, the book treats of the dissemination of Montesquieu's writings, opinions of him, and the use made of his work during the American Enlightenment.

A few words concerning the sources of my information will be appropriate. Books, essays, pamphlets, printed speeches, library catalogs, booksellers' advertisements, and college curricula were all turned to account. I went through the writings and letters of leaders of American thought in the colonial and later period. Sources of prime importance also were the accounts of debates in the various conventions. For popular opinion, I examined important newspapers published in different sections of the country. Research among these newspapers, some of different political complexion, others avowedly nonpartisan, with few exceptions covered either many continuous years of their existence, or the period from their inception up to Jefferson's accession to the presidency, or in some cases even their life span. This investigation, as representative and complete as possible, yielded results which are both interesting and significant.[4]

Since the publication of these findings, I have continued my study of Montesquieu in America. The problem, as I now clearly see, not only is conceptual but also heavily involves institutional history. In regard to the latter aspect, I am much indebted to a remarkable article by Sergio Cotta.[5] He opened my eyes to the importance of the writings of Sir Edward Coke to early American legal thought.

Around 1760 Americans began to be preoccupied with the relationship of the colonies to English parliamentary power. Theories of government, rights, and liberty engrossed their attention. A succession of parliamentary acts in the years following provoked the colonists to anger and caused both resentment and resistance. Worsening relations with England led to the meeting of the First Continental Congress in 1774. Two years later, the Second Continental Congress declared the independence of the American colonies. The Declaration prompted the drawing up of state constitutions. The Constitutional Convention of 1787 framed a constitution for the people of the United States. And the new federal government began its operations in March 1789.

Did Montesquieu influence the American Constitution? Let me set forth, as succinctly as possible, the reasons which lead me to my own conclusions.[6]

Colonials and later Americans were surprisingly well acquainted with Montesquieu. The booksellers' advertisements in the newspapers make it quite clear that Americans had ample opportunity to buy books by great English and French writers. Most often the booksellers advertised Montesquieu's writings in English although some could be purchased in French. The advertisements in the press contained few offerings of his *Lettres persanes* or of his *Considérations sur les causes de la grandeur des Romains et de leur décadence*. But the *Esprit des lois* was repeatedly and consistently advertised in English translation. This book, in English, was early for sale: in Charleston in 1756, at Annapolis in 1762, at Williamsburg in 1765, and in Boston certainly by 1771. It was a "better seller" in the American colonies in 1774.[7]

Books of Montesquieu were in the libraries of such leaders of thought as Franklin, John Adams, Jefferson, James Wilson, John Witherspoon, and John Marshall. To judge by the numerous citations of the *Spirit of Laws* in their papers and speeches, although one cannot always point with certainty to the book's presence in their libraries, many other influential Americans—among them George Mason, James Otis, John Dickinson, Samuel Adams, Nathaniel Chipman, Richard Henry Lee, Edmund Randolph, Alexander Hamilton, and James Madison—were familiar with the masterpiece. Montesquieu's books were also to be found in circulating libraries and in some college libraries. The *Spirit of Laws* was recommended to law students. At Princeton and Yale it was used as a textbook.

The American gazettes disseminated Montesquieu's ideas. Both before and after the Revolution editors printed extracts, sometimes entire chapters, from his masterpiece. Occasionally they did not even bother to acknowledge their source. During the colonial period and under the government of the Continental Congress, it was quoted in books, newspaper articles, magazines, pamphlets, sermons, and speeches. By 1787 the *Spirit of Laws* had become an "American" classic. It was cited in the Constitutional Convention at Philadelphia in the debates on the Constitution and in the state ratifying conventions. It was referred to and quoted in *The Federalist,* the collection of important papers written to encourage the adoption of the great charter. Revolutionist and Loyalist, Anglican and Quaker, Federalist and Republican, advocate and adversary of the Constitution all reinforced and adorned their articles and addresses by citing this treatise. Throughout the century it was used as an authoritative handbook of political information. Montesquieu was held in high esteem. If generally admired and respected, he was, nevertheless, the object of isolated attacks. But instances of iconoclasm were few indeed. Jefferson, absent in France during the Constitutional Convention, was his only real detractor.

By the time of the Declaration of Independence Jefferson had copied and filled twenty-eight pages of his *Commonplace Book* with extracts from the *Spirit of Laws,* more space than he devoted to any other author. But later on Jefferson changed his opinion of the French writer. His antagonism, first manifested openly in 1790 to my knowledge, appears to have been motivated by political and ideological considerations. Montesquieu's "blind admiration for everything English was precisely Jefferson's bugbear," writes Gilbert Chinard, "and there is little doubt that he considered Montesquieu as a sort of political opponent and the chief support of his most ardent enemies [the Federalists]."[8]

On September 16, 1810, Jefferson wrote to William Duane, Philadelphia printer and editor, that Montesquieu's "predilection for monarchy, and the English monarchy in particular, has done mischief everywhere, and here also, to a certain degree." Concerning ideological differences between the two *philosophes,* one example will suffice. In a letter to Nathaniel Niles on March 22, 1801, Jefferson spoke of "the falsehood of Montesquieu's doctrine, that a republic can be preserved only in a small territory," and he said, "The reverse is the truth." Madison would have agreed (see *The Federalist,* Number 10). In another letter to Duane, on August 12, 1810, the Virginian criticized the *Spirit of Laws* "as a book of paradoxes; having, indeed, much of truth and sound principle, but abounding also with inconsistencies, apochryphal facts and false inferences." And he added, "It is a correction of these which has been executed in the work I mention." Jefferson had fixed on a course of action to belittle Montesquieu. The work of "correction" to which he refers was a French manuscript by Destutt de Tracy. Jefferson saw to its translation and publication in the United States. This work—*A Commentary and Review of Montesquieu's Spirit of Laws,* published by William Duane in Philadelphia—appeared anonymously in 1811.[9] The author of the Declaration of Independence called it "the most valuable political work of the present age." He expressed the hope that it would "become the elementary book of the youth at all our colleges," and his correspondence offers evidence that he did what he could to bring this about. "Such a reduction of Montesquieu to his true value," Jefferson said, "had been long wanting in political study."

This is a good place to call attention to the chief subjects on which men appealed to Montesquieu's authority in the decades between 1760 and 1800. Before 1774, the year of the First Continental Congress, most of the citations had to do with the English constitution. His reputation in America was established by the chapter on this constitution in *De l'Esprit des lois,* first published in English translation in 1750.[10] Americans appealed to the celebrated chapter because in it Montesquieu insisted on the separation of the executive, legislative, and judicial powers of government as the indispensable condition of liberty. In addition to the subjects of separation of powers and political liberty, the French thinker was apparently most cited on confederate republics and on virtue as the principle of republican government. Opponents of the American Constitution cited his dictum that a republic could exist only on a small territory. But defenders of the Constitution parried their thrusts by quoting him on the advantages of a federal republic. Most of the controversy among scholars concerning Montesquieu and American political thought has revolved around the subject of separation of powers, and to this I turn.

Cotta calls attention to the fact that in the chapter on the constitution of England there are two types of tripartition of powers: the one concerning the executive, the legislative and the judicial; the other the chief of the executive, the body of nobles, and the body of representatives. The purpose of the first tripartition, Cotta writes, it to ensure the liberty of the individual against the powers of the state. The second establishes the conditions for the exercise of powers by any government wishing to be free. This double tripartition, he adds, corresponds therefore to two different notions of liberty: civil liberty and political liberty.[11] I propose in this essay to deal only with the first type of tripartition. The second type to which Cotta refers pertains to a mixed or balanced form of government.[12]

Separation of the powers of government into executive, legislative, and judicial branches is, as everyone knows, a fundamental principle of the American Constitution. If Montesquieu exerted a definite influence in America, it was on this tripartition. It is certain that there was a tendency here toward such separation long before the *Spirit of Laws* first appeared in French (1748). In my book *Montesquieu in America,* I point to two official protests against violation of the principle. The first, in Maryland in 1720, had to do with the uniting of executive and judicial powers; the second, in New Jersey in 1744, involved the union of legislative and judicial functions. To give Montesquieu credit for the great principle incorporated in our Constitution, simply on the basis of ideological resemblance, would be foolhardy. On the other hand, one cannot disavow his influence because of the colonial tendency toward this tripartition, or because the principle was followed after a fashion in state constitutions adopted immediately after the Declaration of Independence.

The doctrine elaborated by Montesquieu is, as I believe, unique:

> The political liberty of the subject is a tranquility of mind arising from the opinion each person has of his safety. In order to have this liberty, it is requisite the government be so constituted as one man need not be afraid of another.
>
> When the legislative and executive powers are united in the same person, or in the same body of magistrates, there can be no liberty; because apprehensions may arise, lest the same monarch or senate should enact tyrannical laws, to execute them in a tyrannical manner.
>
> Again, there is no liberty, if the judiciary power be not separated from the legislative and executive. Were it joined with the legislative, the life and liberty of the subject would be exposed to arbitrary control; for the judge would be then the legislator. Were it joined to the executive power, the judge might behave with violence and oppression.
>
> There would be an end of everything, were the same man or the same body, whether of the nobles or of the people, to exercise those three powers, that of enacting laws, that of executing the public resolutions, and of trying the causes of individuals.

It is hardly irrevelant to compare a paragraph in the Virginia constitution of 1776 with the preceding passage:

> The legislative, executive, and judiciary departments, shall be separate and distinct, so that neither exercise the powers properly belonging to the other: nor shall any person exercise the powers of more than one of them, at the same time; except that the Justices of the County Courts shall be eligible to either House of Assembly.

Nor is it inappropriate to compare Article 30 of A Declaration of Rights in the Massachusetts constitution of 1780:

> In the government of this Commonwealth, the legislative department shall never exercise the executive and judicial powers, or either of them: The executive shall never exercise the legislative and judicial powers, or either of them: The judicial shall never exercise the legislative and executive powers, or either of them: to the end it may be a government of laws and not of men.

The last clause is from James Harrington's *Commonwealth of Oceana* (1656). Whence came the inspiration for the rest?

Montesquieu's formulation of a theory of tripartite separation of powers as essential to civil liberty cannot be found in John Locke or any other predecessor. This type of separation does figure in Sir William Blackstone's *Commentaries on the Laws of England* (1765–69), but here the eminent English legal scholar was himself influenced by Montesquieu. Blackstone was of course widely read in the United States. And one may well wonder why Americans did not quote Blackstone on this instead of appealing to a Frenchman. For one thing, the theory is "lost" in the *Commentaries*. Elements or components of it are scattered here and there in the pages of this big book. It is not treated at any length. Colonial Americans, harassed by what they believed to be unjust ministerial demands and encroachments on their rights by the mother country, found it convenient to cite the *Spirit of Laws*. Its precise statement on the necessity of separation of powers as the prerequisite of liberty was ready to hand. The tripartition that Montesquieu stressed was, of course, diametrically opposite to the combining of powers in the cabinet form of government which was then emerging in England. The British jurist did not accentuate separation of powers.

Blackstone did emphasize in the *Commentaries*—and this was his central message—the sovereignty of Parliament. The implications of this were more than enough to drive American colonists to Montesquieu. Confronted with acts and issues involving constitutional points, it was both easy and advantageous for them to refer to the French thinker's concise exposition of the broad principles of the English constitution—a constitution not to be found in a single document. To my knowledge, one could find an elucidation of this sort at that time only in the famous chapter 6, book II, of the *Spirit of Laws*.

Many scholars have taken issue with the French thinker's treatment of this constitution. He has been censured by some for his "false views" of it. In an introduction to Montesquieu's masterpiece published in New York in 1900, even Mr. Justice Holmes went so far as to say, "His England—the England of the threefold division of power into legislative, executive and judicial—was a fiction invented by him, a fiction which mislead Blackstone and Delolme." Years later, when Sir Frederick Pollock, the distinguished English legal scholar, learned of this statement, he wrote Holmes, "It is true that the English Constitution does not lend itself to formulas. But as formulas go I don't think M. was far out of the middle of the 18th century. Not only in Blackstone's time but down to the end of the century (if not later) 'the distribution of real political power between the Crown and the two Houses of Parliament was still undefined' as I say in . . . my little *History of the Science of Politics*. . . . But no one thought of the King as a cogwheel: certainly not the fathers of the American Constitution, who knew a good deal more than they read in Blackstone. Montesquieu's error was not in observation but in supposing that the balance of powers could be stable."[13] Another scholarly opinion in support of Montesquieu's understanding of the British system of government is apposite. "If we say that

Montesquieu was interested in the mixed form of government, with the separation of powers as an incidental device to maintain the mixed constitution, it can be argued that his mistake was not great. It may be added that Englishmen in the eighteenth century, notably Blackstone in his *Commentaries* . . . did not believe that Montesquieu had misinterpreted the British Constitution."[14] Pertinent to this last sentence is an opinion expressed by a well-informed colonial. Charles Carroll of Carrollton, a signer of the Declaration of Independence, while engaged in a newspaper polemic, wrote that "so far from being *crude*," what he had "quoted as the notions of Montesquieu, enlarged upon, and explained by the writer of a pamphlet . . . are judicious, and discover a perfect knowledge of our [English] constitution."[15]

The constitution of England as explained by Montesquieu has never had its counterpart in reality. The Founding Fathers could not have derived the tripartition that is of concern to us from England because it has never existed there. Madison took care to make this clear in *The Federalist,* Number 47: "On the slightest view of the British Constitution, we must perceive that the legislative, executive, and judiciary departments are by no means totally separate and distinct from each other." Montesquieu's chapter poses many problems. For one thing, confusion may arise from an unjustified assumption on the part of readers that the author's purpose was to describe this constitution. This he did not pretend to do. Rather than a description, Montesquieu, in treating of this unwritten constitution, appears to have given what in law is called a construction, that is, an interpretation, not directly expressed. "In strictness, interpretation is limited to exploring the written text, while construction goes beyond and may call in the aid of extrinsic considerations. . . . [A construction is] the process of bringing together and correlating a number of independent entities, so as to form a definite entity."[16] The words of the French publicist himself suggest a construction.

At the beginning of book II, chapter 6, "Of the Constitution of England," Montesquieu writes, "The political liberty of the subject is a tranquility of mind arising from the opinion each person has of his safety. In order to have this liberty, it is requisite the government be so constituted as one man need not be afraid of another." This definition is immediately followed by the three oft-quoted paragraphs which assert the necessity of a tripartite separation of the powers of government as a safeguard. In the preceding chapter, which serves as an introduction to 11.6, he had remarked that the constitution of England has political liberty as its direct object, and that he would examine the principles on which this liberty is founded. Montesquieu concluded his examination of these principles in chapter 6 with this statement: "It is not my business to examine whether the English actually enjoy this liberty or not. Sufficient it is for my purpose to observe that it is established by their laws; and I inquire no further."

The most original thing in the French publicist's doctrine of tripartition, I believe, is the position occupied by the judiciary. I do not need to explain the source or sources of his thinking concerning this third power. But he did insist that there could be no liberty were it not separated from the legislative and executive. Yet oddly enough, Montesquieu wrote, "Of the three powers . . . mentioned, the judiciary is in some measure next to nothing: there remain, therefore, only two." He may have meant by this that the judiciary had, to use Alexander Hamilton's words, "neither FORCE nor WILL but merely judgment." So much for the conceptual aspect of the Montesquieu problem. American institutional history is another facet, another side of it. I can only refer to this here.[17]

Eighteenth-century Americans certainly did not consider the judiciary "in some measure next to nothing." They had good reasons not to do so. Only two need be mentioned in this place. One was the ancient belief that no man should be both judge and jury. The other had to do with the confiscations of Tory properties by legislatures during the War of the Revolution. Concerning the latter, J. Franklin Jameson wrote, "The legislatures were so hot against the Tories and so eager in the pursuit of their spoils that they quite overstepped constitutional bounds in their enactments against them. Among the lawyers there grew up the idea, virtually a new idea, that courts might set aside laws if they conflicted with the constitution of the state."[18] The reader should also look at Gordon S. Wood's section on the "The Enhancement of the Judiciary."[19]

I have mentioned Sir Edward Coke. This English jurist was "the chief guide of the older lawyers" until the Revolution.[20] Raoul Berger writes, "The Framers did not pluck the concept of judicial review from the void. It harked back to Coke's 1610 statement in Bonham's case: 'when an Act of Parliament is against common right and reason . . . the common law will control it and adjudge such act to be void.' "[21] And again to quote Berger, "The case for judicial review does not . . . hinge upon whether there existed an established *practice* of judicial review, but rather on the Founders' *belief* that existing precedents, apparently fortified by Coke and Holt, furnished a means to curb Congressional excesses and enforce Constitutional limits."[22] The year 1803 and the decision in the case of *Marbury* v. *Madison* were not far away. This was the first case in which the Supreme Court annulled an act of Congress. This case, however, involved the court's own jurisdiction. The decision in 1857 in the Dred Scott Case, when the Supreme Court declared an act of Congress unconstitutional, was the first in which the court itself was not involved. The trilateral equality which in 1789 had been established in law had now been established in fact. Would that Montesquieu could have observed the development of his third power in the United States! But enough with regard to the institutional side of the Montesquieu problem.

The eminent French critic Gustave Lanson long ago wrote that influence exists when something intervenes to cause a definite change in direction.[23] If this be the test, Montesquieu did not exert any influence on the Constitution. But there is another criterion to be considered, and it is this: a foreign writer will not have influence in another country unless people there are ready to receive his ideas. If they are, the seed will fall on fertile ground, will take root and begin to grow. In that case the writer may direct or help direct thought or practice.

Colonial charters did not contain provisions for tripartite separation of powers, but colonials had made such separation an important article of their political credo long before 1776. Whenever the name of an author was mentioned in the countless discussions of the separation of power into executive, legislative, and judicial branches that I noticed in the years between 1760 and 1800, that name, with one exception, was always Montesquieu.

James Madison, "Father of the Constitution," called this principle of separation "the sacred maxim of free government." He himself believed that Montesquieu was the author of this maxim. "The oracle who is always consulted and cited on this subject," Madison wrote, "is the celebrated Montesquieu. If he be not the author of this invaluable precept in the science of politics, he has the merit at least of displaying and recommending it most effectually to the attention of mankind."[24]

The French thinker's doctrine that made tripartition of powers the sine qua non of liberty helped give a definite and permanent form to American constitutional thought. He supplied the verbal formula for a strongly marked trend. He provided the rationale, and the broad outlines of a structure, for a native concept that had long been in the process of development. This is how Montesquieu influenced the Founding Fathers and the American Constitution.

Eight
Voltaire in the South

 The University of North Carolina was hit by a tidal wave of infidelity at the end of the eighteenth century. Speaking of the university's history around 1796 and the years following, one minister said, "Strong bands of sympathy and gratitude united our people to the French nation, and as a consequence French opinions and French infidelity rolled like a devastating tide over the land. The writings of Voltaire, Volney, and Paine were in the hands of almost all, and the public mind was poisoned."[1] When a fire destroyed his house at Bizarre in 1813, John Randolph of Roanoke wrote, "I lost a valuable collection of books. In it was a whole body of infidelity, the Encyclopedia of Diderot and D'Alembert. Voltaire's works, in seventy volumes, Rousseau . . . Hume."[2] The Virginian, Henry Adams noted, "was as deistical in his opinions as any of them."[3] But our concern here is not primarily with deism but with the writings of Voltaire.

Surprisingly enough, there is no single written account dealing with Voltaire's impact on the South in the eighteenth century. Mary-Margaret H. Barr limited her study to New England and the Middle Atlantic area.[4] John F. McDermott wrote on "Voltaire and the Freethinkers in Early Saint Louis."[5] But there is no monograph on Voltaire and the southeastern part of the United States. Scholars have unearthed many pieces of information on the subject. They have drawn certain conclusions based on their findings. Our knowledge, however, remains fragmented.

There follow some facts concerning the acquaintance with Voltaire in Maryland, Virginia, and Charleston, South Carolina, in the last four decades of the century. I make no claim to a systematic or exhaustive investigation.

Charles Carroll of Carrollton, the prominent Maryland Roman Catholic, interestingly enough, was an admirer of the Sage of Ferney. Carroll wrote to his father from France in 1759, "I intend . . . to buy their best authors, as for example Boileau, Rousseau, Voltaire."[6] In 1771, after his return to Maryland, Carroll wrote to a European correspondent, "Has Voltaire published any late tracts, I mean since the year 1768? I have all his works to that time. If he has . . . oblige me by sending them to me."[7] In 1773 Carroll spoke of having "received Voltaire's *L'Evangile du jour* in four volumes, and *Les Questions sur L'Encyclopedie* in seven volumes last year."[8]

In 1765 another Carroll, Charles Carroll, barrister, who lived in Annapolis, had "sent for Voltaire's *Age of Louis XIV* in English."[9] It was not always necessary to send to Europe, however, for the author's writings. In Annapolis, William Rind, a bookdealer, advertised a long list of books for sale in the *Maryland Gazette* on July 3, 1760. Among these were "Voltaire's Age of Lewis XIV, his General History of Europe, and Life of Charles XIIth." In the issue of this paper for August 26, 1762, Rind offered the "Letters on the English Nation."[10] Baltimore bookdealers advertised writings of the author in the 1790s. "Voltaire's Philosophical Dictionary, 1 dol." was available in 1794.[11] This book, along with "Voltaire's Works, 5 vols. handsomely bound and gilt," was also offered to Baltimore readers by a different bookseller in 1795.[12] The "Works" in fact were offered for sale in this city on several other occasions.[13] "Voltaire's Charles 12th, Lon. 1796" was also available.[14] James David Hart mentions one resident of Baltimore, Mr. Parkin, who "had seventy volumes of Voltaire's works in his home."[15]

Voltaire's histories seem to have enjoyed a decided vogue. J. T. Wheeler, in a study of Maryland colonial libraries, found that the *Age of Louis XIV*, the *History of Charles XII*, and the *General History of Europe* frequently appeared in the inventories, in English. One of his conclusions is of particular interest: Voltaire's historical works were the most read of foreign books.[16] The author was quoted and referred to in the public press. The Annapolis *Maryland Gazette* printed "A Prayer" from the *Treatise on Tolerance* in its issue for January 31, 1765. In Baltimore, a magazine reprinted the chapter in *Zadig* entitled "The Nose."[17] English adaptations of three of Voltaire's plays, *Zaïre, Mahomet,* and *L'Ecossaise,* were performed in Maryland on a number of occasions between 1782 and 1796. *Zara,* adapted by Aaron Hill from *Zaïre,* was the play most often performed. All the performances except two, apparently, took place in Baltimore.[18]

The duc de la Rochefoucault-Liancourt's remark on Virginia is familiar to many. "Fond as the inhabitants are of dissipation, a taste for reading is more prevalent among the gentlemen of the first class than in any other part of America."[19] Such statements are easy to make but hard to document. A latter-day scholar, Thomas J. Wertenbaker, was of a different mind, though he too stressed the important role of books: "The commonly accepted belief that the well-to-do Virginian was a 'playboy,' wasting his time and his inheritance in gambling, cockfighting, drinking, feasting, and dancing, is entirely erroneous. It is true that there was much extravagance . . . but there was also a keen interest in intellectual and cultural matters."[20] What part did Voltaire play in the intellectual life of the Old Dominion?

Williamsburg was one of the South's "crucibles of culture," to use a phrase of Wertenbaker. The College of William and Mary had been there since the end of the seventeenth century. There were booksellers in the town and the *Virginia Gazette* was published here. *The Virginia Alamanack for the Year of Our Lord God 1765,* by Theophilus Wreg, was itself a humble instrument in the service of culture. In the back of it there is listed "A Collection of the Most Esteemed Modern Books" in various fields of knowledge which were for sale at the Williamsburg Printing Office. In the collection were "Voltaire's Works, complete," his "General Hist. and State of Europe," "Charles the XIIth" and

"Select Pieces." It also included the *Henriade,* "Candidus, or All for the Best, in two Parts," an edition of the author's "Letters" and "Gerard on Taste, with three Dissertations on the same Subject by Voltaire, Alembert and Montesquieu." Likewise from the 1760s is a broadside in the Rare Book Room of the Library of Congress of "A Catalogue of Books to be sold at the Post Office, Williamsburg." Among the books offered were "Voltaire's select Essays from the Encyclopedie" and his "Letters." On November 25, 1775, Dixon and Hunter printed in the *Virginia Gazette* a long list of books which they had for sale. It included "Voltaire's Miscellaneous Poems, 3 V." Further investigation would without doubt turn up many other sales notices of the author's writings. In September 1796 Parson Weems, book agent for the Philadelphia publisher Mathew Carey, wrote to Carey from Norfolk that "Voltair's . . . Life different works" were among books that "will sell well" in Norfolk.[21] Here are some facts concerning the dissemination of the author's writings in Virginia.

One investigator made a study of about a hundred libraries of the colonial period. One of his conclusions is of interest and to some degree pertinent: "Voltaire . . . is occasionally found in the libraries, his historical works, *Candide,* and the essay on toleration making infrequent appearances."[22] The historical works included the *History of Charles XII of Sweden* and the *Age of Louis XIV.* Lord Botetourt, a colonial governor of Virginia, had "6 [vols.] Oeuvres de Voltaire" in his library.[23] Here are the findings of an examination of two of these libraries which lie within the scope of the present study. "Councillor" Robert Carter, of Westmoreland County, owned "Voltaire's Select Pieces."[24] Colonel William Fleming, doctor and soldier, had the *Age of Louis XIV* and "Candid."[25] Washington himself was interested in Voltaire's histories. At the close of the Revolutionary War he sent for "Charles the XIIth of Sweden," "Lewis the XVth" [sic] and "Voltaire's Letters."[26] John Parke Custis, a stepson of Washington, owned "Voltaire's works 36 vols."[27] Jefferson, in 1771, recommended "Voltaire's works, Eng." for Robert Skipwith's library.[28]

William Short, Jefferson's secretary while in France, owned an edition of Voltaire's *Oeuvres complètes* in ninety-two volumes. Some of his works gave great pleasure to John Randolph. His testimony is eloquent and to the point. He mentioned several titles which "have made up more than half of my worldly enjoyment. To these ought to be added . . . Voltaire (*Charles XII, Mahomed* and *Zaïre*). . . . One of the first books I ever read was Voltaire's *Charles XII.*"[29] To a nephew Randolph also wrote this bit of criticism: "Voltaire is a most sprightly, agreeable writer, but not always to be depended upon for facts. His Charles XII and Peter are his most accurate works. The Siècle de Louis XIV is, upon the whole, not an unfaithful history; and, as a picture of the manners of that age, is *unique*."[30] And one of Thomas Jefferson's libraries is a story in itself.

Congress bought from Jefferson his second library, his first having been destroyed by fire at Shadwell in 1770. This library consisted of over six thousand books. The purchase price was $23,950. One of the objections raised to buying it was that it contained the writings of Voltaire "and other literary apostles of the French Revolution."[31] Jefferson did indeed have many books by and on Voltaire. The large amount of Voltaire material in the catalog of Jefferson's second library offers ample evidence of the Virginian's interest.[32] He wrote to James Monroe from Paris in 1785 an opinion concerning Voltaire.[33] He quoted the French author in a letter to Charles Bellini, written in Paris this same year: "I find the general fate of humanity here [in Paris and Europe] most deplorable. The truth of Voltaire's observation offers itself perpetually, that every man here must be either the hammer or the anvil."[34] But Gilbert Chinard, a biographer of Jefferson and editor of his *Commonplace Book,* affirms that

A study of Jefferson's correspondence fails to reveal that Voltaire had made any lasting impression upon his mind, nor even that he had read him to any considerable extent. From *L'Essai sur les Moeurs* and Le *Siècle de Louis XIV* he collected a large number of precise facts, using Voltaire as a sort of dictionary of inventions, but never paying any attention to his ideas, nor even hinting that Voltaire had ever expressed any ideas at all. The only mention of Voltaire found in the published works is a discussion of the well-known and ridiculous theory of the French "philosophe" on fossils.[35]

So, in Chinard's view, "As far as the evidence at hand permits us to draw a conclusion, it may be said that the most famous writer of the eighteenth century had little influence upon Jefferson."[36]

Precise information concerning the contents of many private libraries is often lacking. There are, however, other ways of ascertaining acquaintance with a writer. James Madison is a case in point. I cannot say what books of Voltaire were on the shelves of his library. But according to George R. Havens, he was cited by Madison, though less often than some other French writers. Havens points out that in *The Federalist,* Madison spoke of the advantages of a variety of religious sects as a safeguard against persecution and writes that this was a favorite idea of his.[37]

Finally, it must not be forgotten that the popular newspaper itself was a minor source of information about Voltaire. The editors reprinted interesting details concerning him from foreign sources.[38] A reader might find there "An Oriental Tale. By Voltaire."[39] Or a quotation or extract from Voltaire on some subject such as the one on liberty sent in to the *Virginia Gazette* by "Sidney," who called the author "one of the most celebrated writers of the present age."[40] Williamsburg, where this newspaper was published, was one of the South's important cultural centers. But Williamsburg, wrote Wertenbaker, "was never more than a village." Charleston was the largest city in the South. In 1790 it was larger than Baltimore. It was a city where French influences were strong.

The first known American edition of a work by Voltaire, according to Barr, was published in Charleston in 1777.[41] This was his *Commentary* on *An Essay on Crimes and Punishments* by Cesare Beccaria. I have never studied South Carolina newspapers. But Edward D. Seeber of Indiana University did work on Charleston newspapers in the last half of the eighteenth century. And I am indebted to him for the Voltaire references which he found in these papers and which are utilized here. He informed me that Voltaire's writings were frequently on sale and that his escapades in Europe were often reported in the foreign news columns. Some of his findings from a study of the *South Carolina Gazette* are of particular interest: the *Age of Louis XIV*, the *History of Charles XII, King of Sweden, The Temple of Taste*, and *Letters Concerning the English Nation* were advertised in 1755 and *The Temple of Taste* again in 1757. The author was on occasion quoted in the gazettes. In 1767 the *South Carolina Gazette* printed the article "God" from the *Philosophical Dictionary*. According to Frederick P. Bowes, "Voltaire's argument that the theatre was a beneficial influence on morals and society" was also quoted in the same newspaper in 1773.[42] The *Charleston Evening Gazette* for September 25, 1786, printed a "Prayer by the Late Mons. Voltaire." Toasts were drunk to the memory of the writer and other "illustres philosophes" at French celebrations.[43] Dr. Joseph B. Ladd, of Charleston, using the pen name "Arouet," published several of his poems in the *City Gazette*. By 1770 the Charleston Library Society had acquired a number of books by Voltaire, some of which were in French.[44] In 1773 the society ordered an edition of his complete works in English.[45] John Mackenzie left books for the College of Charleston "when erected." They included the *Philosophical Dictionary* and the *History of Charles XII*.[46]

Surprisingly enough in view of the city's interest in things French, Charlestonians had the opportunity to see performances of Voltaire's dramatic works only on the rarest of occasions. Between April 1794 and 1800, *Zara*, the English adaptation of *Zaïre*, was performed only twice. In this same period, *Mahomet* was played once but it is not clear whether the performance was in French or English.[47]

The opinion expressed on the French thinker by one Charlestonian is of particular interest. In 1773, Henry Laurens wrote this in a letter from Geneva:

I know too little of Voltaire to presume to enter upon particulars relative to his history; but in general I may say that he seems to enjoy blessings which neither King nor church nor the combined force of ignorance and envy can rob us of, a sound conscience and peace of mind. His passage, therefore, be his errors in judgment what they may, must be smooth; and I have too much charity if it does not also prove safe. The mistakes of the most brilliant reptile fancy cannot defeat the schemes of unerring Wisdom.[48]

I regret not being able to point to other expressions of opinion by Carolinians. It is known, for example, that John C. Calhoun, as a boy, read the *History of Charles XII, King of Sweden*.[49] Archibald Murphey read this same history in North Carolina in the 1790s.[50] And Samuel Johnston, governor of North Carolina, had in his library Voltaire's *Works* in thirty-six volumes, published in London in 1770.[51]

Let me quote disclosures of Jay B. Hubbell's very extensive research on the South. I have drawn upon his work only for the two items of information just cited. Here are his conclusions concerning Voltaire:

By far the most widely advertised French writer was Voltaire. . . . His three most advertised books were his life of Charles XII of Sweden, his book on England, and *The Age of Louis XIV;* but many other titles are found, usually in translation. *Candide,* strangely enough, I have noted as a separate title only once—in the *Georgia Gazette* for May 26, 1763. The Colonial newspapers often advertised his works in English in thirty-five volumes or twenty-six in French.[52]

My own conclusions are necessarily brief because of the scattered nature of my findings. I am confident that a methodical study of Voltaire in the South both before and after the period 1760–1800 would reveal much interesting data concerning the reception of the author's writings and attitudes toward him. With regard to his fortune in the forty-year period itself, several observations may be safely advanced. His writings were rather well advertised in the newspapers. The newspapers also reprinted from time to time information about Voltaire. And one could find in them quotations from his writings. The presence of large amounts of Voltaire materials in some of the libraries, and specifically in those of such statesmen as Charles Carroll of Carrollton, Samuel Johnston and Thomas Jefferson is impressive. Impressive too were the Voltaire holdings of the Charleston Library Society. The many different works of the author to be found in libraries here and there, from plays to poems, are also noteworthy. He was read by most in English translation. It is obvious that the historical works, especially the *History of Charles XII* and the *Age of Louis XIV*, had the widest appeal. Books such as the *Letters Concerning the English Nation* and the *Philosophical Dictionary* were, apparently, to be found less often on library shelves, and *Candide* only rarely. I think one can say that Voltaire was as well if not better known in the South than were Montesquieu and Rousseau.

Opinions of Voltaire which have been uncovered are all too few to make any sort of generalization. But I have been struck by the apparent lack of abuse of the French writer in the South. We shall never know, of course, how many shared Henry Laurens's tolerant view. It is true that there was obvious fear of his "infidelity" at the University of North Carolina at the end of the century. And a closer examination would doubtless reveal other censorious passages. But from the evidence at hand I surmise that they would not be comparable in quantity to the vituperations of the author, because of the anti-Christian bias in his writings, that I have encountered in my research in other parts of the country. Barr has documented examples of such in a chapter entitled "Typical American Reactions."[53] The fundamental religious and political differences between North and South may well account for dissimilar attitudes towards Voltaire.

Nine

Diderot, D'Alembert, and the Encyclopedia

 In 1751 Benjamin Franklin was busy in Philadelphia with, among other things, the publication of a *Pocket Almanack* and *Poor Richard Improved*. In this same year in Paris, the first two volumes of the *Encyclopedia* were rolling from the press under the watchful eye of Denis Diderot. The first volume appeared at the end of June 1751, and the second followed promptly seven months later. The appearances of Diderot's folio volumes marked an epoch.

The *Encyclopédie; ou, Dictionnaire raisonné des sciences des arts et des métiers* has been called the first of the great modern encyclopedias. As its editor in chief, Diderot's purpose, as he himself made clear, was "to assemble the knowledge scattered over the face of the earth; to explain its general plan to the men with whom we live, and to transmit it to those who will come after us, so that the labors of past centuries may not be useless to future times." The *Encyclopédie* was also an arsenal of philosophic thought in the Age of Reason. This great work, wrote Ira Wade, "organized definitely the knowledge of the eighteenth century; it created a close organization of the more liberal thinkers of the century; and, lastly, it welded the political, social and religious doctrines and theories into a compact whole."[1]

Diderot himself was almost unknown when he began to work on the vast project, which occupied most of his time between 1746 and 1771. He supervised the publication of its first seventeen volumes of text and first eleven volumes of plates—plates which were to become blueprints of the modern world. The long and complicated story of the publication of the *Encyclopédie* need not detain us.[2] The general reader knows, of course, that D'Alembert, already famous as a mathematician, wrote the *Encyclopédie*'s "Preliminary Discourse" and assisted Diderot until 1758. And that the two men were aided by a host of collaborators. The successful completion by Diderot of his part in the enterprise, in the face of powerful opposition, was possible only because of his intelligence, his courage, and his unwearying labor. He devoted the best years of his life to this monumental undertaking, which inspired the compilation of other encyclopedias. I shall mention only one. Charles-Joseph Panckoucke undertook a rearrangement and a reworking by subjects of Diderot's *Encyclopédie*. Panckoucke's *Encyclopédie méthodique, ou par ordre de matières* began to come from the press in 1782.[3] And its last volume was not published until fifty years later. Darnton calls this the "second Encyclopedia of the Enlightenment."

Important as it was for the advancement of knowledge and the philosophic cause, Diderot's work on the *Encyclopédie* constituted only one phase of his extraordinary literary and philosophical activity. Indeed, the reputation today of Diderot and that of D'Alembert do not depend upon the encyclopedic venture. Diderot's fame, especially, now rests on a number of writings, several of which were not even published during his lifetime.

In her book *The Domestic Manners of the Americans* (London, 1832), Frances Trollope let fly an opinion on Diderot in eighteenth-century America. Diderot, Rousseau, and Voltaire, she wrote, "were read by the old federalists, but now they seem known more as naughty words, than as great names." Travelers are entitled to their opinions. The question is whether the facts warranted the inclusion of Diderot in her statement. Howard Mumford Jones, after a study of newspapers in New York in the last half of the eighteenth century, remarked, "It is, however, curious that Diderot and D'Alembert seldom figured in the book lists."⁴ Following a similar examination of Philadelphia news-papers, he wrote, "There is curiously little interest in Diderot; his name appears in 1784, and 'The Nun' is twice advertised at the close of the century."⁵ It may surprise some to learn that this translation of Diderot's novel, *La Religieuse,* was on sale in America at so early a date.

Some years ago, J. Robert Loy wrote an article on "Diderot aux Etats-Unis."⁶ With regard to the eighteenth century, he spoke of the difficulties Americans had in obtaining his writings and of their habit of grouping Diderot with other *philosophes* without taking care to differentiate between them. Loy surmised that the French author was probably considered to be an atheist, a dreamer, and a builder of doctrinal systems rather than a man of action. I wish to examine more closely the fortune of Diderot in America in the last forty years of the century. I wish also to show something of the reception of the writings of D'Alembert, and finally, of the *Encyclopédie* itself.

One of the Founding Fathers, at least, knew Diderot personally. Benjamin Rush, physician and signer of the Declaration of Independence, wrote that "Mr. Diderot entertained me in his library."⁷ How many Americans were acquainted with his writings? H. M. Jones's remark that the French writer seldom figured in the New York book lists seems to have been true generally. He found, as was seen, two advertisements of one of his novels in Philadelphia papers at the close of the century. I can only point to an advertisement of French books, the same one alluded to above by Jones, for sale by Daniel Boinod in Philadelphia. Boinod's list included Diderot but no titles were specified.⁸ The dearth of Diderot offerings by the booksellers is understandable. Several of his works were not published until the end of the eighteenth century and a few were first published only in the nineteenth. But the booksellers' advertisements constitute only one source of information regarding dissemination of the author's writings.

Diderot was well represented in the 1804 catalog of Caritat's circulating library in Manhattan. It included an edition of his

Oeuvres, Jacques le fataliste in French and in English, *La Reli-gieuse,* also in French and English, and "The natural son; a novel; in two volumes [unintelligible]."[9] Both *Jacques le fataliste* and *La Religieuse* were first published in French in 1796. It is reasonable to assume that some if not all of these books were acquired before 1800. Writings of Diderot were also occasionally to be found in libraries here and there. In the library of the American Philosophical Society there is an undated letter in English from Louis Guillaume Le Veillard to Benjamin Franklin. "I send you," wrote Le Veillard, "the Book of M. Diderot called *L'Interpré-tation de la nature* where you will find those ridiculous explana-tions of the causes of *the Aurora Borealis.*" For interesting infor-mation on this book the reader may wish to consult I. Bernard Cohen, "A Note Concerning Diderot and Franklin," in *Early American Science,* edited by Brooke Hindle (New York: Science History Publications, 1976). John Adams owned Diderot's *Oeuvres de théâtre,* two volumes, listed as having been published in Paris in 1771.[10] Thomas Jefferson's second library contained a number of Diderot's writings, the titles of which are reprinted here as they appear in the catalog of this library.[11] As for James Madison, according to one scholar, "There is evidence that he was thoroughly familiar with the works of . . . Diderot."[12] James Kent, the eminent jurist, had in his library the first eight volumes of an edition of the author's *Oeuvres* published in Paris in 1798.[13] St. John de Crèvecoeur, author of the *Letters from an American Farmer,* knew something of Diderot but only through his read-ing of Raynal.[14] The Harvard library possessed a 1749 edition of the *Lettre sur les aveugles.*[15] And the Library Company of Philadel-phia had some of Diderot's writings on its shelves.[16] Diderot's name appeared only rarely in magazines and newspapers.[17] A Philadelphia paper printed in translation almost half a column from his piece *Regrets sur ma vieille robe de chambre.*[18] In 1797 a New York magazine reprinted extracts from Diderot's eulogy of Richardson and from his novel *The Nun.*[19] Theater-goers had the opportunity to see one of his plays. In the decade 1789–99, different English adaptations of Diderot's *Le Père de famille* were performed a number of times in Boston, Hartford, New York, Philadelphia, and Charleston.[20] This play was also apparently used in the teaching of declamation.[21] Zoltán Haraszti found that John Adams did not comment on the works of Diderot as he was wont to do with the writings of other *philosophes*.[22] He occasionally mentioned his name. "I know," wrote Adams in 1790, "that encyclopedists and economists, Diderot and d'Alembert, Voltaire and Rousseau, have contributed to this great event [the French Revolution] more than Sidney, Locke, or Hoadly, perhaps more than the American Revolution."[23] In Adams's correspondence after 1800, one finds more than one reference to *Jacques le fataliste*, which had obviously impressed him, and barbed references to the author himself. In a letter to Benjamin Rush in 1807 Adams spoke, for example, of "a miserable piece of Sophistry, worthy of Diderot." Timothy Dwight, president of Yale, included the *philosophe* in an attack on French philosophy.[24] William Cobbett lashed out against "the savage and impious Diderot, who hoped to see 'the last of kings strangled with the guts of the last of the priests.' "[25] And finally, Samuel Miller, the Presbyterian minister and intellectual historian of his day, wrote about the fictional writings of Diderot and Voltaire which, he said, "were of different kinds, and possessed different degrees of literary merit; but chiefly designed, like most of the other writings of those far-famed infidels, to discredit Religion, both natural and revealed, and to destroy the influence of those institutions which have proved so conducive to human happiness. The novels of Diderot, in particular, abound in every species of licentiousness, and have a most pernicious tendency."[26]

From all indications, it seems clear that Diderot's writings did not enjoy any wide dissemination here. The diffusion of his books could not begin to compare with the spread of those of Voltaire, Rousseau, and Montesquieu. He was read by a few of the "old federalists" such as Adams and Cobbett but not by nearly so many as Frances Trollope implied. It is also obvious, as Loy affirmed, that Diderot was often grouped with other *philosophes* and castigated, along with them, as an infidel and fomenter of revolution. And finally, American interest in Diderot, however slight, appears to have been as much literary as philosophical.

In the first sentence of his well known *Eloge de D'Alembert* (1784), read before the Académie des Sciences, Condorcet enumerated the many learned bodies in Europe to which D'Alembert belonged and concluded his list by mentioning membership in "la société philosophique de Boston." He meant the American Academy of Arts and Sciences. But oddly enough, the distinguished mathematician and philosopher was never elected a member of the American Philosophical Society in Philadelphia.[27] To my knowledge, no monograph has been written on D'Alembert in the United States. What did Americans know of him and his many writings?

Talking of his student days at Yale in the early 1790s the Reverend Lyman Beecher wrote that "most of the class before me were infidels, and called each other Voltaire, Rousseau, D'Alembert."[28] That collection of French prose extracts published in 1792 for the use of Harvard students, *L'Abeille françoise,* bore on its title page a quotation from D'Alembert: "Les hommes ne se haïront plus quand ils s'entendront tous."[29] And Moreau de Saint-Méry, in a book intended primarily for the instruction of French-speaking youth but which he hoped Americans might also profitably use in learning French, wrote that "les ouvrages de d'Alembert prouvent, irrésistiblement, qu'on peut être tout à la fois & grand Géomètre, & Homme d'esprit & de goût."[30]

In the public press D'Alembert seems to have been mentioned only rarely. A not unfavorable reference was made to him by "A Country Clergyman" in the *Virginia Gazette* on July 18, 1771. He was referred to as one of the teachers of the atheistic school in Europe by Judge Jacob Rush in a grand jury charge, in which he attacked French philosophers. The jurist's remarks appeared in a Philadelphia paper, the *Gazette of the United States,* September 18,

1798. D'Alembert and Voltaire were branded as "either deists or atheists" in a belaboring of Jefferson printed in the *Columbian Centinel* on July 5, 1800. Adrian H. Jaffe found only one mention of D'Alembert in an investigation of American magazines.[31] H. M. Jones, in the two studies mentioned above, commented that D'Alembert seldom figured in the book lists published in the newspapers and that in Philadelphia papers he had found only one advertisement for D'Alembert. This was in 1787. Sales notices of his writing were indeed infrequent but there were a few others. In Philadelphia, Daniel Boinod included D'Alembert's name in an advertisement of French books for sale in 1784 but specified no titles.[32] A Boston bookdealer advertised "Dalembert's works" in 1786.[33] In 1795 Moreau de Saint-Méry, the Philadelphia bookdealer, included D'Alembert's *Académie Française* and *Mélanges* in a catalog of books for sale.[34] And as early as 1765, D'Alembert's essay on taste could be purchased at the Williamsburg Printing Office.[35]

I have found few books by the author in private and other types of libraries. But from references made to him, various individuals had some knowledge of certain of his writings. Charles Carroll, barrister, sent to England for a copy of "Jean D'Alembert's *Analysis of Montesquieu's Spirit of Laws.*"[36] The Harvard library owned two sets of his *Mélanges de littérature, d'histoire, et de philosophie,* listed as a work in four volumes, published in Amsterdam in 1764. It also had an edition of this title in English bearing a London imprint of the same year, as well as his *An Account of the Destruction of the Jesuits in France.*[37] In 1772 D'Alembert was named secretary of the Académie Française and in this capacity began to compose eulogies of academicians who had died since the beginning of the eighteenth century. A translation of some of these, *Select Eulogies of Members of the French Academy,* was published in two volumes in London in 1799. This book was on the shelves of two institutional libraries.[38] John Adams once betook himself to a meeting of another academy at which the philosopher spoke. He made this entry in his *Diary* for April 29, 1778: "Apres diner, went to the Academy of Sciences and heard Mr. D'Alembert pronounce Eulogies upon divers Members deceased."[39]

D'Alembert was interested in the American scene. He wrote to Frederick, king of Prussia, from Paris in 1777, "Nous sommes ici fort occupés des insurgens [American], et fort impatiens de voir quel sera le succès de la campagne décisive qui va s'ouvrir."[40] He translated Turgot's famous epigram on Franklin, "Eripuit coelo fulmen, sceptrumque tyrannis," and sent the French verses to Doctor Franklin.[41] What of American opinion with regard to D'Alembert?

The only appreciation of his work encountered was expressed by Samuel Miller. He pointed out his contributions to physics, mathematics and astronomy. He quoted the French writer in a discussion of medicine and he cited his *Eléments de musique théorique et pratique suivant les principes de M. Rameau.*[42] Timothy Dwight made passing and insignificant references to D'Alembert in a baccalaureate address at Yale College.[43] Dwight censured him and other *philosophes,* as was seen in the discussion on Diderot, for "loose and undefined Atheism." But the heaviest attack of all came from John Adams.

Adams reported that D'Alembert owed his place in the Académie des sciences to the influence of persons who could "make members at pleasure."[44] And in commenting on a remark of D'Alembert in a letter to Frederick, Adams exploded. The French thinker had written that "had he been present when God created the world, he could have given Him some good advice." This was too much. Adams gave full vent to his anger against D'Alembert: "Thou Louse, Flea, Tick, Ant, Wasp, or whatever Vermin thou art, was this Stupendous Universe made and adjusted to give you Money, Sleep, or Digestion?"[45] Haraszti was at a loss to account for Adams's animosity.[46]

For some conservatives, D'Alembert was a *philosophe* and that was enough. It is interesting to note, however, that here and there efforts were made to absolve him from the then all too common accusations of atheism. In the appendix to the Reverend

Uzal Ogden's book *Antidote to Deism,* there is reprinted a paragraph of foreign origin entitled "D'Alembert." The *philosophe* is here reported to have said "that he had *carefully examined christianity,* and found nothing in it repugnant to reason."[47] Another writer, who attempted to defend D'Alembert from the charge of atheism, was fulsome in his praise of the mathematician's character.[48]

D'Alembert's career was a most distinguished one. His work in science was acclaimed in Europe. His services were coveted by Frederick the Great and by Catherine, empress of Russia. But in America he was known only to a handful of people and then for reasons that had nothing to do with the work on which his celebrity was based. Only Samuel Miller, to my knowledge, voiced appreciation of his contributions to science. D'Alembert's writings were less widely disseminated in the United States than even those of Diderot.

Brissot de Warville, French lawyer and journalist, visited Cambridge, Massachusetts in 1788. He was much moved by what he discovered in a tour of the Harvard library. "The heart of a Frenchman," he wrote, "palpitates on finding the works of Racine, of Montesquieu, and the Encyclopaedia, where, 150 years ago, arose the smoke of the savage calumet."[49] As late as 1826, according to H. M. Jones, another foreign traveler, this time to New Orleans, "finding there a complete set of the French Encyclopaedia, observed that the books were difficult or impossible to get in the United States."[50] Was this really the case? There is an obvious discrepancy between the observations of these two travelers. What were the facts of the matter as regards the eighteenth century? Gilbert Chinard wrote an essay on "L'Encyclopédie et le rayonnement de l'esprit encyclopédique en Amérique."[51] Actually, his concern was more with the diffusion of the encyclopedic spirit than with the dissemination of the *Encyclopédie* itself. I would like to add, as a complement to his essay, my own gleanings concerning the reception here of "the greatest publishing venture" of the century.

Jones found only two advertisements of the *Encyclopédie* in his study of the Philadelphia newspapers, mentioned above. Both were in 1787. Daniel Boinod, a bookseller in this city, had, however, advertised it in the *Independent Gazetteer* on November 27, 1784. Bookdealers' advertisements of it in the newspapers, admittedly, were few in number. An edition in twenty-eight volumes published in Italy had been advertised in Virginia newspapers about 1780. As governor of Virginia, Jefferson bought this edition for the use of the public.[52] The *Columbian Centinel* (Boston) for May 24, 1794, carried an announcement of the sale of a French library, which contained the *Encyclopédie*. It was also to be had from Moreau de Saint-Méry, the Philadelphia bookdealer, in 1795.[53] The great work was not translated into English in the eighteenth century. But even back in the 1760s, "Voltaire's select Essays from the Encyclopedie" appeared in a catalog of books for sale at the Williamsburg Post Office.[54] In 1772 an octavo volume, *Select Essays from the Encyclopedy,* was published in London and a copy of this was on the shelves of the Library Company of Philadelphia.[55] Our concern, however, is with the dissemination of the *Encyclopédie* itself. Who possessed this expensive work?

Benjamin Franklin owned it.[56] In 1780 John Adams paid a Parisian bookseller 360 livres for an edition in thirty-nine volumes.[57] The work was in Thomas Jefferson's second library, also in thirty-nine volumes.[58] James Madison had a copy, and in the preparation of his memorandum "Of Ancient & Modern Confederacies" he referred five times to the *Encyclopédie*.[59] It was in the library of William Short, and also in John Randolph's.[60] Others either owned copies or had access to the work. Haraszti noted that "the first twenty pages of d'Alembert's *Discours préliminaire* was translated or paraphrased by John Quincy Adams on the margins."[61] In support of a point he was making, Alexander Hamilton quoted from the article "Empire" of the *Encyclopédie* in Number 22 of *The Federalist*.[62] Joel Barlow was familiar with it.[63] Charles Brockden Brown, the novelist, "read through a considerable library [French refugees] had brought with them, including the voluminous 'Encyclopédie.' "[64] But familiarity with the work was not limited to a well-known few.[65] The *Encyclopédie* was in institutional libraries. The Charleston Library Society ordered the work in 1773.[66] It was in the Harvard Library.[67] Incidentally, the Harvard librarian, Thaddeus Mason Harris, underwent its influence. In 1793 Harris published "A Selected Catalogue of Some of the Most Esteemed Publications in the English Language, Proper to Form a Social Library." He wrote in this catalog that he had adopted in it the principles of classification of books (memory, reason, imagination) delineated "by the immortal Bacon and since illustrated and enlarged by the learned D'Alembert."[68] A set of the *Encyclopédie* was also on the shelves of the New York Society Library.[69] Such a spread of a many-volumed and expensive work is rather impressive. Ownership of other sets could doubtless be found. It was, for example, among the books of Father Gabriel Richard, of Michigan.[70] But my concern is with the eastern section of the United States.

We shall never know how much solid use Americans made of the *Encyclopédie* and its volumes of plates, a mine of designs and practical information on a multitude of subjects then not easily obtainable. Unfortunately, contemporary comment as to the helpfulness of the magnificent plates is lacking. But there are a number of reactions from the orthodox and conservatives to the volumes of text themselves, and these were unfavorable. In short, they charged that the work was part of a vast conspiracy to undermine Christianity and to promote atheism. President Timothy Dwight of Yale believed Voltaire to be the leader of the plot and named Frederick II, Diderot, and D'Alembert, "all men of talents, atheists," as accomplices. The first step in the conspiracy, he said, was "the compilation of the Encyclopedie; in which with great art and insidiousness the doctrines of Natural as well as Christian Theology were rendered absurd and ridiculous; and the mind of the reader was insensibly steeled against conviction and duty."[71] One other opinion, similar in nature to Dwight's, will suffice to illustrate the conservative attitude. The Reverend Samuel Miller wrote:

> It is probable that they were prompted to this undertaking by the fame and success of Mr. Chamber's work [*Cyclopedia*]; and also by a premeditated and systematic design to throw all possible odium on revealed religion. . . . A leading feature of the Encyclopédie is the encouragement which it artfully gives throughout to the most impious infidelity; and though much valuable science is undoubtedly diffused through its pages, yet it is so contaminated with the mixture of licentious principles in morals and religion, that nothing but its great voluminousness prevents it from being one of the most pernicious works that ever issued from the press.[72]

Let me conclude with a few observations concerning the fortune of Panckoucke's *Encyclopédie méthodique* in the United States. I wish to do so because one or two of the remarks made by contemporaries about Panckoucke's enterprise, mentioned earlier, have some bearing on attitudes toward Diderot's *Encyclopédie*.

Jefferson was the most enthusiastic American promoter of the *Encyclopédie méthodique*. In a letter written in 1783, he referred to "this valuable depository of science" and suggested to Panckoucke "the expediency of appointing some agent in Philadelphia who may open a subscription for this work, deliver the copies to the subscribers and receive the money from them."[73] This encyclopedia had its place in his second library. The Virginian urged friends and acquaintances to subscribe, corresponded with them about it. To one he wrote from Paris in 1784, "I know of no other work here lately published or now on hand which is [as?] interesting."[74] His correspondence shows that Franklin, Francis Hopkinson, James Madison, James Monroe, and the College of William and Mary were subscribers.[75] Madison called the *Encyclopédie méthodique* "a complete scientific library."[76] Hamilton, no friend of Jefferson's, also had the work in his library.[77] As enthusiastic as he was about this encyclopedia, Jefferson was sorely disappointed by the errors in J.-N. Démeunier's article, "Etats Unis," in one of its volumes. "He has still left in . . . a great deal of falsehood, and he has stated other things on bad information. I am sorry I had not another correction of it."[78] The only other comment on the *Encyclopédie méthodique* encountered was that of Samuel Miller. He wrote that it was begun by some of the literati of France who were not pleased either with the plan or execution of Diderot's *Encyclopédie*. And, Miller added, "it is scarcely necessary to say that this last work [the *Encyclopédie méthodique*], executed by many of the persons who were engaged in the preceding, bears, like that, an anti-religious complexion; and that, while it displays much genius, learning, industry, and perseverance, its general tendency is highly unfavorable to the interests of virtue and piety."[79]

Miller's ambivalent attitude toward both the *Encyclopédie* and the *Encyclopédie méthodique* was rather characteristic of eighteenth-century American thought with regard to things French. Much could be learned from France. But the fear of French "infidelity" and its moral consequences was very real. A fine subject for a new and lengthy *Entretien entre D'Alembert et Diderot* in the Elysian fields!

Ten

A Citizen of New-Heaven:
The Marquis de Condorcet

 In the spring of 1778 John Adams dined at the home of the duchesse d'Enville in Paris. Among the guests on this occasion was the marquis de Condorcet. Afterwards, he made this notation in his diary: "Mr. Condorcet, a Philosopher with a face as pale or rather as white as a Sheet of paper, I suppose from hard Study."[1] Irascible "Honest John" Adams would have much more to say about him in the future.

Franklin, Thomas Paine, Jefferson,[2] William Short, and Gouverneur Morris also knew Condorcet personally. Not surprisingly, Morris, in his own diary, mentioned the philosopher's wife: "Go to Supper [March 17, 1791] at Made. D'Angivilliers. Made. de Condorcet is here. She is handsome and has *une Air spirituelle* [*sic*]."[3]

Condorcet is generally considered the last of the important *philosophes,* and he has received much attention from many scholars. Indicated in my notes is a major recent study which contains a very extensive bibliography of writings by and on him.[4] Mathematician, pioneer social scientist, and political theorist, he became perpetual secretary of the Académie des sciences in 1776 and a member of the Académie Française in 1782. As secretary of the Academy of Sciences, he eulogized the deceased Franklin on November 13, 1790.[5]

Condorcet was one of France's leading Americanists. He wrote, to cite only one example of his lively interest in the American experiment, *De l'Influence de la Révolution d'Amérique sur l'Europe* (1786).[6] A later supplement to this little work included a translation of, and his comments on, the Constitution drawn up at Philadelphia. The American Philosophical Society elected him a member in 1775. A bust of Condorcet still occupies a prominent position in the society's reading room.[7] In 1785 he was made an honorary citizen of New Haven.[8] This explains the pseudonym used by him in his *Lettres d'un Bourgeois de New-Heaven à un Citoyen de Virginie, sur l'inutilité de partager le pouvoir législatif entre plusieurs corps.*[9] The typographical error in the title could hardly have been more appropriate for one of his lofty idealism.

Circumstances warranted American publication of certain of his writings. Here is the list: *Lettres d'un Citoyen des Etats-Unis, à un Français, sur les affaires présentes* (Philadelphie [that is, Paris], 1788); *Sentiments d'un Républicain, sur les Assemblées provinciales et les Etats-Généraux* (Philadelphie [that is, Paris], 1788), a continuation of the preceding; *The Life of Voltaire . . . To which are added Memoirs of Voltaire, written by himself. Translated from the French* (Philadelphia: W. Spotswood, 1792); *A Letter from M. Condorcet, a Member of the National Convention, to a Magistrate in Swisserland* (New York: Printed for the Booksellers, 1793); and *Outlines of an Historical View of the Progress of the Human Mind*, Translated from the French (Philadelphia: Printed by Lang and Ustick, for M. Carey . . . , 1796).

John Adams had some writings of Condorcet in his library.[10] Jefferson owned many of his works, and in French, including the *Essai sur l'application de l'analyse à la probabilité des décisions rendues à la pluralité des voix.*[11] Jefferson, Franklin, John Jay, and Robert Morris received in 1786 as gifts Condorcet's *Vie de Turgot.*[12] Jefferson wrote to Madison from Paris in 1788 that he was sending him two pamphlets of Condorcet "wherein is the most judicious statement I have seen of the great questions which agitate this nation [France] at present."[13] These were the two French items published in Philadelphia the same year. Madison later sent these pamphlets on to Edmund Randolph, telling him that they "contain more correct information than has been communicated to the public through any other channel."[14] Previously, Madison had sent to Randolph Condorcet's "essai [*sic*] on the probability of decisions resulting from plurality of voices."[15] Jefferson wrote again to Madison from Paris in January 1789 that he was getting for him Condorcet's *Essai sur la constitution et les fonctions des assemblées provinciales* (Paris, 1788). Dr. Benjamin Rush showed familiarity with the French thinker in his *Two Essays on the Mind* (New York: Brunner/Mazel, 1972). To cite only one other person at this point, Philip Freneau, poet and journalist, "was steeped in the philosophy of Rousseau and Condorcet," according to an investigator.[16]

Books by Condorcet were available in Philadelphia libraries and elsewhere. According to its 1789 catalog the Library Company of Philadelphia contained two copies of an English translation of his *Vie de Turgot*. Its next catalog shows that this library had later acquired a copy in English of his *Vie de Voltaire* and *Outlines of an Historical View of the Progress of the Human Mind.*[17] Moreau de Saint-Méry, the Philadelphia bookseller, offered in his 1795 catalog various writings of Condorcet in French.[18] The *Records of the Union Library of Hatborough* (Pennsylvania) show the purchase in 1797 of "Condorcet on the Mind." The *Outlines,* and a copy of the French original of this book, as well as the *Vie de Turgot* were to be had in New York City.[19] Barr found that "Condorcet's *Life of Voltaire* in both English and French was listed in Boston and Philadelphia library and booksellers' catalogs thirty times from 1792 to the close of the century."[20]

Excluded from this survey are booksellers' advertisements noted in newspapers of Condorcet's writings. These advertisements contained offerings of his books published in English in the United States, and other things, such as his *Vie de Turgot,* which were not.

One finds mention of Condorcet in various newspapers. John Adams referred to him occasionally in his *Discourses on Davila,* which originally appeared in issues of the *Gazette of the United*

States in 1790. In passing references, he was praised in the *General Advertiser*, October 17, 1792, and in the *Baltimore American and Daily Advertiser*, December 4, 1800; and derided in the *Gazette of the United States*, September 18, 1798, and July 12, 1800. He was also quoted. The *National Gazette*, December 5, 1792, under the heading "Thoughts on Constitutions," printed in translation almost an entire column from his pen. The *General Advertiser*, January 18, 1793, reprinted "From the Chronique de Paris, by Condorcet," a good half-column of his reflections on Robespierre. This Philadelphia newspaper also reprinted *A Letter from M. Condorcet to a Magistrate in Swisserland* on January 28, 1793. Loughrey found that the *Newport Mercury* was the only Rhode Island paper to quote from Condorcet. This was an extract from his *Life of Voltaire*.[21] This book too was quoted at some length in a reprint published in the *Maryland Journal and Baltimore Advertiser*, February 4, 1796. The original French of the quotation in English appeared in a footnote. There was also a citation of the author in English and French on the importance of the invention of printing in the annihilation of slavery.

Condorcet was in many respects far ahead of his time. He advocated, for instance, equal rights for women. According to David Williams, these demands for granting full legal and constitutional rights to women were first formulated in the second of the *Lettres d'un bourgeois de New-Heaven* and *Sur l'admission des femmes au droit de cité*.[22] Another scholar, Mary S. Benson, concluded that "his argument [for the political rights of women] though ably developed seems to have been quite unnoticed in America."[23]

It goes without saying that Condorcet, like other *philosophes*, opposed the institution of slavery. Signing himself as secretary of the Académie des sciences, he wrote a letter in December 1773 to Dr. Franklin, then in London. In this letter he put five questions to the American Philosophical Society and bespoke Franklin's help in obtaining answers to them.[24] All but one of the inquiries were scientific in nature. The other, the fourth, had to do with free blacks in the English colonies. Bernard Faÿ has translated these questions, and here is his rendition of the latter:

> I should be glad to know if there are in the English Colonies Negroes who having obtained their liberty have lived without mixing with the white people? If their black children born free and educated as such have retained the genius and character of the Europeans? If men of genius and parts have been observed among them?[25]

Franklin replied to Condorcet's letter in March 1774, giving him short answers to his questions and informing him that he had transmitted the inquiries to the society. With regard to the query concerning Negroes Franklin told him, "I think they are not deficient in natural Understanding, but they have not the Advantage of Education."[26]

In 1781 Condorcet's *Réflexions sur l'esclavage des nègres* was published at Neufchâtel. Jefferson bought two copies of a Paris edition of 1788 and began a translation of this little work, but did not complete it.[27] Years later, and almost as if in reply to his fourth question, Jefferson wrote to Condorcet from Philadelphia on August 30, 1791. In this letter, somewhat in the tenor of Franklin's short answer, Jefferson said,

> I am happy to be able to inform you that we have now in the United States a negro [Benjamin Banneker], the son of a black man born in Africa, and of a black woman born in the United States, who is a very respectable mathematician. I procured him to be employed under one of our chief directors in laying out the new federal city on the Potowmac, & in the intervals of his leisure . . . he made an Almanac . . . which I inclose to you. . . . he is a very worthy & respectable member of society. He is a free man. I shall be delighted to see these instances of moral eminence so multiplied as to prove that the want of talents observed in them is merely the effect of their degraded condition, and not proceeding from any difference in the structure of the parts on which intellect depends.[28]

Condorcet's most famous work is of course *L'Esquisse d'un tableau historique des progrès de l'esprit humain.* Published posthumously in 1795, an English translation, *Outlines of an Historical*

View of the Progress of the Human Mind, was printed in London in the same year. As indicated above, this translation was reprinted in Philadelphia in 1796.[29] James Kent, the Columbia law professor, owned a French edition.[30] William Duane, the Philadelphia newspaper editor, had two copies in English.[31] William Dunlap, the dramatist, noted in his *Diary* on July 21, 1797: "Read Condorcet on the Human mind to my Wife." And on August 2 this: "Finish reading Condorcet."[32] Jefferson compiled a list of books for study by those whose reading was placed under his direction. On this list one finds "Condorcet, Progrès de l'esprit humain."[33] Many persons possessed or had access to the book, in French or English.

The dramatic story of the composition of *L'Esquisse d'un tableau historique des progrès de l'esprit humain,* and of the writer's arrest and death shortly afterward, has been told many times and needs no retelling here. Condorcet calls his book an *Esquisse* (outlines or sketch) because he had projected a complete tableau. It consists of ten stages or epochs, the tenth being the future.[34] In this work the scientistic author sets forth his version of the heavenly city of the eighteenth-century *philosophes*—a city that shall be built on a double foundation of progress and the indefinite perfectibility of humankind. Neither the idea of progress nor belief in indefinite perfectibility proceeded from him,[35] but in the *Outlines* they are preeminent.

"John Adams Flays a Philosophe: Annotations on Condorcet's *Progress of the Human Mind*" is the title of an essay by Zoltán Haraszti.[36] According to Haraszti, Adams read the work at least twice, in 1798 and 1811, and his comments run over four thousand words. In short, Adams, musing on the *Outlines,* considered Condorcet a visionary. This book aside, he never hesitated to treat the *philosophe* with scorn as a political thinker. He never ceased censuring him as a champion of a unicameral legislature. And he ridiculed the idea of the "Perfectibility of Man," had much to say on this subject.[37] The philosophical notion of indefinite perfectibility bothered the religious-minded Adams no end.

He told Jefferson in 1814, "I am a believer, in the probable improvability and improvement, the ameliorability and amelioration in human Affairs; though I never could understand the doctrine of the perfectibility of the human mind."[38] The Reverend James Madison, president of William and Mary College, was more sure of himself. In 1800 he had written to Jefferson:

> The old-fashioned Divines look out for a millenium; the modern Philanthropist for the epoch of infinite Perfectibility. Both equally distant, because equally infinite. The advancement of man to this state of Perfection, is like those two geometrical lines, which are continually approaching, & yet will never touch. Condorcet appears to me the ablest, & at the same Time, equally as visionary as Godwin, or any other.[39]

Jefferson gave his own view in this passage from a letter he wrote to Du Pont de Nemours in 1816:

> Although I do not, with some enthusiasts, believe that the human condition will ever advance to such a state of perfection as that there shall no longer be pain or vice in the world, yet I believe it susceptible of much improvement, and most of all, in matters of government and religion; and that the diffusion of knowledge among the people is to be the instrument by which it is to be effective.[40]

The doctrine of human perfectibility elicited several objections from the discerning and orthodox Samuel Miller.[41] To mention only one, it is inconsistent with the scriptural account of creation and the present state of human beings. He contrasts the millenium of scripture and the millenium dreamt of by Condorcet and others. Miller admits, however, that the doctrine is "too flattering to the pride of man not to have considerable currency among certain classes of society."

There was, apparently, much discussion of progress and perfectibility by the Connecticut Wits (John Trumbull, Timothy Dwight, David Humphreys, and Joel Barlow).[42] Fisher Ames, a Massachusetts political leader, and Benjamin Silliman, a scientist and Yale professor, spoke sarcastically of Condorcet and perfectibility.[43]

According to one scholar, "The doctrine of the indefinite perfectibility of man and of institutions . . . became the dominant motif of the Enlightenment and of the revolutionary democratic movements in America and France."[44] This is a sweeping statement. Not every *philosophe* believed in indefinite perfectibility. The doctrine, furthermore, came to be bruited about only late in the eighteenth century, too late to have been as influential as the statement implies. With regard to the United States, I can only point to two other mentions of the idea. In an oration delivered before the Tammany Society, the orator spoke of the "perfectable nature of man" without mentioning Condorcet.[45] Charles Brockden Brown, the novelist, "came to believe in the perfectibility of man."[46] So much for the *Outlines* and this notion. As for the book's basic idea of progress, belief in progress was already a fundamental concept in eighteenth-century American thought.[47]

Here are some expressions of opinion on Condorcet himself, and his work. Franklin, in a letter to Benjamin Rush in 1774, called him "a very respectable Man." Bitterly anti-French Federalists such as William Cobbett and Robert Treat Paine vilified him. Cobbett railed against his atheism, characterized him as "pre-eminent in infamy."[48] Paine rebuked him for his "absurd philanthropy."[49]

Federalists of the stamp of John Adams and Noah Webster were more objective. Adams, in a letter written in 1809, said, "I was personally acquainted with Mr. Turgot, the Duke de la Rochefoucauld, and Mr. Condorcet. They were as amiable, as learned, and as honest men as any in France."[50] And to James Madison he wrote in 1817, "I was personally treated with great kindness by these three great and good men. . . . Condorcet's Observations on the twenty-ninth book of the Spirit of Laws; Helvetius, too, in his Letters to Montesquieu . . . Condorcet's Life of Turgot; his Progress of the Human Mind . . . appear to me the most pedantical writings that ages have produced."[51] As noted elsewhere, Webster believed that the Frenchman's theories were "founded on artificial reasoning, not on the nature of man; not on fact and experience."[52] An enthusiast for the French-Revolutionary cause, the fiercely republican-minded Elihu Palmer held him in high esteem. In an Independence Day oration he proclaimed that "the names of Paine, Volney, Barlow, Condorcet, and Godwin will be revered by posterity, and these men will be ranked among the greatest benefactors of the human race."[53]

In the Republican camp, Philip Freneau, editor of the *National Gazette* (Philadelphia), "did not hesitate to publish attacks against Condorcet" in the first numbers of this newspaper, said Gilbert Chinard.[54] According to him, these numbers were nonpartisan. William Short, Jefferson's secretary in France, wrote to Hamilton from Paris in 1791 that "Condorcet . . . is considered as a man of knowlege [*sic*] in these matters [of currency], though I think too theoretical in all."[55] Madison told John Adams in 1817 that "the idea of a Government 'in one centre,' as expressed and espoused by this Philosopher [Condorcet] and his theoretic associates, seems now to be every where exploded."[56]

The Sage of Monticello said, "Diderot, D'Alembert, D'Holbach, Condorcet, are known to have been among the most virtuous of men."[57] And Jefferson told Short, who had been instrumental in obtaining Houdon's bust of Condorcet from a member of the family, "I am glad the bust of Condorcet has been saved and so well placed [in the American Philosophical Society]. His genius should be before us."[58]

Eleven

French Deism, Empiricism, Ideology, and Physiocracy

 In 1815 the United States purchased Jefferson's second library. It became the substratum of the Library of Congress. In the discussions in Congress over this library, Cyrus King, a Massachusetts Federalist, opposed its acquisition in these words, recorded in the *Annals of Congress:*

> It might be inferred from the character of the man who collected it, and France, where the collection was made, that the library contained irreligious and immoral books, works of the French philosophers, who caused and influenced the volcano of the French Revolution, which had desolated Europe and extended to this country. He [King] was opposed to a general dissemination of that infidel philosophy, and of the principles of a man [Jefferson] who had inflicted greater injury on our country than any other, except Mr. Madison.[1]

This caustic criticism of the *philosophes* is only one of many censures on the same theme. In 1801 Joseph Dennie, the essayist, had published in *The Portfolio* a piece entitled "The Imported French Philosophy" in which he said, "Those who have been professors of the new philosophy of France, and their servile devotees in America, taint everything they touch." The acrimony of conservatives goes back at least to the time of the American Revolution. It was then, wrote Timothy Dwight, that Americans had intercourse with "Frenchmen, disciples of Voltaire, Rousseau, d'Alembert, and Diderot; men holding that loose and undefined atheism which neither believes nor disbelieves the existence of a God, and is perfectly indifferent whether he exists or not."[2] The fear of French "infidel philosophy" greatly increased during the French Revolution. This apprehension was widely expressed. "The fact is," said the writer of a piece printed in the *Connecticut Courant,* January 19, 1795, "that a spirit of Infidelity is spreading far and wide; and, what is new, at least in this country, it pervades a large portion of the lower classes of the people. This evil, I consider as naturally connected with the wild, and libertine principles, which the French Revolution has engendered in the world." Charles Nisbet was president of Dickinson College. "From the first, he regarded it [the French Revolution] not only with suspicion, but with fixed aversion, and even abhorrence. He considered it, from the outset, as originating with the infidel philosophers of France, for the overthrow of religion and of all government."[3] And Noah Webster wrote:

> By French principles are now meant, principles of Atheism, irreligion, ambition, and Jacobinism. The citizens of this part of America are firmly persuaded that French conquests, or attempts to reform Europe by the sword, are inconsistent. . . . They believe the opinion, that man can be governed by his *reason improved,* without the usual aids of religion and law, to be not merely a chimera, but a dangerous doctrine, calculated to undermine the foundation of morals and all social confidence and security.[4]

The reader will find many things of interest with regard to American attitudes toward the French Revolution in Charles Downer Hazen's old but well-documented study, *Contemporary American Opinion of the French Revolution.*[5]

Cyrus King's diatribe calls for one further comment. His implied charge of Jefferson's guilt by association with France and things French was, of course, far from new. Such partisan accusations aside, it has been long and frequently asserted that Jefferson was heavily influenced by French philosophy. But Gilbert Chinard, himself a Frenchman, wrote, "The idea that Jefferson had been influenced more than any other American of his generation . . . by French thought has so long been accepted both by his friends and his enemies that we have not come to a different conclusion without some misgivings . . . such an influence, if it really existed, was limited and should be studied historically."[6] Another Jefferson scholar, Adrienne Koch, believed, however, that Jefferson *was* influenced by French philosophers.[7]

In this section I want to comment briefly on the American reaction to French deism and at some length on the reaction to Volney. I wish also to speak of the reception of the philosophical doctrines of empiricism, ideology, and physiocracy.

Deism

Much has been written on deism in the times of the Founding Fathers and earlier. I refer the reader especially to two important sources of information.[8] The deism of the *philosophes* was abhorred by many orthodox Americans. There is, moreover, no dearth of evidence as to the inroads it made in colleges and elsewhere. The deism of Voltaire was the object of repeated attacks.[9] Timothy Dwight, a Congregational minister and grandson of Jonathan Edwards, dedicated his poem *The Triumph of Infidelity* (1788) to Voltaire. I have observed that while Rousseau was excoriated for his deistic beliefs by Dwight, Cobbett, and others, he was also called upon to provide ammunition against the deists. Some American writers used his famous comparison of Jesus Christ and Socrates in the *Emile* as such. From the evidence accumulated, I find it rather difficult to believe that the *philosophes*, with the possible exception of Voltaire and Volney, could have exerted any appreciable influence on the deistic movement in this country.

Deism, or natural religion, has a long history in the United States. With regard to the eighteenth century, which Samuel Miller denominated "The Age of Infidel Philosophy," one can trace its growth from the early imports of books by English rationalists to the founding in New York City in November 1800 of a weekly deistic newspaper, *The Temple of Reason*. It is noteworthy that Herbert Morais began his study of the rise of deism in colonial America with the year 1713. It is also to be noted that Timothy Dwight's *The Nature and Danger of Infidel Philosophy* (1798) contains far more references to English than to French deists. In this little book, composed of two baccalaureate addresses to graduating classes at Yale, Dwight does take a few shots at Voltaire and D'Alembert, but does not mention any of Voltaire's important "coadjutors," as he would later call and name them in his *Travels in New England and New York* (1822). Who would care to argue that Voltaire, more or less singlehandedly, could have changed a whole climate of opinion? Or that French thought was largely responsible for the great damage done to orthodoxy by deism following the outbreak of the French Revolution? It would seem almost axiomatic that a writer would exert little or no influence in a foreign country if his ideas were basically the same as those already to be found in the writings of that country.

I conclude this brief discussion of rationalism and "infidel philosophy" with some remarks on the fortune here of one of Volney's books, *Les Ruines, ou méditations sur les révolutions des empires* (1791). A biographer of Volney, who was a deist or an atheist, calls it a "strange book, with four distinct parts . . . very unequal in value: a prose poem, an abridgment of the philosophy of Helvétius and Holbach, a sentimental history of the Constituent Assembly, and a picture, drawn in broad outlines, of the religious development of humanity."[10] This book was published in English translation in New York in 1796 and in Philadelphia in 1799. A copyright had also been granted for an edition in the latter city in 1795. A new English translation of *Les Ruines* appeared in Paris in 1802. Joel Barlow usually receives the credit for this translation. But it was Thomas Jefferson, according to Gilbert Chinard, who translated the eloquent invocation and the first twenty chapters of the book, which were later touched up by Barlow, who translated the remaining half.[11]

The Ruins; or, Meditations on the Revolutions of Empires, on the authority of Frank Luther Mott, was the only French "over-all best seller" in eighteenth-century America.[12] It is difficult today to understand the great success here of this anticlerical work, which has also been called a study in comparative religion. The book's romanticism, iconoclasm, and the novelty of its approach to religion may explain its appeal to so many people. But this is only a surmise. "Of all the books that ever were published," Elihu Palmer wrote, "Volney's Ruins is pre-eminently entitled to the appelation of *Holy Writ, and ought to be appointed to be read in Churches* . . . by the universal consent and approbation of all those who love nature, truth, and human happiness." Palmer and Ethan Allen were two of the country's most rabid deists. *Reason the Only Oracle of Man* (1784), published under Allen's name, contains no overt indication of French deistic influence. This is obviously not the case with Palmer's *Principles of Nature*, whence comes the preceding quotation.[13] Peter Gay calls Palmer's book the "Bible" of American deism. Volney, along with Paine, Barlow, Condorcet, and Godwin, said Palmer in an Independence Day oration, "will be ranked among the greatest benefactors of the human race."[14]

Another book by Volney was published in English translation in Philadelphia in 1796. This was *The Law of Nature; or, Principles of Morality, Deduced from the Physical Constitution of Mankind and the Universe*. It also appeared in abbreviated pamphlet form in the same city the following year.

At the University of North Carolina near the end of the century, according to a minister of the time, whom I have previously cited, "The writings of Voltaire, Volney, and Paine were in the hands of almost all, and the public mind was poisoned."[15] The writer of an article appearing in Boston's *Columbian Centinel*, July 9, 1800, who called himself an "old fashioned" American and who blasted Jefferson's liberal views, refused to consider "Voltaire, Godwin and Volney the greatest philosophers of the age."

Volney, disillusioned with France and Europe, had come to

the United States in 1795 with the intention of establishing residency. In addition to Jefferson, whom he knew as a friend, he was acquainted with a number of Americans, among them Franklin, Benjamin Rush, and James Monroe. He met Washington. The American Philosophical Society elected him a corresponding member in 1797.

During the administration of John Adams, Volney was forced to return to France, having become suspect in this country. He had traveled widely during his three-year stay. His book *Tableau du climat et du sol des Etats-Unis d'Amérique* was published in Paris in 1803. Charles Brockden Brown, the novelist, translated this important work into English. In its preface, Volney presented his version of the circumstances that led to his departure, and expressed his disillusionment with the United States: "I have observed, with much regret, none of that friendly and brotherly good-will, in this people, towards us. . . . There is nothing in the social forms and habits of the two nations that can make them coalesce."[16]

Empiricism

John Locke's epoch-making *Essay Concerning Human Understanding* was first published in French in 1770. This essay exerted more influence in eighteenth-century France than any other foreign philosophical work. Locke rejected the notion of innate ideas, posited sensation as the source of knowledge. His denial of abstract ideas had many repercussions, and his empiricism appealed to those whose fixed purpose was to challenge any assertion without proof. The *philosophes,* especially, found this most useful in their attacks on church and state. Under Locke's sway, Condillac published his *Essai sur l'origine des connaissances humaines* in 1746.[17] And in his *Traité des sensations* (1754), Condillac went even further than Locke in postulating a theory of empiricism.[18]

Locke's influence, as is well known, was long felt in America.[19] But the French thinker fared differently. Condillac's "Origin of

Human Knowledge, 8vo." was, in truth, among the more frequently used books in the Harvard Library.[20] The Library Company of Philadelphia had this book in its collection.[21] And it was also available in Caritat's circulating library in New York.[22]

John Adams owned five of Condillac's books in French, including an edition in two volumes of the *Traité des sensations*. Jefferson's 1815 library contained, of works by Condillac, only his *Le Commerce et le gouvernement* and copies of his *Logique* in both English and Spanish. William Duane, editor of the *Aurora General Advertiser*, had three different English editions of "Condillac's Works" and also his "La Langue des Calculs."[23]

Few contemporary comments on Condillac have come to my attention. Samuel Miller paid tribute to him, among others, as one who, "with great learning and ingenuity," treated the philosophy of language.[24] In a discussion of education, John Adams wrote to Jefferson in 1814, that he had "turned over [read] Locke, Milton, Condillac, Rousseau and even Miss. Edgeworth as a bird flies through the Air." He also said that "Condelacs course of Study has excellent Parts."[25] Dr. Benjamin Rush, in an 1805 lecture, declared that for the most part the opinions and observations of Locke, Condillac, and others on "a science of the mind" were to be found in Aristotle and Plato.[26] All in all, Condillac seems to have had little or no impact on American thought. Elihu Palmer, in his *Principles of Nature*, wrote of Locke's empiricism, and of sensation as the source and cause of all ideas.[27] But nowhere in his long book does Palmer even mention Condillac. He does refer, however, in other matters, to Holbach, Rousseau, Voltaire, and often to Volney.

Ideology

Ideology, founded on Condillac's empiricism, was the philosophy of revolutionary and postrevolutionary France. Van Duzer writes, "Proceeding on the premises, first, that sensations are the primary data of cognition, and secondly, that all ideas are resolvable compounds of sensations, Condillac sought to remake philosophy into an analytical methodology for testing the validity of ideas."[28] Destutt de Tracy coined the term *Idéologie* in 1796, and the word as first used meant the "science of ideas." It later came to mean "science of man." But, as B. G. Garnham points out, "*Idéologie* goes beyond the study of man himself to become a science of methods applicable in many fields—legislation, political economy, education, medicine, mathematics and so on."[29] Tracy[30] and Cabanis were prime leaders in this new movement, whose adherents were known as *idéologues* or *idéologistes*.[31] The *idéologues* succeeded the *philosophes,* and they served as a "bridge" between the *philosophes* and such nineteenth-century social thinkers as Saint-Simon and Comte.[32]

Franklin was friendly with some of the ideologists, especially with Cabanis, when he was in Paris.[33] In his twilight years, John Adams made teasing remarks about "Idiologians" and "Idiology" in letters to Jefferson.[34] Aldridge has studied Paine's relations with the *idéologues*.[35] But Jefferson is the important link between Ideology and the United States.[36] He considered Tracy "the ablest writer living on intellectual subjects, or the operations of the understanding."[37] Even John Adams had good things to say about one of Tracy's books.[38]

Chinard found that Tracy's influence here was deep and extensive, more so than François Picavet had suspected when he published *Les Idéologues* (Paris: F. Alcan, 1891).[39] "To see Idéologie at its best and in its purest form," Chinard writes, "it would be necessary to study it in America; in France its career was much more toubled and stormy."[40]

Tracy was elected an associate member, and Cabanis a corresponding member, by the American Philosophical Society.

Physiocracy

A glowing picture of Du Pont de Nemours as man, philosopher, admirer of Jefferson, and devotee of America emerges from Gilbert Chinard's study of the Physiocrat.[41] Chinard gainsays, however, any influence of the French economist on Jefferson. It was Parrington who, more than anyone else to my knowledge, disseminated the notion of Physiocratic influence in the United States: "Landing first in Virginia in the early seventeen-seventies, it [French revolutionary theory] met with a hospitable reception from the generous planter society and spread widely there the fashion of Physiocratic agrarianism."[42] And Parrington believed that "the strongest creative influence on the mature Jefferson came from the Physiocratic group, from Quesnay, Condorcet, Mirabeau, Du Pont de Nemours, the brilliant founders of an economy that was primarily social rather than narrowly industrial or financial."[43] But G. K. Smart, who made an extensive study of Virginia libraries, said, "Of the French Physiocrats mentioned by Parrington as influential in Virginia after the 1770's, such a complete dearth exists as to make his conclusions questionable."[44]

François Quesnay, a physician, was the founder of Physiocracy ("government according to natural order"). Gournay and Turgot, in addition to those named above, were also important representatives of this school of economic thought. The Physiocrats believed that the land was the only source of wealth. They opposed tariff barriers on agricultural production, something they considered unnatural. *Laissez faire, laissez passer.* Physiocracy was the principal economic doctrine of eighteenth-century France.

Franklin had met the leading Physiocrats on an early visit to France. Scholars have found that while there are similarities between Franklin's thinking on certain principles and that of members of this economic school, there are also differences."[45]

Dr. George Logan, whom his biographer calls an "Agrarian Democrat" and "a good Physiocrat," had been "urged" by Franklin "to read the French *économistes*—Mercier de la Rivière, Le Trosne, Turgot, all the disciples of Quesnay."[46] Turgot's name occurs occasionally in booksellers' advertisements in city gazettes. I would like to say a word or two about him, not as a political economist, but as a political theorist. And in this connection a few remarks about the Abbé de Mably may also be appropriate.

Zoltán Haraszti, in his chapter on "Turgot's Attack on the American Constitutions," writes, "Of all the French thinkers of the eighteenth century, Adams regarded Turgot as the most dangerous adversary of good government."[47] To parry this attack, Adams composed *A Defence of the Constitutions of Government of the United States of America* (London: C. Dilly and John Stockdale, 1787–88). The New Englander vigorously defended bicameral legislatures and the principle of balance of powers against "Mr. Turgot's idea of a perfect commonwealth, a single assembly . . . possessed of all authority, legislative, executive, and judicial."[48] Adams was never reluctant to express an opinion: "In general, the theory of government is as well understood in America as it is in Europe; and by great numbers of individuals is everything, relating to a free constitution, infinitely better comprehended than by the Abbé De Mably or Mr. Turgot, amiable, learned, and ingenius, as they were."[49]

Mably, a brother of Condillac, held ideas that paralleled those of the Physiocrats, but he also differed with them.[50] My concern, however, is with Mably as political theorist. In 1784 he published his *Observations sur le gouvernement et les lois des Etats-Unis d'Amérique*.[51] The book consisted of four letters addressed to John Adams. An English translation of it appeared in the same year. Haraszti has a chapter on Adams's reaction to Mably.[52] Others also challenged the *Observations*. William Vans Murray, a Marylander, wrote a book entitled *Political Sketches,* which he inscribed to John Adams. Mably was the subject of the first sketch, in which Murray defended the government of the United States against the French thinker's "erroneous conclusions, and fanciful conjectures."[53] Philip Mazzei, a friend and neighbor of Jefferson's, undertook a very lengthy refutation of Mably's errors in the *Observations*. Mazzei's book, written in Italian, was translated into French and published in Paris in 1788 under the title *Recherches historiques et politiques sur les Etats-Unis de l'Amérique septentrionale.*[54] In this book "par un Citoyen de Virginia," Mazzei also felt obligated to document Raynal's ignorance of and mistakes in writing about the United States in the latter's *Philosophical History of the Two Indies.* James Kent, Columbia law professor and jurist, owned a French edition of Mably's complete works. On the flyleaf of one volume, he wrote, "The Abbé in this work [*De la législation ou principes des loix?*] in the study of history, appears to be a wild and contemptible philosopher. He dares not indulge his wishes for full equality, but is at all events for the sumptuary and agrarian laws."[55] James Madison, nevertheless, had made use of Mably in his memorandum "Of Ancient and Modern Confederacies," which he prepared prior to the Constitutional Convention of 1787.[56] And Madison's memorandum was the source of Washington's own notes on this subject.

There is little doubt that the rationalism of Voltaire and Volney was a factor that contributed to the spread of natural religion in the United States. But it does not appear that Condillac's empiricism, or Ideology, or Physiocracy were of much consequence here, at least in the eighteenth century. In concluding this brief but valid account of the reception of these philosophies, I think it appropriate to point out that the Founding Fathers set great store by practical experience. The evidence bears this out.

Aldridge cites Franklin's remark that "true philosophy could be founded only on patient and accurate observation, which must always take precedence over conjectures and suppositions."[57] Chinard reminds us that Jefferson had little use for metaphysical speculation.[58] Adrienne Koch concludes that however much Jefferson loved ideas, "His intellectual life . . . is primarily practical, drawing upon the basic source of human experience. . . . Jefferson's understanding of ideology [for instance] was not a speculative discipline for its own sake at all. He tried to put ideology into practice. . . . For Jefferson those ideas were significant which related to the needs, the sweat, and the labor of human life."[59] One has only to leaf through *The Federalist,* that political classic of a new and proud nation, to be made aware of the numerous references and appeals to experience.[60] Noah Webster imparted emphasis to the point: "On political subjects, I have no hesitation in saying, that I believe the learning of our eminent statesmen to be the superior of most European writers; and their opinions far more correct. They have all the authors on these subjects, united with much experience which no European country can have had."[61] To sum up, theories can come to the aid of experience, but they must be compatible with it.

Conclusion

 Social and political changes in eighteenth-century France were cataclysmic in nature, in America less so. The "junction" of French and American intellects in the second half of this century was a momentous one. My concern has been with important thinkers of that time in both countries. Some American leaders became personally acquainted with French *philosophes* and writers while they were in France. They and others also came to know French authors by virtue of their literary presence in America. The reception of their writings during the Enlightenment is manifest in these pages. No summary of this information is needed. Nor is any restatement of the opinions expressed by prominent Americans in this meeting of minds necessary. Data on which judgments may be based are clear to the eye. Some observations, however, are appropriate.

In America politics, religion, and cultural relations with France were intertwined from the beginning. The interest of Americans in the French language, for instance, waxed and waned as diplomatic relations between the two countries improved or worsened. American distrust of France before 1776 had hindered the study of French. The Franco-American Alliance of 1778 and the comradeship engendered in the War of Independence accelerated its learning. French enjoyed much prestige here in the last quarter of the century. It commanded attention, far more than any other foreign language. But the repeal of the treaties with France in 1798 caused it to suffer eclipse.

Americans were not, however, discouraged from their reading of French publications by untoward political events. Readership increased from the 1780s onward. The majority of the readers resided in or near the cities or towns. They had easy access to bookstores and libraries of various sorts. "Cultural cleavage," of course, existed. There were different levels of readers, with differing literary preferences.

With respect to the reading of French literature, including the philosophic, by the Founding Fathers and particular individuals, enough has been said. But I must reiterate that for many, if not most, theories had to be compatible with experience. Speculation was of little value in a new country.

I am wary of assertions about the influence of various French writers on Americans in the formative years of the country's history. Pronouncements should be based on a broad and sound knowledge of American reading and the reading public in the early years. They should be founded on all kinds of documentary evidence, including the popular newspaper and the magazines. In his book *Problems and Methods of Literary History* (New York: Biblo and Tannen, 1969), André Morize has a chapter on questions of success and influence with which every interested person should be familiar. In his view, "if it is indisputable that [literary] success is not synonymous with influence, it is no less evident that success is usually the starting-point of influence. Success proves the adoption of a work by a social group, which finds in it an answer to its aspirations, an expression of its unanimous opinion. . . . [but] The influence of a work is something more than its general diffusion. There may be acquaintance and curiosity without the real permeation that is influence. This is particularly true of the work of a foreigner." For present purposes it is unnecessary to continue to discuss these questions. On the basis of my findings and with Morize's criteria in mind, I reach the following conclusions concerning the literary presence of a few French authors in eighteenth-century America.

In the novelistic genre, Fénelon's *Télémaque*, Le Sage's *Gil Blas*, Rousseau's *La Nouvelle Héloïse*, and Bernardin de Saint-Pierre's *Paul et Virginie* had success. *La Nouvelle Héloïse* may have been a "starting-point of influence" on the early American novel.

Rousseau's pedagogical novel *Emile* had a vogue but not success. This book, incidentally, along with Saint-Pierre's *Etudes de la nature*, was used to resist atheism. In the field of history, three books enjoyed success: Voltaire's *Histoire de Charles XII* and *Le Siècle de Louis XIV*, and Rollin's *Histoire ancienne*. Montesquieu's *L'Esprit des lois* easily met Morize's requirement of "the real permeation that is influence." Rousseau's *Du Contrat social* did not. Writings of Voltaire and Volney exerted some influence, immeasurable, on the deistic movement in the United States. With the upsurge of deism in the 1790s, Volney's *Les Ruines,* in English of course, became the only French "over-all best seller" in this country in the eighteenth century. But the "infidel philosophy" of Voltaire and Volney also exerted a strong negative influence. Their writings outraged innumerable Americans. We shall never know which influence, the positive or the negative, outweighed the other. My conclusions as to the reception here of the writings of Buffon, Helvétius, and Diderot, of Condillac's empiricism, of Ideology and Physiocracy, have already been expressed. Condorcet, the man, had a *succès d'estime*.

Americans were ambivalent about France. This ambivalence had been of long duration. On the one hand, it was thought that much could be learned from theoreticians in various subjects. On the other hand, there was the deep-seated Protestant fear of Catholicism, then of French infidelity and its ethical consequences. Many Americans blamed the coming of the French Revolution on the writings of the *philosophes*. Others demonstrated enthusiasm. Controversy in the United States over French Enlightenment philosophy occurred for the most part from 1789 to 1801. Partisan politics and strong feelings ran riot. Hostility between the two nations at the end of the century brought to a close the first period of French-American cultural relationship. Such attitudes, reactions, and enmity can becloud the reception of a foreign literature and the effects of divers philosophies. But every endeavor to make an appraisement of the role of French literature and thought in the American Enlightenment is accompanied by difficulties. These essays tell the story.

Notes

Preface

1. See his 1958 address: Gilbert Chinard, "La Littérature comparée et l'histoire des idées dans l'étude des relations franco-américaines," in *Comparative Literature: Proceedings of the Second Congress of the International Comparative Literature Association*, 2 vols. (New York: Johnson Reprint, 1970), 2:349–69. For a checklist of his writings see *Princeton University Library Chronicle* 26 (1965): 150–96. For a biographical memoir consult Antonio Pace, "Gilbert Chinard (1881–1972)," in *Year Book of the American Philosophical Society*, 1972, 132–38.

2. *L'Esprit révolutionnaire en France et aux Etats-Unis à la fin du XVIIIe siècle* (Paris: E. Champion, 1925), trans. Ramon Guthrie as *The Revolutionary Spirit in France and America: A Study of Moral and Intellectual Relations Between France and the United States at the End of the Eighteenth Century* (New York: Harcourt, Brace, 1927). Reviews: Carl Becker, *American Historical Review* 30 (1924–25): 810–12; Gilbert Chinard, *Revue de littérature comparée* 6 (1926): 371–76; G. L. Van Roosbroeck, *Romanic Review* 18 (1927): 158–60; Henry Commager, *New Republic* 54 (1928): 355–56.

3. *America and French Culture, 1750–1848* (Chapel Hill: University of North Carolina Press, 1927; rpt. ed., Durham, N. C.: Seeman Press, 1965). Reviews: Carl Becker, *American Historical Review* 33 (1927–28): 883–85; Henry Commager, *New Republic* 54 (1928): 355–56; Robert E. Spiller, *Saturday Review of Literature*, July 28, 1928, 8; Bernard Faÿ, *Revue de littérature comparée* 10 (1930): 353–60.

Introduction

1. Charles A. Beard and Mary R. Beard, *The Rise of American Civilization*, 2 vols. (New York: Macmillan, 1927), 1:124.

2. See my *Rousseau in America 1760–1809* (University: University of Alabama Press, 1969), 18–21.

3. James Truslow Adams, *Revolutionary New England, 1691–1776* (Boston: Atlantic Monthly Press, 1923), 288.

4. *L'Idée du bonheur dans la littérature et la pensée françaises au XVIIIe siècle,* 4th ed. (Paris: A. Colin, 1969).

5. Garry Wills, *Inventing America: Jefferson's Declaration of Independence* (Garden City, N.Y.: Doubleday, 1978).

6. James Breck Perkins, *France in the American Revolution* (New York: Burt Franklin, 1970), 418–19.

7. For annual annotated bibliographies of books, articles, and reviews, French > American and American > French, see *Romanic Review* 29 (1938)–39 (1948); *French American Review* 2 (1949), 3 (1950); and *Bulletin de l'Institut Français de Washington, nouvelle série,* 1951–54. See too the various publications of the Institut Français de Washington itself. A number of these were crowned by L'Académie Française. Consult also the *Franco-American Review* 1–2 (1936–38) and the *American Society Legion of Honor Magazine* 1 (1930–). The latter magazine is an especially good source of articles pertaining to almost every aspect of French and American culture. A new periodical, the *French-American Review,* began publication in 1976. This is a scholarly journal of comparative literature, concerned with the history of French and American literary relations.

8. Louis B. Wright, *The Atlantic Frontier: Colonial American Civilization, 1607–1763* (Ithaca, N.Y.: Cornell University Press, 1959), 335.

9. But see also Adrienne Koch, *The American Enlightenment: The Shaping of the American Experiment and a Free Society* (New York: George Braziller, 1965), 19–20, and her article "Aftermath of the American Enlightenment," *Studies on Voltaire and the Eighteenth Century* 56 (1967): 735–63.

10. Saul K. Padover, *The World of the Founding Fathers: Their Basic Ideas on Freedom and Self-Government* (New York: Thomas Yoseloff, 1960), 27.

11. See Stanley Elkins and Eric McKitrick, "The Founding Fathers: Young Men of the Revolution," *Political Science Quarterly* 76 (1961).

Padover, in *The World of the Founding Fathers,* writes that "most of the delegates [to the Constitutional Convention of 1787] were in their early middle age, averaging slightly under 45" (p. 29).

One. The Enlightenment

1. From a wealth of writings on the Enlightenment generally, I select for mention here only two books: Ernst Cassirer, *The Philosophy of the Enlightenment,* trans. Fritz C. A. Koelln and James P. Pettegrove (Princeton, N.J.: Princeton University Press, 1951; Boston: Beacon Press, 1955), and Peter Gay, *The Enlightenment: An Interpretation,* 2 vols. (New York: Knopf, 1966, 1969).

2. Herbert Dieckmann, *Essays in Comparative Literature* (St. Louis: Washington University Studies, 1961), 43–44. See also the section "Theories on the Origins of the Enlightenment," in Ira O. Wade, *The Intellectual Origins of the French Enlightenment* (Princeton, N.J.: Princeton University Press, 1971), 28–57.

3. See J. H. Brumfitt, *The French Enlightenment* (London: Macmillan, 1972).

4. *Ethics* 53 (1943): 257.

5. See Richard M. Gummere, *The American Colonial Mind and the Classical Tradition: Essays in Comparative Culture* (Cambridge, Mass.: Harvard University Press, 1963), and Charles F. Mullett, "Classical Influences on the American Revolution," *Classical Journal* 35 (1939): 92–104.

6. Daniel J. Boorstin, *America and the Image of Europe: Reflections on American Thought* (New York: Meridian Books, 1960), 63–78.

7. Henry Steele Commager, "America and the Enlightenment," in *The Development of a Revolutionary Mentality* (Washington, D.C.: Library of Congress, 1972), 7.

8. Henry Steele Commager, "Leadership in Eighteenth-Century America and Today," *Daedalus* 90 (1961): 657. Much earlier Commager had written, "The sources of American revolutionary philosophy are English, not French, and the development of American institutions has been a realistic phenomenon, dominated by geographic conditions and by economic considerations" (*New Republic* 54 [1928]: 356).

9. In *Intellectual History in America: Contemporary Essays on Puritanism, the Enlightenment, and Romanticism*, ed. Cushing Strout, 2 vols. (New York: Harper and Row, 1968), 1:, 64–93. With regard to this introductory phase, see also Theodore Hornberger, "Benjamin Colman and the Enlightenment," *New England Quarterly* 12 (1939): 227-40; David Levin, ed., *The Puritan in the Enlightenment: Franklin and Edwards* (Chicago: Rand McNally, 1963); Stow Persons, "The Cyclical Theory of History in Eighteenth Century America," *American Quarterly* 6 (1954): 147–63; and Harold B. Wohl, "Charles Chauncy and the Age of Enlightenment in New England" (Ph.D. diss., Iowa State University, 1957).

10. Russel B. Nye, *The Cultural Life of the New Nation, 1776–1830* (New York: Harper and Row, 1960), 5.

11. Bernard Bailyn, "Political Experience and Enlightenment Ideas in Eighteenth-Century America," *American Historical Review* 67 (1961–62): 339.

12. For further information consult Peter Gay, "The Enlightenment," in *The Comparative Approach to American History*, ed. C. Vann Woodward (New York: Basic Books, 1968), 34–46; Henry F. May, "The Problem of the American Enlightenment," *New Literary History* 1 (1970): 201–14, and *The Enlightenment in America* (New York: Oxford University Press, 1976); Donald H. Meyer, *The Democratic Enlightenment* (New York: G. P. Putnam's Sons, 1976); and *American Quarterly* (special issue, "An American Enlightenment," ed. Joseph Ellis), vol. 28, no. 2 (Summer 1976). See, among other articles in this issue, David Lundberg and Henry F. May, "The Enlightened Reader in America." Their article gives statistical information on the reception in America, from 1700 to 1813, of certain major authors of the European Enlightenment.

Two. *The World of the Founding Fathers and France*

1. Henry Thomas Buckle, *History of Civilization in England*, new impression, 3 vols. (London: Longmans, Green, 1902), 2: 213–14.

2. Gilbert Chinard, *La Déclaration des droits de l'homme et du citoyen et ses antécédents américains* (Washington, D.C.: Institut Français de Washington, 1945); "Notes on the American Origins of the

'Déclaration des Droits de l'Homme et du Citoyen,' " *Proceedings of the American Philosophical Society* 98 (1954): 383–96.

3. R. R. Palmer, *The Age of the Democratic Revolution: A Political History of Europe and America, 1760–1800,* 2 vols. (Princeton, N.J.: Princeton University Press, 1959), vol. 1.

4. Durand Echeverria, *Mirage in the West: A History of the French Image of American Society to 1815* (Princeton, N.J.: Princeton University Press, 1957).

5. See also, among others, Charles Downer Hazen, *Contemporary American Opinion of the French Revolution,* extra vol. 14 (1897) of *Johns Hopkins University Studies in Historical and Political Science;* and Cushing Strout, *The American Image of the Old World* (New York: Harper and Row, 1963).

6. For this figure and the following population statistics I am indebted to the *Encyclopedia of American History . . . Updated and Revised,* ed. Richard B. Morris (New York: Harper and Row, 1965).

7. Frank J. Klingberg, *The Morning of America* (New York: D. Appleton–Century, 1941), 294. For maps showing the space of the country, colonies, and cities see Lester J. Cappon, editor-in-chief, *Atlas of Early American History: The Revolutionary Era, 1760–1790* (Princeton, N.J.: Princeton University Press, 1976).

8. Merle E. Curti, *The Growth of American Thought,* 2d ed. (New York: Harper, 1951), 39.

9. Carl Bridenbaugh, *Cities in Revolt: Urban Life in America, 1743–1776* (New York: Alfred A. Knopf, 1955).

10. Michael Kraus, *The Atlantic Civilization: Eighteenth-Century Origins* (Ithaca, N.Y.: Cornell University Press, 1949), 30, 31.

11. For example, Klingberg, *The Morning of America,* and Evarts B. Greene, *The Revolutionary Generation, 1763–1790* (New York: Macmillan, 1943).

12. Howard Mumford Jones reckoned the total number of Huguenot immigrants here at about fifteen thousand (*America and French Culture* [Chapel Hill: University of North Carolina Press, 1927], 102).

13. Gilbert Chinard, "The American Philosophical Society and the World of Science (1768–1800)," *Proceedings of the American Philosophical Society* 87 (1943): 1–11. Chinard's article supersedes J. G.

Rosengarten, "The Early French Members of the American Philosophical Society," *Proceedings of the American Philosophical Society* 46 (1907): 87–93.

14. Brissot de Warville, *New Travels in the United States of America, Performed in 1788* (Dublin: W. Corbet, 1792), 107.

15. *The Autobiography of Lyman Beecher,* ed. Barbara M. Cross, 2 vols. (Cambridge, Mass.: Harvard University Press, Belknap Press, 1961), 1:27.

16. V. L. Collins, *President Witherspoon: A Biography,* 2 vols. (Princeton, N.J.: Princeton University Press, 1925), 2:207.

17. See Gilbert Chinard, ed., *The Treaties of 1778 and Allied Documents,* introduction by James Brown Scott (Baltimore: Johns Hopkins Press, 1928); and William C. Stinchcombe, *The American Revolution and the French Alliance* (Syracuse, N.Y.: Syracuse University Press, 1969).

18. *Les Combattants français de la guerre américaine, 1778-1783* (Washington, D.C.: Imprimerie Nationale, 1905; rpt. Baltimore: Genealogical Publishing Co., 1969). See also Thomas Balch, *The French in America During the War of Independence of the United States, 1777–1783,* 2 vols. (Philadelphia: Porter and Coates, 1891–95), vol. 2.

19. *The Writings of George Washington,* ed. John C. Fitzpatrick, 31 vols. (Washington, D.C.: U.S. Government Printing Office, 1931–44), 26:7.

20. *French American Review* 1 (1948): 123–25.

21. Donald Greer, *The Incidence of the Emigration During the French Revolution* (Cambridge, Mass.: Harvard University Press, 1951), 92. See also Frances S. Childs, *French Refugee Life in the United States, 1790–1800: An American Chapter of the French Revolution* (Baltimore: Johns Hopkins Press, 1940); and *Moreau de St. Méry's American Journey* [1793–98], trans. and ed. Kenneth Roberts and Anna M. Roberts (Garden City, N.Y.: Doubleday, 1947).

22. See Louis Réau, *L'Art français aux Etats-Unis* (Paris: Henri Laurens, 1926), for the source of these remarks on Houdon and Saint-Mémin. On L'Enfant and Houdon, consult particularly Elizabeth S. Kite, comp., *L'Enfant and Washington, 1791–1792* (Baltimore: Johns Hopkins Press, 1929), and Gilbert Chinard, ed., *Houdon in America* (Baltimore: Johns Hopkins Press, 1930).

23. Consult John G. Roberts, "The American Career of Quesnay de Beaurepaire," *French Review* 20 (1947): 463–70.

24. See Frank Monaghan, *French Travellers in the United States, 1765–1932* (New York: New York Public Library, 1933); Lee W. Ryan, *French Travelers in the Southeastern United States, 1775–1800* (Bloomington, Ind.: Principia Press, 1939); and Genevieve G. Hubbard, "French Travellers in America, 1775–1840: A Study of their Observations" (Ph.D. diss.; American University, 1936). I have not seen the latter. According to Ryan, Hubbard is concerned with impressions of the entire country.

25. See "French Newspapers in the United States Before 1800," *Papers of the Bibliographical Society of America* 14, pt.2 (1920): 45–126; Samuel J. Marino, "The French-Refugee Newspapers and Periodicals in the United States 1789–1825" (Ph.D. diss., University of Michigan, 1962); and Allen J. Barthold, "French Journalists in the United States, 1780–1800," *Franco-American Review* 1 (1936): 215–30.

26. Consult F. C. Green, *Eighteenth-Century France: Six Essays* (London: J. M. Dent and Sons, 1929), 48, 69.

27. See Alfred O. Aldridge, *Franklin and His French Contemporaries* (New York: New York University Press, 1957), and his article "Benjamin Franklin and the Philosophes," *Studies on Voltaire and the Eighteenth Century* 24 (1963): 43–65.

28. Aldridge, "Franklin and the Philosophes," 46–48.

29. Kenneth N. McKee, "The Popularity of the 'American' on the French Stage During the Revolution," *Proceedings of the American Philosophical Society* 83 (1940): 480.

30. Consult Claude-Anne Lopez, *Mon Cher Papa: Franklin and the Ladies of Paris* (New Haven, Conn.: Yale University Press, 1966).

31. *The Writings of Benjamin Franklin,* ed. Albert H. Smyth, 10 vols. (New York: Macmillan, 1905–7), 9:77. When news of Franklin's death on April 17, 1790, reached Paris, the National Assembly decreed a three-day period of mourning. For details, see Gilbert Chinard, *L'Apothéose de Benjamin Franklin* (Paris: Librairie Orientale et Américaine, 1955).

32. Marie Kimball, *Jefferson: The Scene of Europe, 1784 to 1789* (New York: Coward-McCann, 1950); Edward Dumbauld, *Thomas Jefferson,*

American Tourist (Norman: University of Oklahoma Press, 1946); Howard C. Rice, *Thomas Jefferson's Paris* (Princeton, N.J.: Princeton University Press, 1976.)

33. *The Papers of Thomas Jefferson*, ed. Julian P. Boyd (Princeton, N.J.: Princeton University Press, 1950–), 10:600.

34. Gilbert Chinard, "Jefferson Among the Philosophers," *Ethics* 53 (1943):160. See also Chinard's book *Trois Amitiés françaises de Jefferson d'après sa correspondance inédite avec Madame de Bréhan, Madame de Tessé, et Madame de Corny* (Paris: Belles Lettres, 1927).

35. *A Diary of the French Revolution, by Gouverneur Morris, 1752–1816, Minister to France During the Terror*, ed. Beatrix C. Davenport, 2 vols. (Boston: Houghton Mifflin, 1939). See also the chapter on Morris in Charles C. Tansill, *The Secret Loves of the Founding Fathers* (New York: Devin-Adair, 1964).

36. *Diary and Autobiography of John Adams*, ed. L. H. Butterfield et al., 4 vols. (Cambridge, Mass.: Harvard University Press, Belknap Press, 1961); see vols. 2 and 3. Consult also the chapter "John Adams and the 'Philosophes,'" in Alfred Iacuzzi's *John Adams Scholar* (New York: S. F. Vanni (Ragusa), 1952), 174–212, and Zoltán Haraszti, *John Adams and the Prophets of Progress* (Cambridge, Mass.: Harvard University Press, 1952).

37. *Letters of Mrs. Adams, the Wife of John Adams*, ed. Charles Francis Adams, 2 vols., 2d ed. (Boston: C. C. Little and J. Brown, 1840), 2:55–56.

38. Thomas O'Brien Hanley, *Charles Carroll of Carrollton: The Making of a Revolutionary Gentleman* (Washington: Catholic University of America Press, 1970).

39. The source of my remarks pertaining to the medical careers of Bond, and of Jones and Morgan farther on, are the articles on these men in the *Dictionary of American Biography*.

40. Frederick B. Tolles, *George Logan of Philadelphia* (New York: Oxford University Press, 1953), 39.

41. *The Journal of Dr. John Morgan of Philadelphia, from the City of Rome to the City of London, 1764* (Philadelphia: J. B. Lippincott, 1907), 216–29.

42. *The Autobiography of Benjamin Rush*, ed. George W. Corner (Princeton, N.J.: Princeton University Press, 1948), 67–73.

43. *The Selected Writings of Benjamin Rush,* ed. Dagobert D. Runes (New York: Philosophical Library, 1947), 393–94.
44. Ibid., 373–95.
45. M. L. Welch, "The American Colony in Pre-Revolutionary Paris," *American Society Legion of Honor Magazine* 23 (1952): 47.
46. Elkanah Watson, *Men and Times of the Revolution; or, Memoirs of Elkanah Watson,* ed. Winslow C. Watson (New York: Dana, 1856), 88.
47. Foster Rhea Dulles, *Americans Abroad: Two Centuries of European Travel* (Ann Arbor: University of Michigan Press, 1964).
48. Yvon Bizardel, *Les Américains à Paris pendant la Révolution* (Paris: Calmann-Lévy, 1972).
49. *Discours à l'Assemblée Nationale, prononcé par M. William Henry Vernon, au nom des citoyens unis de l'Amérique* (Paris: Baudouin, 1790).
50. "The Grand Tour Diary of Robert C. Johnson, 1792–1793," ed. Vernon F. Snow, *Proceedings of the American Philosophical Society* 102 (1958): 84.
51. For the source of these remarks, see Yvon Bizardel's article "French Estates, American Landlords," trans. Francine Yorke, *Apollo* 101 (February 1975): 108–15.
52. See Yvon Bizardel, *American Painters in Paris,* trans. Richard Howard (New York: Macmillan, 1960).
53. Irving Brant, *The Fourth President: A Life of James Madison* (New York: Bobbs-Merrill, 1970), 266, 396.
54. Consult Robert F. Durden, "Joel Barlow in the French Revolution," *William and Mary Quarterly,* 3d ser., 8 (1951): 327–54.
55. *The Adams-Jefferson Letters,* ed. Lester J. Cappon, 2 vols. (Chapel Hill: University of North Carolina Press, 1959), 2:467.
56. *The Revolution in France, Considered in Respect to Its Progress and Effects* (New York: George Bunce, 1794), 3d page unnumbered.
57. *Correspondence Between the Hon. John Adams . . . and the Late Wm. Cunningham, Esq.* (Boston: True and Greene, 1823), 35.
58. Cushing Strout, *The American Image of the Old World* (New York: Harper and Row, 1963), 42.
59. R. R. Palmer, in his book *The World of the French Revolution* (New York: Harper and Row, 1971), has a chapter entitled "The English-Speaking Countries: The Revolution Acclaimed and Detested"; see

pp. 219–32. See also Esther E. Brown, *The French Revolution and the American Man of Letters,* University of Missouri Studies 24 (1951), a study of the reactions of Jefferson, John Adams, Joel Barlow, Noah Webster, Timothy Dwight, and Philip Freneau—three Republicans and three Federalists—to the Revolution.

60. Nathan Schachner, *The Founding Fathers* (New York: G. P. Putnam's Sons, 1954), 132.

61. Consult Alexander De Conde, *The Quasi-War: The Politics and Diplomacy of the Undeclared War with France 1797–1801* (New York: Scribner, 1966). On the XYZ Affair, see pp. 36–73.

62. Herbert M. Morais, *Deism in Eighteenth Century America* (New York: Columbia University Press, 1934), 148. See also Gilbert Chinard, "Jefferson Among the Philosophers," *Ethics* 53 (1943): 255.

63. John Fiske, *Essays Historical and Literary,* 2 vols. (New York: Macmillan, 1902), 1:175.

Three. The Fathers' Knowledge of French

1. Henry S. Randall, *The Life of Thomas Jefferson,* 3 vols. (New York: Derby and Jackson, 1858), 2:192n.

2. *The Writings of Benjamin Franklin,* ed. Albert H. Smyth, 10 vols. (New York: Macmillan, 1905), 1:216.

3. Moses Coit Tyler, *Patrick Henry* (Boston: Houghton Mifflin, 1887), 16.

4. *Familiar Letters of John Adams and His Wife Abigail, During the Revolution,* ed. Charles Francis Adams (Boston: Houghton Mifflin, 1875), 136.

5. Carl Becker, *The Declaration of Independence: A Study in the History of Political Ideas* (New York: Harcourt, Brace, 1922), 27.

6. See Howard Mumford Jones's chapter on "The French Language in America" in his *America and French Culture, 1750-1848* (Chapel Hill: University of North Carolina Press, 1927). This book was reprinted by the North Carolina State University Print Shop, Raleigh, 1965.

7. Maurice Le Breton, *The French in Boston in the Eighteenth Century* (Bordeaux: Y. Cadoret, 1929), 19.

8. F. O. Vaille and H. A. Clark, *The Harvard Book,* 2 vols. (Cambridge, Mass.: Welch, Bigelow, 1875), 1:115.

9. *The Literary Diary of Ezra Stiles,* ed. F. B. Dexter, 3 vols. (New York: Charles Scribner's Sons, 1901), 2:296–97.
10. Howard C. Rice, "Cotton Mather Speaks to France: American Propaganda in the Age of Louix XIV," *New England Quarterly* 16 (1943): 208.
11. V. L. Collins, *President Witherspoon: A Biography,* 2 vols. (Princeton, N.J.: Princeton University Press, 1925), 2:206.
12. L. G. Tyler, "Education in Colonial Virginia," *William and Mary College Quarterly* 6 (1897): 81.
13. *The Papers of Thomas Jefferson,* ed. Julian P. Boyd (Princeton, N.J.: Princeton University Press, 1950), 15:204.
14. A. I. Katsch, "The Teaching of Hebrew in American Universities," *Modern Language Journal* 30 (1946): 576.
15. Josiah Quincy, *The History of Harvard University,* 2 vols. (Boston: Crosby, Nichols, Lee, 1860), 2:281.
16. Le Breton, *The French in Boston,* 21.
17. Ibid., 47.
18. *Maryland Journal and Baltimore Advertiser,* March 14, 1786.
19. *Massachusetts Centinel,* September 5, 1787.
20. John Clarke, *Letters to a Student in the University of Cambridge, Massachusetts* (Boston: Samuel Hall, 1796), 76f.
21. Samuel Eliot Morison, *Three Centuries of Harvard 1636–1936* (Cambridge: Harvard University Press, 1946), 82. See also Bernard Faÿ, "La Langue française à Harvard, 1636–1936," in *Harvard et la France* (Paris: La Revue d'Histoire Moderne, 1936), 177.
22. See C. F. Castaneda, "Modern Language Instruction in American Colleges, 1779–1800," *Catholic Educational Review* 23 (1925):92. For a comprehensive survey of instruction in French, consult especially George B. Watts, "The Teaching of French in the United States: A History," *French Review* 37, pt. 2 (1963): 11–165. Watts also refers to important bibliography on the subject.
23. R. A. Guild, *Early History of Brown University* (Providence: Snow and Farnham, 1897), 350–51.
24. Collins, *President Witherspoon,* 2:206.
25. Watts, "Teaching of French," 66.
26. See H. M. Jones, "The Importation of French Literature in New York City, 1750–1800," *Studies in Philology* 28 (October 1931): 250,

and "The Importation of French Books in Philadelphia, 1750–1800," *Modern Philology* 32 (1934): 157.

27. See, for example, Robert F. Seybolt, "The Teaching of French in Colonial New York City," *Romanic Review* 10 (1919).

28. See Mary S. Benson, *Women in Eighteenth-Century America: A Study of Opinion and Social Usage* (New York: Columbia University Press, 1935).

29. Robert Withington, "The Marquis of Chastellux on Language and Peace," *New England Quarterly* 16 (1943): 317.

30. *Papers of Thomas Jefferson*, 8:459.

31. Gilbert Chinard, *Trois amitiés françaises de Jefferson* (Paris: Les Belles Lettres, 1927), 118.

32. Collins, *President Witherspoon*, 1:196, 2:109, 206–7.

33. "Narrative of the Prince de Broglie," *Magazine of American History* 1 (1877): 378.

34. Samuel Eliot Morison, *John Paul Jones: A Sailor's Biography* (Boston: Little, Brown, 1959), 320. For a specimen of Jones's written French, see p. 373.

35. Kate Mason Rowland, *The Life of George Mason, 1725–1792*, 2 vols. (New York: G. P. Putnam's Sons, 1892), 1:368.

36. *The Private Journal of Aaron Burr*, comp. and ed. W. H. Samson, 2 vols. (Rochester, N.Y.: Genesee Press, 1903), 2:483.

37. *Works of Fisher Ames*, ed. Seth Ames, 2 vols. (Boston: Little, Brown, 1854), 1:20.

38. Harry Ammon, *James Monroe: The Quest for National Unity* (New York: McGraw-Hill, 1971), 158.

39. E. C. Shoemaker, *Noah Webster, Pioneer of Learning* (New York: Columbia University Press, 1936), 41.

40. Bernard Faÿ, "Benjamin Franklin Bache, A Democratic Leader in the Eighteenth Century," *Proceedings of the American Antiquarian Society*, n.s., 40 (1930):291.

41. See David L. Clark, *Charles Brockden Brown, Pioneer Voice of America* (Durham, N.C.: Duke University Press, 1952), 68–69.

42. See *Diary of William Dunlap (1766–1839)*, ed. Dorothy C. Barck, 3 vols. (New York: New-York Historical Society, 1930), 1:63, 226, 334.

43. For information regarding advertisements of grammars, dictionar-

ies, and other teaching aids, see Jones, "Importation of French Books," 158n; and Seybolt, "Teaching of French," 371.

44. Faÿ, "La Langue française à Harvard," 178. For information concerning Nancrède, see the *Dictionary of American Biography*.

45. Le Breton, *The French in Boston*, 75. For information on *Le Courier* and other French language papers, and related bibliography, consult Samuel J. Marino, "The French-Refugee Newspapers and Periodicals in the United States 1789–1825" (Ph.D. diss., University of Michigan, 1962).

46. George G. Raddin, Jr., *An Early New York Library of Fiction* (New York: H. W. Wilson, 1940), 22.

47. Years ago I published an article on "The Founding Fathers' Knowledge of French," *French Review* 20 (1946). I desire to express my thanks to the editor of the *French Review*, Stirling Haig, for his kind permission to revise and use this article, or any portion of it, in whatever way I wish. I have utilized the article in writing this essay.

48. Jules Jusserand, *With Americans of Past and Present Days* (New York: C. Scribner's Sons, 1916), 199.

49. See *A Catalogue of the Washington Collection in the Boston Athenaeum* (Cambridge, Mass.: University Press, 1897).

50. *The Writings of George Washington*, ed. John C. Fitzpatrick, 31 vols. (Washington: U.S. Government Printing Office, 1931–44), 16:372. For the other references see 3:36, 27:338, 28:522, and 35:511.

51. *Writings of Benjamin Franklin*, 5:254.

52. *The Works of Benjamin Franklin*, ed. Jared Sparks, 10 vols. (Boston: Hilliard, Gray, 1840), 10:414–15.

53. Ibid., 1:126.

54. As clear examples see three letters to Madame Brillon in *Letters from Dr. Franklin*, vol. 46 (1), nos. 42, 43 and 50. The American Philosophical Society.

55. See the delightful book by Claude-Anne Lopez, *Mon Cher Papa: Franklin and the Ladies of Paris* (New Haven: Yale University Press, 1966). For specimens of Franklin's written French consult also *Writings of Benjamin Franklin*, 1:189–90, 192–93, and 9:364–65; Lopez, *Mon Cher Papa*, p. 76; and Dorothy Medlin, "Benjamin Franklin and the French Language: A Letter to Madame Brillon," *French-American Review* 1 (1977): 232–39.

56. *Diary and Autobiography of John Adams*, ed. L. H. Butterfield et al., 4 vols. (Cambridge, Mass.: Harvard University Press, Belknap Press, 1961), 4:59–60.

57. *Writings of Benjamin Franklin*, 9:338.

58. See, for all these questions, *Diary and Autobiography of John Adams*, respectively, 2:352; 4:78; 2:354, 361, 370, 384; and 4:79. For further information concerning Adams's French, consult Alfred Iacuzzi, *John Adams Scholar* (New York: S. F. Vanni [Ragusa], 1952), 3–12.

59. See J. M. Carrière, "Mr. Jefferson Sponsors a New French Method," *French Review* 19 (1945–46): 394–405.

60. *The Writings of Thomas Jefferson*, definitive ed., ed. Albert E. Bergh, 20 vols. (Washington: Thomas Jefferson Memorial Association, 1907), 1:3.

61. Ibid., 7:ii.

62. See Gilbert Chinard, *Volney et l'Amérique* (Baltimore: Johns Hopkins Press, 1923), and also his *Jefferson et les Idéologues* (Baltimore: Johns Hopkins Press, 1925).

63. *Papers of Thomas Jefferson*, 15:622.

64. Kenneth Umbreit, *Founding Fathers* (New York: Harper and Brothers, 1941), 67.

65. *Papers of Thomas Jefferson*, 10:127.

66. For specimens see Carrière, "Mr. Jefferson," 400–401.

67. Consult George R. Havens, "James Madison et la pensée française," *Revue de littérature comparée* 3 (1923): 604–15.

68. Irving Brant, *James Madison*, 6 vols. (Indianapolis: Bobbs-Merrill, 1941–61), 1:63.

69. *Writings of Benjamin Franklin*, 6:236.

70. *Old Family Letters, Copied from the Originals for Alexander Biddle*, 2 vols. (Philadelphia: J. B. Lippincott, 1892), 1:16.

71. *The Autobiography of Benjamin Rush*, ed. George W. Corner (Princeton, N.J.: Princeton University Press, 1948), 42–43.

72. *Letters of Benjamin Rush*, ed. L. H. Butterfield, 2 vols. (Princeton, N.J.: Princeton University Press, 1951), 1:531.

73. Ibid., 1:493.

74. John C. Hamilton, *The Life of Alexander Hamilton*, 2 vols. (New York: D. Appleton, 1840–41), 1:3.

75. Daniel Walther, *Gouverneur Morris: Witness of Two Revolutions* (New York: Funk and Wagnalls, 1934), 9–10.

76. Broadus Mitchell, *Alexander Hamilton* (New York: Macmillan, 1957), 94.

77. *A Diary of the French Revolution by Gouverneur Morris,* ed. Beatrix Cary Davenport, 2 vols. (Boston: Houghton Mifflin, 1939), 1:xv, xli.

78. See, for instance, Faÿ, "La Langue française à Harvard," 180–81.

79. Consult, for a case in point, Samuel Eliot Morison, *Three Centuries of Harvard, 1636–1936* (Cambridge, Mass.: Harvard University Press, 1946), 186.

Four. French Literature

1. George G. Raddin, *An Early New York Library of Fiction, with a Checklist of the Fiction in H. Caritat's Circulating Library* (New York: H. W. Wilson, 1940).

2. Harvey Gates Townsend, *Philosophical Ideas in the United States* (New York: American Book Co., 1934), 18.

3. *The Papers of Thomas Jefferson,* ed. Julian P. Boyd (Princeton, N.J.: Princeton University Press, 1950), 1:76–81.

4. *The Catalogue of the John Adams Library in the Public Library of the City of Boston* (1917) lists some four hundred or more titles of books in French, not to speak of translations from the French. Concerning this library, see Zoltán Haraszti, *John Adams and the Prophets of Progress* (Cambridge, Mass.: Harvard University Press, 1952), 14–25. See also Alfred Iacuzzi, *John Adams Scholar* (New York: S. F. Vanni, 1952).

5. George R. Havens, "James Madison et la pensée française," *Revue de littérature comparée* 3 (1923): 615.

6. *Memoirs and Letters of James Kent,* ed. William Kent (Boston: Little, Brown, 1898), 27.

7. *Diary of William Dunlap,* ed. Dorothy C. Barck, 3 vols. (New York: New-York Historical Society, 1930) 1:168–69.

8. Paul M. Spurlin, "Readership in the American Enlightenment," in *Literature and History in the Age of Ideas: Essays on the French Enlight-*

enment Presented to George R. Havens, ed. Charles G. S. Williams (Columbus: Ohio State University Press, 1975), 359–74.

9. Russel B. Nye, *The Cultural Life of the New Nation, 1776–1830* (New York: Harper and Brothers, 1960), 250.

10. H. Lehmann-Haupt, *The Book in America: A History of the Making and Selling of Books in the United States,* 2d ed. (New York: Bowker, 1952), 132–33.

11. Albert Schinz, "La Librairie française en Amérique au temps de Washington," *Revue d'histoire littéraire de la France* 24 (1917):568–84.

12. Michael Kraus, *The Atlantic Civilization: Eighteenth-Century Origins* (Ithaca, N.Y.: Cornell University Press, 1949), 81.

13. Evarts B. Greene, *The Revolutionary Generation, 1763–1790* (New York: Macmillan, 1943), 136.

14. For an analysis, See Albert Schinz, "Un 'Rousseauiste' en Amérique (*L'Abeille française,* de Joseph Nancrède)," *Modern Language Notes* 35 (1920): 10–18.

15. Forrest Bowe, *French Literature in Early American Translation: A Bibliographical Survey of Books and Pamphlets Printed in the United States from 1668 Through 1820,* ed. Mary Daniels (New York: Garland, 1977).

16. Howard Mumford Jones, "The Importation of French Literature in New York City, 1750–1800," *Studies in Philology* 28 (October 1931), and "The Importation of French Books in Philadelphia, 1750–1800," *Modern Philology* 32 (1934).

17. Frank Luther Mott, *American Journalism,* 3d ed. (New York: Macmillan, 1962), 113n.

18. David Lundberg and Henry F. May, "The Enlightened Reader in America," *American Quarterly* 28 (Summer, 1976). My own findings and remarks are independent of those of these two investigators.

19. E.g., *Universal Asylum and Columbian Magazine* 6 (March 1791); *American Monthly Review* 3 (1795); 367–73; and *American Universal Magazine* 4 (1797–98): 422.

20. Consult the Evans, Bristol, Shipton, and Mooney indexes of American imprints through 1800.

21. See, for instance, the *Boston Gazette,* November 30, 1761, and the *Maryland Gazette,* August 26, 1762. It was advertised in the *South Carolina Gazette* as early as 1753. I am indebted to my friend Edward

D. Seeber for certain facts he gleaned from a study of South Carolina newspapers.

22. Joseph T. Wheeler, "Books Owned by Marylanders, 1700–1776," *Maryland Historical Magazine* 35 (1940): 351.

23. George K. Smart, "Private Libraries in Colonial Virginia," *American Literature* 10 (1938): 35. Smart cannot say whether in French or in English.

24. *William and Mary College Quarterly Historical Magazine* 3 (1895): 251.

25. Herbert W. Schneider, *Samuel Johnson, President of King's College,* 4 vols. (New York: Columbia University Press, 1929), 2:317. Johnson himself read the work in French in 1728–29 (1:507).

26. Samuel Eliot Morison, *Three Centuries of Harvard 1636–1936* (Cambridge, Mass.: Harvard University Press, 1946), 81.

27. John Clarke, *Letters to a Student in the University of Cambridge, Massachusetts* (Boston: Samuel Hall, 1796).

28. Rufus W. Griswold, *The Female Poets of America* (Philadelphia: Moss, 1863), 24–27.

29. Emily E. F. Skeel, ed., *Mason Locke Weems: His Works and Ways,* 3 vols. (New York: n.p., 1929), 2:82–83.

30. *Catalogue of the Washington Collection in the Boston Athenaeum* (Cambridge, Mass.: University Press, 1897).

31. James D. Hart, *The Popular Book: A History of America's Literary Taste* (New York: Oxford University Press, 1950), 33.

32. [Lucinda Orr], *Journal of a Young Lady of Virginia, 1782* (Baltimore: John Murphy, 1871), 44–45.

33. Mary S. Benson, *Women in Eighteenth-Century America: A Study of Opinion and Social Usage* (New York: Columbia University Press, 1935), 20.

34. V. L. Collins, *President Witherspoon: A Biography,* 2 vols. (Princeton, N.J.: Princeton University Press, 1925), 2:207. Fénelon's treatise had some effect on Brockden Brown's *Alcuin; or, The Rights of Women.* See David Lee Clark, *Charles Brockden Brown: Pioneer Voice of America* (Durham, N.C.: Duke University Press, 1952).

35. Skeel, *Mason Locke Weems,* 2:167, 186.

36. Consult Madeleine B. Stern, "Saint-Pierre in America: Joseph Nancrède and Isaiah Thomas," *Papers of the Bibliographical Society of*

America 68 (1974): 312–25. This article also contains information concerning Nancrède's publications of *Paul and Virginia.*

37. The *American Universal Magazine,* for example, began serial publication of *Arcadia,* from the third volume of the book, on February 6, 1797.

38. Samuel Miller, *A Brief Retrospect of the Eighteenth Century,* 2 vols. (New York: T. and J. Swords, 1803; reprint ed., New York: Burt Franklin, 1970), 1:41n.

39. Ibid., 2:170.

40. Smart, "Private Libraries," 35. Smart cannot say whether in French or in English.

41. Wheeler, "Books Owned by Marylanders," 350.

42. J. H. Shera, *Foundations of the Public Library: The Origins of the Public Library Movement in New England, 1629–1855* (Chicago: University of Chicago Press, 1949), 136–37.

43. Frank Luther Mott, *Golden Multitudes: The Story of Best Sellers in the United States* (New York: Macmillan, 1947), 316.

44. Ruth Halsey, *Forgotten Books of the American Nursery: A History of the Development of the American Story-Book* (Boston: C. E. Goodspeed, 1911; reprint ed., Detroit: Singing Tree Press, 1969), 132. In 1796 Aaron Burr purchased one of her books, *Annales de la vertu,* for his precocious and beloved daughter, Theodosia, then nine. He regretted his purchase, and wrote to his wife urging "the necessity of reading books before we put them in the hands of children" (134).

45. Benson, *Women in Eighteenth-Century America,* 79.

46. See Lewis P. Waldo, *The French Drama in America in the Eighteenth Century* (Baltimore: Johns Hopkins Press, 1942), 233–34.

47. For an analysis of Harris's *Catalogue,* see Earl L. Bradsher, "A Model American Library of 1793," *Sewanee Review* 24 (1916): 458–75.

48. Halsey, *Forgotten Books,* 134f.

49. David E. Cloyd, *Benjamin Franklin and Education* (Boston: D. C. Heath, 1902), 91. In his *Proposals Relating to the Education of Youth in Pensilvania* (1749), Franklin also cites Rollin's *The Method of Teaching and Studying the Belles Lettres* a number of times. This work was in many libraries.

50. Stephen B. Weeks, "Libraries and Literature in North Carolina in

the Eighteenth Century," *Annual Report of the American Historical Association for the Year 1895* (Washington: Government Printing Office, 1896).

51. Clarke, *Letters*, 64–65.
52. *The Monthly Anthology and Boston Review* 3 (1806):628.
53. See Mary-Margaret H. Barr, *Voltaire in America, 1744–1800* (Baltimore: Johns Hopkins Press, 1941) and my essay on Voltaire later on.
54. Miller, *Brief Retrospect*, 2:137–38.
55. Evarts B. Greene, *The Revolutionary Generation, 1763–1790* (New York: Macmillan, 1943), 139.
56. See Rebecca P. Hein, "Montaigne in America" (Ph.D. diss., University of Michigan, 1966), 12–26.
57. Consult Theophilus Wreg, *The Virginia Almanack for the Year of Our Lord God 1765* (Williamsburg: Joseph Royle, 1765).
58. J. T. Wheeler, "Reading Interests of the Professional Classes in Colonial Maryland, 1700–1776," *Maryland Historical Magazine* 36 (1941): 201, and "Reading Interests of Maryland Planters and Merchants, 1700–1776," *Maryland Historical Magazine* 37 (1942): 41.
59. William Reitzel, "The Purchasing of English Books in Philadelphia, 1790–1800," *Modern Philology* 35 (1937): 162.
60. *Proceedings of the Massachusetts Historical Society* 51 (1917–18): 368.
61. *American Universal Magazine* 4 (1798): 147–55, 229–37.
62. See Lewis P. Waldo, *The French Drama in America in the Eighteenth Century and Its Influence on the American Drama of That Period, 1701–1800* (Baltimore: Johns Hopkins Press, 1942), appendix D, 220–40. Otis Fellows suggests a few additions to Waldo's excellent book in the *Romanic Review* 34 (1943): 268. Consult also Edward D. Seeber, "The French Theatre in Charleston in the Eighteenth Century," *South Carolina Historical and Genealogical Magazine* 42 (1941): 1–7.
63. L. Clark Keating, "Molière in New York," in *Molière and the Commonwealth of Letters: Patrimony and Posterity,* ed. R. Johnson, Jr., E. S. Neumann, and G. T. Trail (Jackson: University Press of Mississippi, 1975), 400. Consult Waldo, *French Drama in America,* 109–15.
64. Reitzel, "Purchasing of English Books," 161f.
65. Collins, *President Witherspoon,* 2:207–8.
66. *William and Mary College Quarterly* 15, (1907): 105.

67. Catalogue of the Library of Chancellor James Kent (1940), mimeographed copy in the William L. Clements Library, University of Michigan, Ann Arbor.
68. John Barker, *Strange Contrarieties: Pascal in England During the Age of Reason* (Montreal: McGill-Queen's University Press, 1975), 242.
69. *Papers of Thomas Jefferson,* 1:78f.
70. See Samuel Eliot Morison, *The Intellectual Life of Colonial New England,* 2d ed. (New York: New York University Press, 1956).
71. Guy R. Lyle, "Imagination in Colonial Literary Taste," *Library Review* 4 (Summer, 1933): 58.
72. Consult Howard C. Rice, "Cotton Mather Speaks to France: American Propaganda in the Age of Louis XIV," *New England Quarterly* 16 (1943): 198–233.
73. Bowe, *French Literature in Early American Translation,* xvii.
74. See *Proceedings of the Massachusetts Historical Society* 51 (1917–18): 363–68.
75. Consult Havens, "James Madison et la pensée française."
76. *Catalogue of the Library of the Late Colonel William Duane* (Philadelphia Auctioneer's Catalog, 1836).
77. Catalogue of the Library of Kent.
78. Shera, *Foundations of the Public Library,* 154.
79. Hart, *The Popular Book,* 53.
80. See Miller, *Brief Retrospect,* 2:171ff.
81. Collins, *President Witherspoon,* 2:206.
82. Clarke, *Letters to a Student,* 76–79.
83. Miller, *Brief Retrospect,* 2:161–63, 193, 195–96, 200.
84. *The Writings of Thomas Jefferson,* library ed., ed. Andrew A. Lipscomb and Albert E. Bergh, 20 vols. (Washington: Thomas Jefferson Memorial Association, 1903–4), 15:166.
85. Mott, *Golden Multitudes,* 7–8, 315, 317.

Five. Buffon

1. Gilbert Chinard, review of *L'Esprit révolutionnaire en France et aux Etats-Unis à la fin du XVIIIe siècle,* by Bernard Faÿ, *Revue de littérature comparée* 6 (1926): 375–76.
2. John C. Greene, "Science and the Public in the Age of Jefferson,"

in *Early American Science,* ed. Brooke Hindle (New York: Science History Publications, 1976), 205.

3. See especially Otis E. Fellows and Stephen F. Milliken, *Buffon* (New York: Twayne, 1972). George R. Havens, reviewing this book in *Diderot Studies* 18 (1975), refers to it as "the first book-length biography of Buffon in English, the special difficulties of the subject having evidently deterred previous writers." Consult also Otis Fellows, "Buffon's Place in the Enlightenment," *Studies on Voltaire and the Eighteenth Century* 25 (1963), 603–29. This article is reprinted in Fellows's *From Voltaire to La Nouvelle Critique: Problems and Personalities* (Geneva: Librairie Droz, 1970), 54–71.

4. See, for example, Edwin T. Martin, *Thomas Jefferson: Scientist* (New York: Henry Schuman, 1952), 152–53.

5. Margaret B. Korty, "Benjamin Franklin and Eighteenth-Century American Libraries," *Transactions of the American Philosophical Society* n.s., 55, pt. 9 (1965): 54.

6. See William F. Falls, "Buffon, Franklin, et deux académies américaines," *Romanic Review* 29 (1938): 37–47.

7. Ibid., 39.

8. Fellows and Milliken, *Buffon,* 146.

9. *The Private Correspondence of Daniel Webster,* ed. Fletcher Webster, 2 vols. (Boston: Little, Brown, 1857), 1:371–72.

10. *Diary and Autobiography of John Adams,* ed. L. H. Butterfield et al., 4 vols. (Cambridge, Mass.: Harvard University Press, Belknap Press, 1961), 3:191.

11. Michael Kraus, *The Atlantic Civilization: Eighteenth-Century Origins* (Ithaca, N.Y.: Cornell University Press, 1949), 160.

12. Albert Schinz, "La Librairie française en Amérique au temps de Washington," *Revue d'histoire littéraire de la France* 24 (1917): 579.

13. *Catalogus Bibliothecae Harvardianae* (Boston: Thomas and John Fleet, 1790).

14. Timothy Dwight, *Travels in New England and New York,* ed. Barbara M. Solomon, 4 vols. (Cambridge, Mass.: Harvard University Press, Belknap Press, 1969), 1:385.

15. Korty, "Benjamin Franklin and Libraries," 35.

16. *William and Mary College Quarterly Historical Magazine,* 2d ser., 5 (1925): 81.

17. Frederick P. Bowes, *The Culture of Early Charleston* (Chapel Hill: University of North Carolina Press, 1942), 64.

18. Saul K. Padover, ed., *The Complete Jefferson* (New York: Duell, Sloan and Pierce, 1943), 1044. Years later, Jefferson abridged Buffon's system of astronomy for Francis Hopkinson, "signer" and satirist. Hopkinson in a letter of thanks whimsically points out the parallels between Buffon's solar system and the American Revolution. See *The Papers of Thomas Jefferson*, ed. Julian P. Boyd (Princeton, N.J.: Princeton University Press, 1950–), 6:443–44.

19. George R. Havens, "James Madison et la pensée française," *Revue de littérature comparée* 3 (1923): 614.

20. Irving Brant, *James Madison*, 6 vols. (Indianapolis: Bobbs-Merrill, 1941–46), 1:278–79; 2:308.

21. See *The Papers of James Madison*, ed. William T. Hutchinson and William M. E. Rachal (Chicago: University of Chicago Press, 1962–), 9:29–47.

22. Korty, "Benjamin Franklin and Libraries," 27.

23. James D. Hart, *The Popular Book* (New York: Oxford University Press, 1950), 33.

24. *Diary of William Dunlap*, ed. Dorothy C. Barck, 3 vols. (New York: New-York Historical Society, 1930), 1:168-69.

25. St. John de Crèvecoeur, *Journey into Northern Pennsylvania and the State of New York*, trans. Clarissa S. Bostelmann (Ann Arbor: University of Michigan Press, 1964), 84.

26. MS in the Library Company of Philadelphia.

27. "Book of Minutes of the Trustees of Union College, Number 1," meeting of December 8–9, 1795.

28. Joseph Nancrède, *L'Abeille françoise; ou, Nouveau recueil de morceaux brillans, des auteurs françois les plus célèbres* (Boston: Belknap and Young, 1792), 252–54.

29. Joseph Perkins, A.M., *An Oration upon Genius, Pronounced at the Anniversary Commencement of Harvard University, in Cambridge, July 19, 1797* (Boston: Manning and Loring for Joseph Nancrède, 1797), 19.

30. "Method of Preserving Birds, and Other Subjects of Natural History," *Columbian Magazine* 1 (1787): 326–27.

31. *Columbian Magazine* 1 (1787): 645.

32. *Columbian Magazine* 2 (December 1788): 749–50. See same in the *Massachusetts Centinel,* August 13, 1788.
33. Buffon, "Description of the Sensations and Ideas of the first Man," *New York Magazine* 1 (1790): 521-23. See also Mary Ellen Loughrey, *France and Rhode Island, 1686–1800* (New York: King's Crown Press, 1944), 83, for a similar quotation in a newspaper the same year.
34. *New York Magazine* 5 (1794): 39–41.
35. *Philadelphia Monthly Magazine* 1 (1798): 38–42.
36. I. Woodbridge Riley, *American Thought from Puritanism to Pragmatism and Beyond* (New York: Peter Smith, 1941), 28.
37. Ernest Earnest, *John and William Bartram: Botanists and Explorers* (Philadelphia: University of Pennsylvania Press, 1940), 32, 41.
38. Ibid., 142, 149.
39. Brooke Hindle, *David Rittenhouse* (Princeton, N.J.: Princeton University Press, 1964), 285.
40. Charles C. Sellers, *Charles Willson Peale* (New York: Charles Scribner's Sons, 1969), 257.
41. James T. Flexner, *America's Old Masters: First Artists of the New World* (New York: Viking Press, 1939), 216.
42. Sellers, *Charles Willson Peale,* 290.
43. Gilbert Chinard, "Eighteenth Century Theories on America as a Human Habitat," *Proceedings of the American Philosophical Society* 91 (1947): 28–57. This article, entitled "La Jeunesse du Nouveau-Monde," appears as one of two essays in Chinard's book *L'Homme contre la Nature* (Paris, Hermann, 1949); Edwin T. Martin, *Thomas Jefferson: Scientist* (New York: Henry Schuman, 1952); Thomas Jefferson, *Notes on the State of Virginia,* ed. William Peden (Chapel Hill: University of North Carolina Press, 1955); Durand Echeverria, *Mirage in the West: A History of the French Image of American Society to 1815* (Princeton: N.J.: Princeton University Press, 1957, 1968); Henry Steele Commager and Elmo Giordanetti, *Was America a Mistake? An Eighteenth-Century Controversy* (New York: Harper and Row, 1967; Columbia, S.C.: University of South Carolina Press, 1968); and Antonello Gerbi, *The Dispute of the New World: The History of a Polemic, 1750–1900,* rev. ed., trans. Jeremy Moyle (Pittsburgh: University of Pittsburgh Press, 1973).

44. Cornelius de Pauw was the author of *Recherches philosophiques sur les Américains*. He wrote also an article denigratory of America which appeared in *Supplément à l'Encyclopédie* 1 (1776). See Echeverria, *Mirage in the West*, 11.

45. Jefferson, *Notes on the State of Virginia*, ed. Peden, 47.

46. *Papers of Thomas Jefferson*, 8:184–85.

47. See Jefferson, *Notes on the State of Virginia*, ed. Peden, 43–72. Extracts from the *Notes* appeared in the *Columbian Magazine* 1 (1787): 366–69, 407–16.

48. Harlow Shapley, "Notes on Thomas Jefferson as a Natural Philosopher," *Proceedings of the American Philosophical Society* 87 (1943): 235.

49. See, for example, the mock epic *The Anarchiad*, book 17; the *Columbian Magazine* 2 (1788): 135–37; *The Federalist*, no. 11; the *Massachusetts Centinel*, October 3, December 8, 1787; February 4, 1789; Nathaniel Chipman, *Sketches of the Principles of Government* (Rutland: J. Lyon, 1793), 60–61; and Timothy Dwight, *Travels in New England and New York*, first published in 1821–22.

50. Gilbert Chinard, "The American Dream," in *Literary History of the United States*, ed. Robert E. Spiller et al., rev. ed. in 1 vol. (New York: Macmillan, 1959), 205.

51. Commager and Giordanetti, *Was America a Mistake?*, 16, 26.

52. Charles Willson Peale, *Discourse Introductory to a Course of Lectures on the Science of Nature* (Philadelphia: Zachariah Poulson, Jr., 1800), 25.

53. Samuel Miller, *A Brief Retrospect of the Eighteenth Century*, 2 vols. (New York: Thomas and John Swords, 1803; reprint ed., New York: Burt Franklin, 1970), 1:115–16. In connection with this quotation, see also 1:496–97. For other references to Buffon in this volume, see pp. 117, 119, 121, 127, 165ff. (disagrees with the naturalist's theory of the origin of the earth because it cannot be reconciled with the biblical account), 174, 187n, and 246.

54. Ibid., 2:413.

Six. The Philosophes

1. Robert Shackleton, *Montesquieu: A Critical Biography* (London: Oxford University Press, 1961), 390.

2. John Lough, "Who Were the Philosophes?" in *Studies in Eighteenth-Century French Literature Presented to Robert Niklaus*, ed. J. H. Fox, M. H. Waddicor, and D. A. Watts (Exeter: University of Exeter, 1975), 139–49.

3. See Durand Echeverria, *Mirage in the West: A History of the French Image of American Society to 1815* (Princeton, N.J.: Princeton University Press, 1957). Echeverria treats at length of America's role in the French Enlightenment.

4. For a concise account of the *philosophes*, their task and their mission, see the essay of Peter Gay, "The Unity of the French Enlightenment," in his book *The Party of Humanity* (New York: W. W. Norton, 1971), 114–32.

5. *Proceedings of the Massachusetts Historical Society* 51 (1917–18): 363.

6. *Catalogus Bibliothecae Harvardianae* (Boston: Fleet, 1790).

7. *Gazette of the United States*, February 1, 1797.

8. Margaret B. Korty, "Benjamin Franklin and Eighteenth-Century American Libraries," *Transactions of the American Philosophical Society*, n.s., 55, pt. 9 (1965): 8.

9. *Proceedings of the Massachusetts Historical Society*, 2d ser., 15 (1901), 15.

10. See Mary Ellen Loughrey, *France and Rhode Island, 1686–1800* (New York: King's Crown Press, 1944).

11. Joseph T. Wheeler, "Reading Interests of the Professional Classes in Colonial Maryland, 1700–1776," *Maryland Historical Magazine* 36 (1941): 190.

12. *The Papers of Thomas Jefferson*, ed. Julian P. Boyd (Princeton, N.J.: Princeton University Press, 1950–), 1:80.

13. *Southern Literary Messenger* 20 (1854): 78.

14. Benjamin Rush, *Essays, Literary, Moral and Philosophical* (Philadelphia: Bradford, 1798), 256.

15. Theophilus Wreg, *The Virginia Almanack for the Year of Our Lord God 1765* (Williamsburg: Joseph Royle, 1765).

16. *William and Mary College Quarterly Historical Magazine* 15 (1906): 103.

17. Loughrey, *France and Rhode Island*, 110.

18. William Reitzel, "The Purchasing of English Books in Philadelphia, 1790–1800," *Modern Philology* 35 (1937): 161.

19. Leonard M. Marsak, "Bernard de Fontenelle: The Idea of Science in the French Enlightenment," *Transactions of the American Philosophical Society,* n.s., 49, pt. 7 (1959): 12. See also Robert Shackleton's edition of *Les Entretiens* (Oxford: Clarendon Press, 1955).

20. Herbert W. Schneider, ed., *Samuel Johnson, President of King's College* (New York: Columbia University Press, 1929), 508.

21. *Virginia Magazine of History and Biography* 33 (1925): 195.

22. Loughrey, *France and Rhode Island,* 110, 105.

23. Macklin Thomas thought that this passage was a possible source of Philip Freneau's idea of beings with multiple senses ("The Idea of Progress in the Writings of Franklin, Freneau, Barlow, and Rush" [Ph.D. diss., University of Wisconsin, 1938], 124n).

24. *American Universal Magazine* 4 (1798): 275–76.

25. See *American Universal Magazine,* August 21, 1797.

26. *Revue d'histoire littéraire de la France* 24 (1917): 579.

27. Loughrey, *France and Rhode Island,* 107.

28. Samuel Miller, *A Brief Retrospect of the Eighteenth Century,* 2 vols. (New York: Thomas and John Swords, 1803; reprint ed., New York: Burt Franklin, 1970), 2:109.

29. John Lough, "Helvétius and Holbach," *Modern Language Review* 33 (1938): 360–84.

30. *Columbian Centinel,* February 27, March 5 and 16, 1796.

31. George C. Raddin, *An Early New York Library of Fiction* (New York: H. W. Wilson, 1940), 21.

32. H. M. Jones, "The Importation of French Literature in New York City, 1750–1800," *Studies in Philology* 28 (October 1931): 242.

33. *Catalogue of Books, Given and Devised by John Mackenzie Esquire, to the Charlestown Library Society, for the Use of the College When Erected* (Charlestown: Robert Wells, 1772).

34. See *Catalogue of the Books, Belonging to the Library Company of Philadelphia* (Philadelphia: Zachariah Poulson, Jr., 1789).

35. *Charter, Bye-Laws, and Names of the Members of the New York Society Library, with a Catalogue of the Books Belonging to the Said Library* (New York: T. and J. Swords, 1793).

36. Kemp P. Battle, *History of the University of North Carolina,* 2 vols. (Raleigh, N.C.: Edwards and Broughton, 1907–12), 1:85. Ac-

cording to J. D. Hart, a student wrote home from Chapel Hill in 1795 that this book "circulated widely" (*The Popular Book* [New York: Oxford University Press, 1950], 35).

37. Loughrey, *France and Rhode Island,* 113.

38. *Lower Norfolk County Virginia Antiquary* 2 (1899); 31n. George K. Smart, in his study "Private Libraries in Colonial Virginia," *American Literature* 10 (1938), found only a "slight" presence of Helvétius.

39. Loughrey, *France and Rhode Island,* 101.

40. Ibid., 84–86.

41. John I. Johnson, *Reflections on Political Society* (New York: Freneau and Menut, 1797), 14–15.

42. *The Works of Benjamin Franklin,* ed. Jared Sparks, 10 vols. (Boston: Hilliard, Gray, 1840), 2:222.

43. Alfred Owen Aldridge, "Benjamin Franklin and the *Philosophes,*" *Studies on Voltaire and the Eighteenth Century* 24 (1963): 58.

44. On Franklin and Madame Helvétius, see Claude-Anne Lopez, *Mon Cher Papa: Franklin and the Ladies of Paris* (New Haven, Conn.: Yale University Press, 1966).

45. See *The Writings of Thomas Jefferson,* ed. Andrew A. Lipscomb and Albert E. Bergh, 20 vols. (Washington: Thomas Jefferson Memorial Association, 1903–4), 14:141–42.

46. *The Commonplace Book of Thomas Jefferson,* ed. Gilbert Chinard (Baltimore: Johns Hopkins Press, 1926). See articles 849–51.

47. *The Adams-Jefferson Letters,* ed. Lester J. Cappon, 2 vols. (Chapel Hill: University of North Carolina Press, 1959), 2:355.

48. *Letters and Other Writings of James Madison,* 4 vols. (Philadelphia: J. B. Lippincott, 1865), 3:577.

49. Allen O. Hansen, *Liberalism and American Education in the Eighteenth Century* (New York: Macmillan, 1926), 254.

50. Noah Webster, *The Revolution in France* (New York: George Bunce, 1794), 60.

51. Noah Webster, *Ten Letters to Dr. Joseph Priestly* (New Haven, Conn.: Read and Morse, 1800), 21.

52. Miller, *Brief Retrospect,* 2:295.

53. Ibid., 2:453.

172 Notes to Pages 83–85

54. Samuel Miller, *Letters from a Father to His Sons in College* (Philadelphia: Grigg and Elliot, 1843), 208–9.

55. W. H. Wickwar, *Baron D'Holbach: A Prelude to the French Revolution* (London: George Allen and Unwin, 1935), 87.

56. Holbach, *Christianity Unveiled; Being an Examination of the Principles and Effects of the Christian Religion*, trans. William M. Johnson (New York: printed at the Columbian Press by Robertson and Gowan, for the Editor, 1795).

57. Evert A. Duyckinck and George L. Duyckinck, *Cyclopoedia of American Literature*, 2 vols. (Philadelphia: Baxter, 1881), 1:607.

58. Uzal Ogden, *Antidote to Deism: The Deist Unmasked*, 2 vols. (Newark: John Woods, 1795), 1:ix–xiii.

59. *Federal Gazette and Baltimore Daily Advertiser*, August 6, 1796.

60. Timothy Dwight, *Travels in New England and New York*, ed. Barbara Miller Solomon, 4 vols. (Cambridge, Mass.: Harvard University Press, Belknap Press, 1969), 4:269.

61. Alan Charles Kors, *D'Holbach's Coterie: An Enlightenment in Paris* (Princeton, N.J.: Princeton University Press, 1976), 106.

62. *Diary of William Dunlap*, ed. Dorothy C. Barck, 3 vols. (New York: New-York Historical Society, 1930), 1:168, 305. Dunlap also notes that in 1798 one of his visitors had received from New York both *Christianity Unveiled* and the *System of Nature* (see 1:344).

63. Leon Howard, *The Connecticut Wits* (Chicago: University of Chicago Press, 1943), 340.

64. George C. Raddin, Jr., *Hocquet Caritat and the Early New York Literary Scene* (Dover, N.J.: Dover Advance Press, 1953), 112.

65. I. Woodbridge Riley, *American Philosophy: The Early Schools* (New York: Dodd, Mead, 1907; reprint ed., New York: Russell and Russell, 1958), 10–11, 17. Riley was also the author of an article, "La Philosophie française en Amérique," published in the *Revue philosophique* 84 (1917): 393–428.

66. *Catalogus Bibliothecae Harvardianae* (Boston: Thomas and John Fleet, 1790).

67. Bernard Faÿ, *Notes on the American Press at the End of the Eighteenth Century* (New York: Grolier Club, 1927), 14.

68. Paul Merrill Spurlin, *Rousseau in America, 1760–1809* (University: University of Alabama Press, 1969).

Seven. *Montesquieu and the American Constitution*

1. See *The Federalist*, particularly nos. 9, 48, 51, and 66.
2. Ibid., no. 51. "In the compound republic of America, the power surrendered by the people is first divided between two distinct governments, and then the portion allotted to each subdivided among distinct and separate departments."
3. Paul Merrill Spurlin, *Montesquieu in America, 1760–1801* (Baton Rouge: Louisiana State University Press, 1940; reprint ed., New York, Octagon Books, 1969). An article, "Montesquieu et l'opinion américaine au dix-huitième siècle," which is a summary of the book, appeared in the *French American Review* 2 (1949): 12–21.
4. For a statistical analysis of this research, see Marie-Louise Dufrenoy, "Montesquieu et la constitution des Etats-Unis," *Journal de la Société de Statistique de Paris* 87 (March–April 1946): 87–91.
5. Sergio Cotta, "Montesquieu, la séparation des pouvoirs, et la Constitution fédérale des Etats-Unis," *Revue internationale d'histoire politique et constitutionelle*, n.s., 1 (1951): 225–47.
6. My paper, "L'Influence de Montesquieu sur la constitution américaine," in *Actes du Congrès Montesquieu* (Bordeaux: Delmas, 1956), 265–72, is an early version of the present essay.
7. Frank Luther Mott, *Golden Multitudes: The Story of Best Sellers in the United States* (New York: Macmillan, 1947), 316.
8. *The Commonplace Book of Thomas Jefferson: A Repertory of His Ideas on Government*, ed. Gilbert Chinard (Baltimore: Johns Hopkins Press, 1926), 35. On the Jefferson-Montesquieu relationship, see pp. 31–35. See also Chinard's *Pensées choisies de Montesquieu tirées du "Commonplace book" de Thomas Jefferson, Etudes françaises, quatrième cahier*, 1925, pp. 15–19, 26–28.
9. Consult Gilbert Chinard, *Jefferson and the Idéologues* (Baltimore: Johns Hopkins Press, 1925), 45–55.
10. With regard to this chapter, consult J. J. Granpré Molière, *La Théorie de la constitution anglaise chez Montesquieu* (Leyden: Presse Universitaire de Leyde, 1972); W. B. Gwyn, *The Meaning of the Separation of Powers, Tulane Studies in Political Science* 9 (1965); and M. J. C. Vile, *Constitutionalism and the Separation of Powers* (Oxford: Clarendon Press, 1967).

11. Cotta, "Montesquieu, la séparation, et la Constitution," 228 and note.
12. See Robert Shackleton, "Montesquieu, Bolingbroke, and the Separation of Powers," *French Studies* 3 (1949): 25–38. With reference to the deliberations in the Constitutional Convention on this type of separation, consult Gilbert Chinard, "Polybius and the American Constitution," *Journal of the History of Ideas* 1 (1940): 38–58.
13. *Holmes–Pollock Letters,* 2d ed., ed. Mark De Wolfe Howe, 2 vols. in 1 (Cambridge, Mass.: Harvard University Press, Belknap Press, 1961), 2:265–66.
14. Francis G. Wilson, *The American Political Mind* (New York: McGraw-Hill, 1949), 69.
15. *Maryland Gazette,* July 1, 1773.
16. *Black's Law Dictionary,* rev. and 4th ed. (St. Paul, Minn.: West, 1968), 386.
17. See B. F. Wright, Jr., "The Origins of the Separation of Powers in America," *Economica* 13 (1933): 169–85; and Vile, *Constitutionalism and the Separation of Powers,* 119–75.
18. *The American Revolution Considered as a Social Movement* (Boston: Beacon Press, 1966), 36.
19. Gordon S. Wood, *The Creation of the American Republic, 1776–1787* (Chapel Hill: University of North Carolina Press, 1969), 453–63.
20. See Charles F. Mullett, "Coke and the American Revolution," *Economica* 12 (1932): 457–71.
21. Raoul Berger, *Congress v. the Supreme Court* (Cambridge, Mass.: Harvard University Press, 1969), 23; see also pp. 27–28. Hamilton, in *The Federalist,* no. 78, quotes Montesquieu on the judiciary and takes judicial review for granted.
22. Berger, *Congress v. the Supreme Court,* 45–46.
23. *Revue d'histoire littéraire de la France* 3 (1896): 47.
24. *The Federalist,* no. 47. In this paper Madison explains Montesquieu's meaning of the precept.

Eight. *Voltaire in the South*

1. Charles Lee Smith, *The History of Education in North Carolina* (Washington: Government Printing Office, 1888), 68.

2. Hugh A. Garland, *The Life of John Randolph of Roanoke,* 2 vols. in 1 (New York: D. Appleton, 1881), 2:9–10.

3. Henry Adams, *John Randolph* (New York: Houghton Mifflin, 1898), 13.

4. Mary-Margaret H. Barr, *Voltaire in America, 1744–1800* (Baltimore: Johns Hopkins Press, 1941).

5. John F. McDermott, "Voltaire and the Freethinkers in Early Saint Louis," *Revue de littérature comparée* 16 (1936): 720–31. See also his book *Private Libraries in Creole Saint Louis* (Baltimore: Johns Hopkins Press, 1938).

6. J. T. Wheeler, "Reading Interests of Maryland Planters and Merchants, 1700–1776," *Maryland Historical Magazine* 37 (1942): 302.

7. Ibid., 305.

8. Ibid., 308.

9. Ibid., 299.

10. In 1762 Rind established, according to J. T. Wheeler, "the earliest known colonial circulating library." This work was among the titles it included. See Wheeler's article "Booksellers and Circulating Libraries in Colonial Maryland," *Maryland Historical Magazine* 34 (1939): 113.

11. *Baltimore Daily Intelligencer,* October 27, 1794.

12. *Federal Intelligencer and Baltimore Daily Gazette,* January 2, 1795.

13. *Maryland Journal,* October 22 and November 26, 1795; March 27, 1781.

14. Ibid., May 2, 1796.

15. James David Hart, *The Popular Book: A History of America's Literary Taste* (New York: Oxford University Press, 1950), 33.

16. J. T. Wheeler, "Books Owned by Marylanders, 1700–1776," *Maryland Historical Magazine* 35 (1940): 347, 350.

17. *General Magazine and Impartial Review* 1 (1798): 17–18. See also the *Maryland Gazette,* December 11, 1766, March 7, 1771; *Maryland Journal,* September 15, 1778, February 4, 1796; and *Baltimore American and Daily Advertiser,* December 4, 1800.

18. Lewis P. Waldo, *The French Drama in America in the Eighteenth Century* (Baltimore: Johns Hopkins Press, 1942), 227–28.

19. François Alexandre Frédéric, duc de la Rochefoucauld-Liancourt,

Travels Through the United States of North America . . . in the Years 1795, 1796, and 1797, 2 vols. (London: R. Phillips, 1799), 2:117.

20. Thomas J. Wertenbaker, *The Golden Age of Colonial Culture*, 2d ed., rev. (New York: New York University Press, 1949), 109.

21. Emily E. F. Skeel, *Mason Locke Weems: His Works and Ways*, 3 vols. (New York: n.p., 1929), 2:36.

22. George K. Smart, "Private Libraries in Colonial Virginia," *American Literature* 10 (1938–39):48.

23. *Tyler's Quarterly Historical and Genealogical Magazine* 3 (1921): 125.

24. Smart, "Private Libraries," 49.

25. *William and Mary College Quarterly Historical Magazine*, 1st ser., 6 (1898): 161.

26. Henry Cabot Lodge, *George Washington*, 2 vols. (New York: Houghton Mifflin, 1889), 2:335–36.

27. *Tyler's Quarterly Historical and Genealogical Magazine* 9 (1927): 102.

28. *The Papers of Thomas Jefferson*, ed. Julian P. Boyd (Princeton, N.J.: Princeton University Press, 1950–), 1:80.

29. William Cabell Bruce, *John Randolph of Roanoke, 1773–1833*, 2 vols. (New York: G. P. Putnam's Sons, 1922), 1:61.

30. *Letters of John Randolph to a Young Relative* (Philadelphia: Carey, Lea and Blanchard, 1834), 43.

31. William D. Johnston, *History of the Library of Congress, 1800–1864* (Washington: Government Printing Office, 1904), 1:74.

32. "La Henriade de Voltaire; Le Saul de Voltaire; Memoires de Voltaire; [Memoires de Voltaire écrits par lui meme, bound up in no. 130]; Vie de Voltaire; Voltaire's history of Charles XII, of Sweden, 12 mo, in his works ch. 44; Soirees de Ferney; Tracts in foreign history, to wit, Voltaire . . . ; Voltaire sur Beccaria; Oeuvres de Voltaire, 58 V 8vo 1775 and 1785; Voltaire's Philosophical Dictionary; Voltaire, Philosophie de l'histoire" (*Catalogue of the Library of the United States* [Washington: Jonathan Elliott, 1815]).

33. "I will send you Voltaire's legacy to the K. of Prussia, a libel which will do much more injury to Voltaire than to the King. Many of the traits in the character of the latter to which the former gives a turn satyrical & malicious, are real virtues" (*The Works of Thomas Jeffer-*

son, ed. Paul Leicester Ford, 12 vols. [New York: G. P. Putnam's Sons, 1904–5], 4:410).

34. *William and Mary College Quarterly Historical Magazine*, 2d ser., 5 (1925): 5.

35. *The Commonplace Book of Thomas Jefferson: A Repertory of His Ideas on Government*, ed. Gilbert Chinard (Baltimore: Johns Hopkins Press, 1926), 48. For the Voltaire extracts in this book, see pp. 334-43 and the appendix.

36. Ibid., 49. *The Literary Bible of Thomas Jefferson: His Commonplace Book of Philosophers and Poets* (Baltimore: Johns Hopkins Press, 1928), also edited by Gilbert Chinard, contains no quotation from Voltaire.

37. George R. Havens, "James Madison et la pensée française," *Revue de littérature comparée* 3 (1923): 612. Cf. Gaillard Hunt, "James Madison and Religious Liberty," *Annual Report of the American Historical Association for the Year 1901*, 2 vols. (Washington: Government Printing Office, 1902), 1:170. "He believed . . . in the untrammeled existence of religious sects and was fond of quoting Voltaire's aphorism: 'If one religion only were allowed in England, the Government would possibly become arbitrary; if there were two, the people would cut each other's throats; but as there are such a multitude, they all live happy and in peace.' "

38. *Virginia Gazette*, March 28, 1766; May 26, 1768; July 1, 1775.

39. Ibid., July 22, 1773.

40. Ibid., January 7, 1775.

41. Barr, *Voltaire in America*, 12.

42. Frederick P. Bowes, *The Culture of Early Charleston* (Chapel Hill: University of North Carolina Press, 1942), 104.

43. *City Gazette*, February 8, 1792; January 11, 1793.

44. *A Catalogue of Books, Belonging to the Incorporated Charlestown Library Society, with the Dates of the Editions* (Charlestown: Robert Wells, 1770). Transcribed here and without the dates are the titles listed: "Voltaire's letters on the English nation, history of Europe, from Charlemagne to Charles V. 3 vols., the age of Lewis XIV, the war in ——, the empire from the reign of Charlemagne, 2 vols., Essai sur l'histoire general, 8 tom., Oeuvres diverses, 12 tom., Histoire de Russie, 2 tom." In an appendix, dated 1772, is "Voltaire's philosophy of history."

45. Bowes, *Culture of Early Charleston*, 63.
46. *A Catalogue of Books, Given and Devised by John Mackenzie Esquire, to the Charlestown Library Society, for the Use of the College When Erected* (Charlestown: Robert Wells, 1772).
47. Edward D. Seeber, "The French Theatre in Charleston in the Eighteenth Century," *South Carolina Historical and Genealogical Magazine* 42 (1941): 6.
48. David D. Wallace, *The Life of Henry Laurens* (New York: G. P. Putnam's Sons, 1915), 440.
49. Jay B. Hubbell, *The South in American Literature, 1607–1900* (Durham, N.C.: Duke University Press, 1954), 413.
50. Ibid., 180.
51. Stephen B. Weeks, "Libraries and Literature in North Carolina in the Eighteenth Century," *Annual Report of the American Historical Association for the Year 1895* (Washington: Government Printing Office, 1896), 203.
52. Hubbell, *South in American Literature*, 98.
53. Barr, *Voltaire in America*, 100–116.

Nine. Diderot, D'Alembert, and the Encyclopedia

1. Ira Wade, *An Anthology of Eighteenth Century French Literature* (Princeton, N.J.: Princeton University Press, 1930), xliv.
2. See Jacques Proust, *Diderot et L'Encyclopédie* (Paris: Armand Colin, 1962). For short accounts consult Joseph Le Gras, *Diderot et L'Encyclopédie*, 5th ed. (Amiens: E. Malfère, 1928); Douglas H. Gordon and Norman L. Torrey, *The Censoring of Diderot's Encyclopédie and the Re-Established Text* (New York: Columbia University Press, 1947); and George R. Havens, *The Age of Ideas: From Reaction to Revolution in Eighteenth-Century France* (New York: Henry Holt, 1955), 292–309.
3. See George B. Watts, "The Encyclopédie méthodique," *PMLA* 73 (1958): 348–66; and especially Robert Darnton, *The Business of Enlightenment: A Publishing History of the Encyclopédie, 1775–1800* (Cambridge, Mass.: Harvard University Press, Belknap Press, 1979).

4. Howard Mumford Jones, "The Importation of French Literature in New York City, 1750–1800," *Studies in Philology* 28 (October 1931): 250.

5. Howard Mumford Jones, "The Importation of French Books in Philadelphia, 1750–1800," *Modern Philology* 32 (1934): 170.

6. J. Robert Loy, "Diderot aux Etats-Unis," *Europe: Revue mensuelle* 41 (January–February 1963): 263–73.

7. *The Autobiography of Benjamin Rush*, ed. G. W. Corner (Princeton, N.J.: Princeton University Press, 1948), 69.

8. *Independent Gazetteer*, November 27, 1784.

9. G. G. Raddin, Jr., *An Early New York Library of Fiction, with a Checklist of the Fiction in H. Caritat's Circulating Library* (New York: H. W. Wilson, 1940), 21, 51, 52.

10. *Catalogue of the John Adams Library in the Public Library of the City of Boston* (Boston: The Trustees, 1917). The first edition I have found was published in Amsterdam in 1772.

11. *Catalogue of the Library of the United States* (Washington: Jonathan Elliott, 1815): "Oeuvres de Theatre de Diderot 12mo; Synonimes de Diderot, Dalembert et Jaucourt, 12mo; Memoires Mathematiques de Diderot, 12mo; Oeuvres Philosophiques de Diderot, 3 v 12mo; [Le Bons Sens, 12mo, Diderot] oeuvres."

12. Edward McNall Burns, *James Madison, Philosopher of the Constitution* (New Brunswick, N.J.: Rutgers University Press, 1938), 187.

13. Catalogue of the Library of Chancellor James Kent (1940), mimeographed copy in the William L. Clements Library, University of Michigan, Ann Arbor.

14. Howard C. Rice, *Le Cultivateur américain: Etude sur l'Oeuvre de Saint John de Crèvecoeur*, Bibliothèque de la Revue de littérature comparée, vol. 87 (1933), 54, 129.

15. *Catalogus Bibliothecae Harvardianae* (Boston: Thomas and John Fleet, 1790).

16. *Catalogue of the Books Belonging to the Library Company of Philadelphia* (Philadelphia: Bartram and Reynolds, 1807). Listed were *Le Père de famille*, (Amsterdam, 1758); *James the Fatalist and His Master*, 3 vols. (London, 1797); and a book published in London in 1776 that contained "The Two Friends of Bourbon."

17. He was mentioned in anecdotal material reprinted from foreign sources in the *Boston Magazine*, April 1, 1784, p. 221, and in the *General Advertiser*, November 17, 1792.

18. *General Advertiser*, November 13, 1790.

19. *New York Magazine or Literary Repository*, n.s., 2 (December 1797): 639, 656–57.

20. Lewis P. Waldo, *The French Drama in America in the Eighteenth Century* (Baltimore: Johns Hopkins Press, 1942), 234–35.

21. Ibid., 166.

22. Zoltán Haraszti, *John Adams and the Prophets of Progress* (Cambridge, Mass.: Harvard University Press, 1952), 18.

23. Ibid., 81.

24. Timothy Dwight, *Travels in New England and New York*, ed. Barbara Miller Solomon, 4 vols. (Cambridge, Mass.: Harvard University Press, Belknap Press, 1969), 4:259.

25. William Cobbett, *The Bloody Buoy, Thrown Out as a Warning to the Political Pilots of America*, 2d ed. (Philadelphia: Benjamin Davies, 1796), 276.

26. Samuel Miller, *A Brief Retrospect of the Eighteenth Century*, 2 vols. (New York: Thomas and John Swords, 1803; reprint ed., New York: Burt Franklin, 1970), 2:162.

27. See J. G. Rosengarten, "The Early French Members of the American Philosophical Society," *Proceedings of the American Philosophical Society* 46 (1907): 87–93.

28. *The Autobiography of Lyman Beecher*, ed. Barbara M. Cross, 2 vols. (Cambridge, Mass.: Harvard University Press, Belknap Press, 1961), 1:27.

29. Albert Schinz, "Un 'Rousseauiste' en Amérique (*L'Abeille française*, de Joseph Nancrède)," *Modern Language Notes* 35 (1920): 12.

30. Moreau de Saint-Méry, *Idée générale ou abrégé des sciences et des arts à l'usage de la jeunesse* (Philadelphia: M. L. E. Moreau de Saint-Méry, 1796), 209.

31. Adrian H. Jaffe, *Bibliography of French Literature in American Magazines in the Eighteenth Century* (East Lansing: Michigan State College Press, 1951).

32. *Independent Gazetteer*, November 27, 1784.

33. *Massachusetts Centinel*, August 2, 1786.

34. Albert Schinz, "La Librairie française en Amérique au temps de Washington," *Revue d'histoire littéraire de la France* 24 (1917): 579.

35. See *The Virginia Almanack for the Year of Our Lord God 1765*, by Theophilus Wreg. "Gerard on Taste, with three Dissertations on the same Subject, by Voltaire, Alembert and Montesquieu."

36. J. T. Wheeler, "Reading Interests of Maryland Planters and Merchants, 1760–1776," *Maryland Historical Magazine* 37 (1942): 299.

37. *Catalogus Bibliothecae Harvardianae* (Boston: Thomas and John Fleet, 1790).

38. See *Catalogue of the Books Belonging to the Library Company of Philadelphia* (Philadelphia: Bartram and Reynolds, 1807) and *Catalogue of Books Belonging to the South Carolina College Library* (Columbia: Daniel and J. J. Faust, 1807).

39. *Diary and Autobiography of John Adams,* ed. L. H. Butterfield et al., 4 vols. (Cambridge, Mass.: Harvard University Press, Belknap Press, 1961), 2:307.

40. *Oeuvres de D'Alembert,* 5 vols. (Paris: A. Belin, 1821–22), 5:386.

41. *The Writings of Benjamin Franklin,* ed. A. H. Smyth, 10 vols. (New York: Macmillan, 1905–7), 1:198. "Tu vois le sage courageux / Dont l'heureux et mâle génie / Arracha le tonnerre aux dieux / Et le sceptre à la tyrannie."

42. Miller, *Brief Retrospect,* 1:36, 40, 44, 55, 61, 62, 203, 363, 422.

43. Timothy Dwight, *The Nature, and Danger, of Infidel Philosophy* (New Haven, Conn.: George Bunce, 1798), 47, 61, 83.

44. *Diary and Autobiography of John Adams,* 4:67.

45. Haraszti, *John Adams and the Prophets of Progress,* 111.

46. Ibid., 112.

47. Uzal Ogden, *Antidote to Deism: The Deist Unmasked,* 2 vols. (Newark: John Woods, 1795), 2:311.

48. James T. Callender, *The American Annual Register; or, Historical Memoirs of the United States for the Year 1796* (Philadelphia: Bioren and Madan, 1797), 220.

49. Brissot de Warville, *New Travels in the United States of America, Performed in 1788* (Dublin: W. Corbet, 1792), 107.

50. H. M. Jones, *America and French Culture, 1750–1848* (Chapel Hill: University of North Carolina Press, 1927), 410.

51. Gilbert Chinard, "L'Encyclopédie et le rayonnement de l'esprit encyclopédique en Amérique," *Cahiers de l'Association internationale des études françaises,* no. 2 (May 1952), 3–22.
52. *The Papers of Thomas Jefferson,* ed. Julian P. Boyd (Princeton, N.J.: Princeton University Press, 1950–), 5:15, 311–12.
53. Schinz, "La Librairie française," 579.
54. Broadside in the Rare Book Room of the Library of Congress.
55. *Catalogue of the Books, Belonging to the Library Company of Philadelphia* (Philadelphia: Zachariah Poulson, Jr., 1789).
56. *The Writings of Benjamin Franklin,* 9:664.
57. *Diary and Autobiography of John Adams,* 2:437.
58. *Catalogue of the Library of the United States.*
59. George R. Havens, "James Madison et la pensée française," *Revue de littérature comparée* 3 (1923): 610ff.
60. Hugh A. Garland, *The Life of John Randolph of Roanoke,* 2 vols. (New York: D. Appleton, 1881), 2:9–10.
61. Haraszti, *John Adams and the Prophets of Progress,* 308.
62. *The Papers of Alexander Hamilton,* ed. H. C. Syrett (New York: Columbia University Press, 1961–), 4:403.
63. Leon Howard, *The Connecticut Wits* (Chicago: University of Chicago Press, 1943), 308.
64. D. L. Clark, ed., *Edgar Huntly* (New York, Macmillan: 1928), viii.
65. In 1790, Dr. George Gilmer of Virginia advised a son studying at Edinburgh that "you should by degrees procure the french encyclopedia" (R. B. Davis, *Francis Walker Gilmer: Life and Learning in Jefferson's Virginia* [Richmond: Dietz Press, 1939], 7). Conceivably, Gilmer's reference could have been to the *Encyclopédie méthodique.* This is, nevertheless, testimony to the prestige enjoyed by Diderot's encyclopedic enterprise. In connection with Gilmer's advice, it is of interest to note the finding of a study made by George K. Smart of libraries of the colonial period in Virginia: "No works of the French Encyclopedists turn up in the lists I have seen." See "Private Libraries in Colonial Virginia," *American Literature* 10 (1938): 43n.
66. Frederick P. Bowes, *The Culture of Early Charleston* (Chapel Hill: University of North Carolina Press, 1942), 63.
67. *Catalogus Bibliothecae Harvardianae.*
68. J. H. Shera, *Foundations of the Public Library* . . . (Chicago: Univer-

sity of Chicago Press, 1949), 113. *The Plan of the French Encyclopaedia* (that is, the *Discours préliminaire*) had been published in London in 1752.

69. *A Catalogue of the Books Belonging to the New York Society Library* (New York: C. S. Van Winkle, 1813).

70. Gabriel Richard Papers, Burton Historical Collection, Detroit Public Library.

71. Timothy Dwight, *The Duty of Americans, at the Present Crisis . . .* (New Haven, Conn.: Thomas and Samuel Green, 1798), 10. This was a sermon. In a note to the passage above, Dwight said that the "articles of Theology were speciously and decently written, but, by references artfully made to other articles, all the truth of the former was entirely and insidiously overthrown to most readers, by the sophistry of the latter." T. G. Fessenden, a believer in the conspiracy, cited a number of examples of the Encyclopedia's cross-references to show "with what *cunning* its authors sought to spread the principles of Atheism, Materialism and Fatalism." See his *Democracy Unveiled* (Boston: David Carlisle, 1805), 25–30nn. For information on the alleged conspiracy, consult Vernon Stauffer, *New England and the Bavarian Illuminati* (New York: Columbia University Press, 1918).

72. Miller, *Brief Retrospect,* 2:266. In 1803 Joseph Dennie, journalist and Federalist, referring to a certain encyclopedia, said, "It displays the Genius, Learning and Taste of the French Encyclopedia, without being polluted by its Atheism or its Politics." See Laura G. Pedder, *The Letters of Joseph Dennie, 1768–1812, Maine Bulletin* 38 (1936): 193.

73. *The Papers of Thomas Jefferson,* 6:258. For a more detailed account of Jefferson's interest in and connection with this undertaking, see George B. Watts, "Thomas Jefferson, the 'Encyclopédie' and the 'Encyclopédie méthodique,'" *French Review* 38 (1965): 318–25.

74. *The Papers of Thomas Jefferson,* 7:518. See also 8:342, 559–60.

75. Ibid., 7:507, 511; 9:357, 439, 482.

76. Adrienne Koch, *Jefferson and Madison: The Great Collaboration* (New York: Knopf, 1950), 19. In a letter dated April 15, 1783, Madison Papers, Library of Congress.

77. Allan McLane Hamilton, *The Intimate Life of Alexander Hamilton* (New York: C. Scribner's Sons, 1911).

78. *The Adams-Jefferson Letters,* ed. L. J. Cappon, 2 vols. (Chapel Hill: University of North Carolina Press, 1959), 1:152. See also the article by Watts in the *French Review* cited above.
79. Miller, *Brief Retrospect,* 2:268.

Ten. A Citizen of New-Heaven: The Marquis de Condorcet

1. *Diary and Autobiography of John Adams,* ed. L. H. Butterfield et al., 4 vols. (Cambridge, Mass.: Harvard University Press, Belknap Press, 1961), 4:66–67.
2. Phillips Russell, in his book *Jefferson: Champion of the Free Mind* (New York: Dodd, Mead, 1956) has a very short but interesting chapter entitled "Jefferson and Condorcet."
3. Gouverneur Morris, *A Diary of the French Revolution,* ed. Beatrix Cary Davenport, 2 vols. (Boston: Houghton Mifflin, 1939), 2:143.
4. Keith Michael Baker, *Condorcet: From Natural Philosophy to Social Mathematics* (Chicago: University of Chicago Press, 1975). Baker has also edited, and published with an introduction, *Condorcet: Selected Writings* (Indianapolis: Bobbs-Merrill, 1976).
5. Consult Alfred Owen Aldridge, *Franklin and His French Contemporaries* (New York: New York University Press, 1957), 223–30. Gilbert Chinard has written in both English and French on the apotheosis of Franklin in France.
6. For further information concerning this interest, see the chapter entitled "The Rediscovery of America" in J. Salwyn Shapiro, *Condorcet and the Rise of Liberalism* (New York: Harcourt, Brace, 1934).
7. An image of the bust and details concerning its provenance are to be found in Gilbert Chinard, *Houdon in America* (Baltimore: Johns Hopkins Press, 1930).
8. *The Literary Diary of Ezra Stiles,* ed. F. B. Dexter, 3 vols. (New York: Charles Scribner's Sons, 1901), 3:161.
9. The *Lettres,* four, were inserted in Philip Mazzei's *Recherches historiques et politiques sur les Etats-Unis de l'Amérique septentrionale,* 4 vols. in 2 (Paris: A. Colle, et se trouvent à Paris chez Froullé, 1788), 1:267–371.
10. *Catalogue of the John Adams Library in the Public Library of the City of Boston* (Boston: The Trustees, 1917), 58–59.
11. See *Catalogue of the Library of Thomas Jefferson,* compiled with anno-

tations by E. Millicent Sowerby, 5 vols. (Washington: Library of Congress, 1952–59).

12. *The Papers of Thomas Jefferson,* ed. Julian P. Boyd (Princeton, N.J.: Princeton University Press, 1950–), 10:354.

13. *The Papers of James Madison,* ed. William T. Hutchinson and William M. E. Rachal (Chicago: University of Chicago Press, 1962–), 11:212.

14. Ibid., 320.

15. Ibid., 215.

16. Samuel E. Forman, "The Political Activities of Philip Freneau," *Johns Hopkins University Studies in Historical and Political Science* 20 (September–October 1902): 98.

17. *Catalogue of the Books Belonging to the Library Company of Philadelphia* (Philadelphia: Bartram and Reynolds, 1807).

18. Albert Schinz, "La Librairie française en Amérique au temps de Washington," *Revue d'histoire littéraire de la France* 24 (1917).

19. G. G. Raddin, Jr., *An Early New York Library of Fiction* (New York: H. W. Wilson, 1940), 17, 21.

20. Mary-Margaret H. Barr, *Voltaire in America, 1744–1800* (Baltimore: Johns Hopkins Press, 1941), 29.

21. Mary Ellen Loughrey, *France and Rhode Island, 1686–1800* (New York: King's Crown Press, 1944), 86–87.

22. David Williams, "Condorcet, Feminism, and the Egalitarian Principle," *Studies in Eighteenth-Century Culture* 5 (1976): 153.

23. Mary S. Benson, *Women in Eighteenth-Century America: A Study of Opinion and Social Usage* (New York: Columbia University Press, 1935), 249. I can point only to Elihu Palmer's quotation of a paragraph from the *Outlines* on this subject. See his *An Enquiry Relative to the Moral and Political Improvement of the Human Species* (New York: John Crookes, 1797), 32.

24. *The Papers of Benjamin Franklin,* ed. Leonard W. Labaree and Whitfield J. Bell, Jr. (New Haven, Conn.: Yale University Press, 1959–), 20:489–91.

25. Bernard Faÿ, "L'Amérique et l'esprit scientifique en France à la fin du XVIIIe siècle," *Revue de littérature comparée* 3 (1923): 396–97. A translation of these queries is also spread on the minutes of the American Philosophical Society.

26. *The Papers of Benjamin Franklin,* 21:151. Franklin sent the queries to

Benjamin Rush in July 1774, and requested him, as one "who understands French," to translate them for the society's use (p. 258). The society has other letters from Condorcet to Franklin and Jefferson on various subjects.

27. See "Jefferson's Notes from Condorcet on Slavery" in *The Papers of Thomas Jefferson* 14:494–98.

28. *The Writings of Thomas Jefferson,* ed. Paul Leicester Ford, 10 vols. (New York: G. P. Putnam's Sons, 1892–99), 5:379. See also Jefferson's letter to Banneker of the same date, pp. 377–78. Henry William De Saussure, in an *Address to the Citizens of South Carolina on the Approaching Election of President and Vice President of the U.S.* (Charleston: W. P. Young, 1800), 16n., refers to Condorcet as a leading member of the society of Les Amis des Noirs and as being an "intimate" friend and correspondent of Jefferson. He mentions Banneker. De Saussure, in favor of slavery, feared that Jefferson would emancipate his slaves.

29. A new translation appeared only in the mid-1950s: *Sketch for a Historical Picture of the Human Mind,* trans. June Barraclough, with an introduction by Stuart Hampshire (London: Weidenfeld and Nicolson, 1955). A new French edition, with a text revised by O. H. Prior and presented by him and Yvon Belaval, was published in Paris in 1970.

30. Catalogue of the Library of Chancellor James Kent (1940), mimeographed copy in the William L. Clements Library, University of Michigan, Ann Arbor.

31. *Catalogue of the Library of the Late Col. William Duane,* auctioneer's catalog, printed in Philadelphia and dated February 25, 1836.

32. *Diary of William Dunlap,* ed. Dorothy C. Barck, 3 vols. (New York: New-York Historical Society, 1930), 1:110, 127.

33. *The Writings of Thomas Jefferson,* 9:481. For whatever reason he was moved to read it, a Mr. Dutton criticized the style and abstractness of the *Outlines* in a poem read at the the Yale College commencement in 1800. See A. O. Aldridge, "Thomas Paine and the Idéologues," *Studies on Voltaire and the Eighteenth Century* 151 (1976): 117.

34. For analyses of and comments on this book, see the section "Marquis de Condorcet: The Taming of the Future," in Frank E. Man-

uel, *The Prophets of Paris* (Cambridge, Mass.: Harvard University Press, 1962); and Keith Michael Baker's *Condorcet: From Natural Philosophy to Social Mathematics,* mentioned above.

35. Consult Robert Nisbet, *History of the Idea of Progress* (New York: Basic Books, 1980), and John Passmore, *The Perfectibility of Man* (London: Duckworth, 1970).

36. Zoltán Haraszti, "John Adams Flays a Philosophe: Annotations on Condorcet's *Progress of the Human Mind,*" *William and Mary Quarterly,* 3d ser., 7 (1950):223–52. An appendix (pp. 252–54) contains Adams's comments on the *Lettres d'un bourgeois de New-Heaven.* The essay, slightly revised, appeared without the appendix as "Condorcet and the Idea of Progress" in Haraszti's book *John Adams and the Prophets of Progress* (Cambridge, Mass.: Harvard University Press, 1952), 235–58.

37. See, for instance, the letters he wrote to Benjamin Rush in 1806. In *Old Family Letters,* copied from the originals for Alexander Biddle (Philadelphia: J. B. Lippincott, 1892), ser. A, pp. 111–26, passim.

38. *The Works of John Adams,* ed. Charles Francis Adams, 10 vols. (Boston: Little, Brown, 1850–56), 10:101.

39. *William and Mary College Quarterly,* 2d ser., 5 (1925): 148.

40. *The Writings of Thomas Jefferson, 10:25.*

41. Samuel Miller, *A Brief Retrospect of the Eighteenth Century,* 2 vols. (New York: Thomas and John Swords, 1803; reprint ed., New York: Burt Franklin, 1970), 2:296–301. See Gilbert Chinard, "Progress and Perfectibility in Samuel Miller's Intellectual History," in *Studies in Intellectual History* (Baltimore: Johns Hopkins Press, 1953), 94–122.

42. See Leon Howard, *The Connecticut Wits* (Chicago: University of Chicago Press, 1943).

43. *Works of Fisher Ames,* ed. Seth Ames, 2 vols. (Boston: Little, Brown, 1854), 2:123; Benjamin Silliman, *An Oration, Delivered at Hartford on the 6th of July, A.D. 1802* (Hartford: Hudson and Goodwin, 1802), 28, 32.

44. Allen Oscar Hansen, *Liberalism and American Education in the Eighteenth Century* (New York: Macmillan, 1926), 20.

45. John I. Johnson, *Reflections on Political Society* (New York: Freneau and Menut, 1797).

46. Charles Brockden Brown, *Edgar Huntly; or, Memoirs of a Sleep-Walker,* ed. David Lee Clark (New York: Macmillan, 1928), viii.
47. See Macklin Thomas, "The Idea of Progress in the Writings of Franklin, Freneau, Barlow, and Rush" (Ph.D. diss., University of Wisconsin, 1938); Edwin Thomas Martin, "Thomas Jefferson and the Idea of Progress" (Ph.D. diss., University of Wisconsin, 1941); and Rutherford E. Delmage, "The American Idea of Progress, 1750–1800," *Proceedings of the American Philosophical Society* 91 (1947): 307–14.
48. William Cobbett, *The Bloody Buoy, Thrown Out as a Warning to the Political Pilots of America,* 2d ed. (Philadelphia: Benjamin Davies and William Cobbett, 1796), 228, 231.
49. Robert Treat Paine, *An Oration . . . in Commemoration of the Dissolution of the Treaties . . . Between France and the United States of America,* 2d ed. (Boston: John Russell, 1799), 12.
50. *The Works of John Adams,* 9:624.
51. Ibid., 10:256. Samuel Miller noted that "the *Life of* M. Turgot, by M. Condorcet, and the *Life of* M. De Voltaire, by the same author, have also been much celebrated and admired, among a certain class of readers" (*Brief Retrospect,* 2:154).
52. Noah Webster, *Ten Letters to Dr. Joseph Priestly* (New Haven, Conn.: Read and Morse, 1800), 21.
53. Elihu Palmer, *An Enquiry Relative to the Moral and Political Improvement of the Human Species* (New York: John Crookes, 1797), 34. See also his *Principles of Nature; or, A Development of the Moral Causes of Happiness and Misery Among the Human Species,* 2d ed. (New York, 1802), 185.
54. Gilbert Chinard, *Honest John Adams* (Boston: Little, Brown, 1933), 239.
55. *The Papers of Alexander Hamilton,* ed. Harold C. Syrett, 26 vols. (New York: Columbia University Press, 1965), 8:439.
56. *The Writings of James Madison,* ed. Gaillard Hunt, 9 vols. (New York: G. P. Putnam's Sons, 1908), 8:390–91.
57. *The Writings of Thomas Jefferson,* library edition, ed. Andrew A. Lipscomb and Albert E. Bergh, 20 vols. (Washington: Thomas Jefferson Memorial Association, 1903–4), 14:140. Letter to Thomas Law, June 13, 1814.
58. Ibid., 15:223. Letter to Short, October 31, 1819.

Eleven. French Deism, Empiricism, Ideology, and Physiocracy

1. William D. Johnston, *History of the Library of Congress* (Washington: Government Printing Office, 1904), 1:86.
2. Timothy Dwight, *Travels in New England and New York*, ed. Barbara Miller Solomon, 4 vols. (Cambridge, Mass.: Harvard University Press, Belknap Press, 1969), 4:259–60.
3. Samuel Miller, *Memoir of the Rev. Charles Nisbet, D.D.* (New York: Robert Carter, 1840), 247. In his course on "Moral Philosophy" at Dickinson, Nisbet derided Voltaire, Raynal, and Rousseau. See pp. 3 and 86 of the MS of these lectures in the Library Company of Philadelphia.
4. Noah Webster, *Ten Letters to Dr. Joseph Priestly* (New Haven, Conn.: Read and Morse, 1800), 8. See also Webster's *The Revolution in France* (New York: George Bunce, 1794), preface, and 30.
5. Charles Downer Hazen, *Contemporary American Opinion of the French Revolution* (Baltimore: Johns Hopkins Press, 1897).
6. *The Commonplace Book of Thomas Jefferson: A Repertory of His Ideas on Government*, ed. Gilbert Chinard (Baltimore: Johns Hopkins Press, 1926), 63. See also Chinard's article "Jefferson Among the Philosophers," *Ethics* 53 (1943):260; and his biography of the third president, *Thomas Jefferson: The Apostle of Americanism*, 2d ed., rev. (Ann Arbor: University of Michigan Press, 1957), 87.
7. Adrienne Koch, *The Philosophy of Thomas Jefferson* (New York: Columbia University Press, 1943; reprint ed. Gloucester, Mass.: Peter Smith, 1957), 19 and 113, for instance.
8. Herbert M. Morais, *Deism in Eighteenth Century America* (New York: Columbia University Press, 1934; reprint ed., New York: Russell and Russell, 1960) and G. Adolf Koch, *Republican Religion: The American Revolution and the Cult of Reason* (New York: Henry Holt, 1933).
9. See, for example, Mary-Margaret H. Barr, *Voltaire in America, 1744–1800* (Baltimore: Johns Hopkins Press, 1941), 107ff.
10. Jean Gaulmier, *Volney* (Paris: Hachette, 1959), 117.
11. Gilbert Chinard, *Volney et l'Amérique d'après des documents inédits et sa correspondance avec Jefferson* (Baltimore: Johns Hopkins Press, 1923), 113. For Volney's impact on Barlow, see Leon Howard, *The Connecticut Wits* (Chicago: University of Chicago Press, 1943).

12. Frank Luther Mott, *Golden Multitudes: The Story of Best Sellers in the United States* (New York: Macmillan, 1947), 305. Gaulmier points out in his book, *Volney*, that *Les Ruines* was also "le plus grand succès de librairie" in France during the Revolution.

13. Elihu Palmer, *Principles of Nature; or, A Development of the Moral Causes of Happiness and Misery Among the Human Species*, 2d ed. (New York, 1802), 148–49.

14. *An Enquiry Relative to the Moral and Political Improvement of the Human Species* (New York: John Crookes, 1797), 34. Palmer was also influenced by Rousseauan deism. See my *Rousseau in America* (University: University of Alabama Press, 1969), 79–80.

15. Charles Lee Smith, *The History of Education in North Carolina* (Washington: Government Printing Office, 1888), 68. For a broad and balanced presentation of clerical attitudes and fears see Gary B. Nash, "The American Clergy and the French Revolution," *William and Mary Quarterly*, 3d ser., 22 (1965): 392–412.

16. Volney, *A View of the Soil and Climate of the United States of America*, trans. C. B. Brown (Philadelphia: J. Conrad, 1804), xvii. With regard to the influence of various *philosophes* on Brown, see Alexander Cowie, *The Rise of the American Novel* (New York: American Book Co., 1948), 70, 91–92.

17. On Condillac and Locke, see R. J. White, *The Anti-Philosophers: A Study of the Philosophes in Eighteenth-Century France* (New York: St. Martin's Press, 1970), 38–45.

18. *Condillac's Treatise on the Sensations*, trans. Geraldine Carr (London: Favil Press, 1930). See translator's introduction, xx–xxvii.

19. Consult P. Emory Aldrich, "John Locke and the Influence of His Works in America," *Proceedings of the American Antiquarian Society*, April 30, 1879, 22–39, and Merle Curti, "The Great Mr. Locke: America's Philosopher, 1783–1861," *Huntington Library Bulletin* 11 (April 1937): 107–51.

20. *Catalogus Librorum in Bibliotheca Cantabrigiensi Selectus, Frequentiorem in Usum Harvardinatum Qui Gradu Baccalaurei in Artibus Nondum Sunt Donati* (Boston: Edes and Gil, 1773).

21. *Catalogue of the Books, Belonging to the Library Company of Philadelphia* (Philadelphia: Zachariah Poulson, Jr., 1789).

22. G. G. Raddin, Jr., *An Early New York Library of Fiction, with a*

Checklist of the Fiction in H. Caritat's Circulating Library (New York: H. W. Wilson, 1940), 17.

23. *Catalogue of the Library of the Late Col. William Duane.* This was an auctioneer's catalog printed in Philadelphia and dated February 25, 1836. There is no way of knowing when Duane (1760–1835) acquired his books.

24. Samuel Miller, *A Brief Retrospect of the Eighteenth Century,* 2 vols. (New York: Thomas and John Swords, 1803; reprint ed., New York: Burt Franklin, 1970), 2:128–29. In a footnote Miller cites specifically the first volume of Condillac's *Cours d'ètudes pour l'instruction du prince de Parme,* and as a work in 16 volumes published in Paris in 1775, which was the case.

25. *The Adams-Jefferson Letters,* ed. Lester J. Cappon, 2 vols. (Chapel Hill: University of North Carolina Press, 1959), 2:438, 439. A *Cours d'étude pour l'instruction des jeunes gens,* by Condillac, was published in Paris in 1796.

26. I. Woodbridge Riley, *American Philosophy: The Early Schools* (New York: Russell and Russell, 1958), 437.

27. Palmer, *Principles of Nature,* 183.

28. Charles Hunter Van Duzer, *Contributions of the Ideologues to French Revolutionary Thought* (Baltimore: Johns Hopkins Press, 1935), 5.

29. B. G. Garnham, "Who Were the Ideologues?" *Studies in the French Eighteenth Century* (Durham, Eng: University of Durham, 1978), 74.

30. On Tracy, consult Emmet Kennedy, *A Philosophe in the Age of Revolution: Destutt de Tracy and the Origins of "Ideology"* (Philadelphia: American Philosophical Society, 1978). Extensive bibliography.

31. See Sergio Moravia, "Les Idéologues et l'âge des Lumières," *Studies on Voltaire and the Eighteenth Century* 154 (1976), 1465–86.

32. Garnham, "Who Were the Ideologues?" 79–80.

33. Consult Emile Cailliet, *La Tradition littéraire des Idéologues* (Philadelphia: American Philosophical Society, 1943).

34. *The Adams-Jefferson Letters,* ed. Cappon, 2:471, 500–501.

35. A. Owen Aldridge, "Thomas Paine and the Idéologues," *Studies on Voltaire and the Eighteenth Century* 151 (1976):109–17.

36. See Gilbert Chinard, *Jefferson et les Idéologues: D'après sa correspondance inédite avec Destutt de Tracy, Cabanis, J.-B. Say, et Auguste*

Comte (Baltimore: Johns Hopkins Press, 1925). Reviewed by George Boas, *Modern Language Notes* 41 (1926): 205–8. The reader should also consult Adrienne Koch, *The Philosophy of Thomas Jefferson*, along with Chinard's book.

37. *The Adams-Jefferson Letters*, 2:491. In a letter dated October 14, 1816.

38. Ibid., 535. Letter dated March 2, 1819.

39. Chinard, *Jefferson et les Idéologues*, 1.

40. Gilbert Chinard, introduction to *La Tradition littéraire des Idéologues* by Emile Cailliet (Philadelphia: American Philosophical Society, 1943), 23.

41. Gilbert Chinard, ed., *The Correspondence of Jefferson and Du Pont de Nemours with an Introduction on Jefferson and the Physiocrats* (Baltimore: Johns Hopkins Press, 1931), xiv–cxxiii.

42. Vernon Louis Parrington, *Main Currents in American Thought: An Interpretation of American Literature from the Beginnings to 1920*, 3 vols. (New York: Harcourt, Brace, 1927), 2:vi–vii.

43. Ibid., 10. For a criticism of these views of Parrington, see Richard Hofstadter, "Parrington and the Jeffersonian Tradition," *Journal of the History of Ideas* 2 (1941): 391–400.

44. George K. Smart, "Private Libraries in Colonial Virginia," *American Literature* 10 (1938): 47.

45. See Malcolm R. Eiselen's chapter on "Franklin and the Physiocrats" in his book *Franklin's Political Theories* (Garden City, N.Y.: Doubleday, Doran, 1928), 62–65; and Alfred Owen Aldridge, *Franklin and His French Contemporaries* (New York: New York University Press, 1957), 24–28.

46. Frederick B. Tolles, *George Logan of Philadelphia* (New York: Oxford University Press, 1953), 68.

47. Zoltán Haraszti, *John Adams and the Prophets of Progress* (Cambridge, Mass.: Harvard University Press, 1952), 139.

48. Adams, *A Defence* 1:372.

49. Ibid., 1:384.

50. See Pierre Teyssendier de la Serve, *Mably et les Physiocrates* (Poitiers: Société Française d'Imprimerie et de Librairie, 1911).

51. Consult J. L. Lecercle, "Mably devant la révolution américaine," *Studies on Voltaire and the Eighteenth Century* 180 (1976): 1287–1306.

52. Haraszti, "The Communism of the Abbé de Mably," in *John Adams and the Prophets of Progress*, 116-38.

53. William Vans Murray, *Political Sketches* (London: C. Dilly, 1787). This sketch was reprinted in the *American Museum or Repository* (Philadelphia) 2 (1787): 221–28.

54. Philip Mazzei, *Researches on the United States*, ed. and trans. Constance D. Sherman (Charlottesville: University Press of Virginia, 1976).

55. *Memoirs and Letters of James Kent LL.D.*, ed. William Kent (Boston: Little, Brown, 1898), 238–39.

56. George R. Havens, "James Madison et la pensée française," *Revue de littérature comparée* 3 (1923): 611.

57. Alfred Owen Aldridge, "Benjamin Franklin and the *Philosophes*," *Studies on Voltaire and the Eighteenth Century* 24 (1963): 52.

58. See Gilbert Chinard, "Jefferson Among the Philosophers," *Ethics* 53, (1943): 265ff.

59. Koch, *The Philosophy of Thomas Jefferson*, 190.

60. See, for example, no. 14, by Madison, eager reader of French.

61. Noah Webster, *Ten Letters to Dr. Joseph Priestly* (New Haven, Conn.: Read and Morse, 1800), 22.

Index